Auto Mobile

Also by Ruth Brandon

Ruth Brandon

Mobile

Macmillan

First published 2002 by Macmillan
an imprint of Pan Macmillan Ltd
Pan Macmillan, 20 New Wharf Road, London N1 9RR
Basingstoke and Oxford
Associated companies throughout the world
www.panmacmillan.com

ISBN 0 333 76666 0

9 8 7 6 5 4 3 2 1

A CIP catalogue record for this book is available from
the British Library.

Printed and bound in Great Britain by
Mackays of Chatham plc, Chatham, Kent

Ruth Brandon's web site address is:
www.ruthbrandon.co.uk

How the Car Changed Life

Auto

Contents

Acknowledgements

In writing this book I have relied even more than usual on other people's generous help. I should especially like to thank: Scott Bottles and his family in San Marino, California; Malcolm Ferguson; Adrian Forty; Larry Gorenflo; Steve Lawson at the AA; the Leroys in Romulus, Michigan; Esther Mes and Melissa Miller at the Harry Ransom Center, Austin, Texas; Robin Read; Linda Skolarus and her staff at the Henry Ford Museum Research Center, Dearborn, Michigan and Dan Erickson and the staff of the Ford Photo Archive. At General Motors, Klaus-Peter Martin, Cymbrie Trepczynski, Ellie Tacke and John Robertson could not have been more generous and helpful. At Macmillan, I have been fortunate in the support and enthusiasm of Stuart Evers, Becky Lindsay, Anya Serota, Tanya Stobbs and Catherine Whitaker. At A. P. Watt I have as always relied upon Caradoc King. But the person to whom, from first to last, I have turned for help and advice is my husband, Phil Steadman. To say this book could never have been written without him is an understatement. It is, among other things, the record of two years' conversation. All errors, needless to say, are entirely my own. I hope he likes it none the less.

List of Illustrations

1. The Cord Phaeton.
2. Poster for the wind yacht *L'Éolienne*, *c.*1834.
3. Trevithick's steam engine.
4. Gottlieb Daimler's motorized bicycle.
5. Ohio, 1905.
6. De Dion's steam quadricycle.
7. Levassor's monument, Porte Maillot, Paris.
8. H. P. Maxim's first horseless carriage.
9. Advertisement for the Daimler Wagonette, 1896.
10. The Bugatti Royale.
11. Mr and Mrs W. K. Vanderbilt, 1904.
12. *L'Effroi*, Paul Gervais, 1904.
13. Detroit freeways, 1950.
14. Henry Ford and Barney Oldfield with a 999.
15. a) and b) Three Cadillacs disassembled and assembled, London, 1908.
16. Advertisement for The Oldsmobile.
17. Model T Ford.
18. The world's first assembly-line, Detroit, 1914.
19. The Rouge, Detroit.
20. Henry Ford.
21. a) and b) Model T on the farm and in the snow.
22. Letchworth High Street, *c.*1930.

58. Harley Earl and friends with the Buick LeSabre.
59. You can do anything in your Buick.
60. The *Cadillac Ranch*.
61. 1959 Cadillac tail light.
62. The Ford Mustang.
63. John DeLorean.
64. Starsky and Hutch's Gran Torino.
65. A restyled DeLorean, with O. J. Simpson.
66. The DeLorean.
67. The Stack, Los Angeles.
68. Los Angeles mural, 'Division of the Barrios'.
69. City Walk, Los Angeles.
70. Automated highway, 1998.
71. Traffic jam.
72. The Big Rollover.
73. Mitsubishi Shogun advertisement.
74. a) and b) Alfa Romeo advertisement
75. Woods 'duo-power' hybrid, 1917.

ACKNOWLEDGEMENTS

5, 13, 15a, 15b, 16, 30, 42, 43, 44, 45, 55, 56, 57, 58, 59, 61, 70 – © 2000 General Motors Corp. Used by permission of GM Media Archives.

14, 18, 19, 21a, 21b, 38, 41 – © Ford Motor Company.

23, 33, 69, 75 – © Ruth Brandon.

39a, 39b, 39c – © Walter P. Reuther Library, Wayne State University.

22, 24 – © Letchworth Garden City Heritage Museum.

17 – © Hulton Getty.   36 – © Karl E. Lustvigsen collection.

40 – Courtesy of the Warden and Fellows of Nuffield College.

60 – © Wayne McSpadden.   62 – © Bettman/Corbis.

68 – Judy Baca, SPARC, Los Angeles.

Chapter One

A Visit to the Motor Show

We have become gods. Anything they could do, so, now, can we. We view the world through television's magic spectacles, converse electronically across oceans, fly, walk on the moon. Though not yet immortal, we have the gift of universal death. And, like gods, we travel the world at will. Perseus rode Pegasus to slay the Chimaera; Hermes with his winged helmet whizzed between immortals; King Solomon positioned his throne on a green silk magic carpet, mortals to his right, spirits to his left, and summoned up the wind. And we, no longer trapped by animal limitations, climb into our cars and leave for the land of heart's desire: escape at the touch of a toe. On the road we are transformed: winged, invincible – free.

No wonder everyone wants a car. And as soon as the money is there, everyone buys one. Before the fall of communism there already existed enough front-seat capacity in America to accommodate the entire population, with the USSR seated in back. In 2001 there were over 23 million private cars on the road in the UK – one for every two and a half Britons. Only fun, food and housing (in that order) consume more of the British family budget than motoring.[1] And this is by no means Europe's highest level of car ownership. In 1997 there were almost six hundred cars for every thousand Italians. Germany, France, Austria, Sweden and Spain all owned more cars per capita than the UK.[2]

This, moreover, is just the start. The car has continents yet to conquer; that it will do so is not in doubt. Everywhere, from kraal to skyscraper, people spend, on average, an hour and ten minutes a day travelling.[3] But where a woman in an African village walks to her vegetable plot, a Texas tycoon jets to his morning meeting. In the time it takes her to cover three miles, he has flown three hundred. The richer you are, the faster and further you go, progressing, in an invariable sequence, from foot to bicycle to bus to train to private car to air or high-speed train. Travel has become the index of prosperity.

In the West, this correlation between income and distance is remarkably exact. In 1960 the average North American earned $9,600 and travelled over twelve thousand kilometres (7,640 miles); by 1990 both income and distance travelled had doubled. And in developing countries, where many still rely on their own or their animals' muscle power and car ownership starts from a very small base, travel volume grows even faster relative to income than in the developed world.[4]

Clearly the car is more than a mere machine. Rather it is what Freud (in *Civilisation and its Discontents*) termed an 'accessory organ': an exo-skeleton, a travelling whelk-shell from which, in safety, to contemplate the surrounding monsters; an extension of home, a refuge from the mob, a private cave of autonomous comforts. So closely do people identify themselves with their cars that those who think of themselves as larger than they are tend to imagine their cars need more space than is actually the case; conversely, those who underestimate their own body size try to squeeze their cars into too narrow a gap.[5] This identification is one of the explanations of road rage. Our perception of 'car space' is related to 'personal space', a zone extending a few feet around our bodies which we feel we own, and whose invasion we resent. This space narrows at the side of our bodies and extends further behind us than in front – the reason, say psychologists Peter Marsh and Peter Collett, 'why we feel particularly uncomfortable when people "creep up behind us" or "look over our shoulder"'. The same discomfort is experienced when other drivers approach too close to our rear bumper, inside the moving boundaries of 'car space'.[6]

Freud, discussing the advances of technology, recognized that these new 'accessory organs' might 'still give . . . trouble at times': a conclusion with which no gridlocked, fume-inhaling driver, her engine overheating along with her temper, would disagree. He concluded, however, that '[man] is entitled to console himself with the thought that this evolution will not come to an end in A.D. 1930'. In other words, something will turn up. There will always be a technical fix. Progress is inevitable, and will lead us out of the mire.

An essentially nineteenth-century world-view; and indeed the great architect of the twentieth-century intellectual world was very much a nineteenth-century man when it came to science and technology, as witness those steam-powered metaphors of repression and bursting libido. But if progress was the nineteenth-century watchword, that of the new-born twenty-first is guilt – the conflict between comfort and its consequences: in this case, between our chair-borne magic carpets and the future of the world we live in. We may take it in our stride, like one friend who, true child of the liberal 60s, described his daily drive to work as 'an indulgence, extra pollution and environmentally irresponsible' (but still persisted in his culpable habits); or defiantly reject it, as do both big business and the representatives of the developing world, who do not see why they should renounce modern amenities because of other people's heedlessness. None the less, guilt dogs us all; and the car is its material embodiment.

In 1930, Freud described the story of science and invention

as 'sound[ing] like a fairy-tale'.[7] But, as he knew better than anyone, fairy-tales are double-edged: nothing in them comes without its price. Perhaps we should look instead to Edith Nesbit, Freud's contemporary and a great teller of fairy-tales. In her stories – *Five Children and It, The Phoenix and the Carpet, The Story of the Amulet* – wishes are magically granted. But they don't turn out as her protagonists hoped and expected.

In Nesbit's book *The Magic City* a special rule applies to those who wish for a piece of machinery: they must keep it and go on using it for the rest of their lives. One wish and you're saddled. There is no escape.

» » »

I'm standing at the entrance to the 1999 London Motor Show at Earl's Court. It seemed the obvious place to begin a book about cars. Olympia has been transformed into a monstrous toyshop for grown-ups. So bright and shiny, so ingeniously constructed and enticingly gadgeted, with their unfurling computerized direction finders, their digital sound, their in-car faxes and electrically retractable roofs; so comfortable, with their ergonomically impeccable headrests and backrests and armrests, their infinitely adjustable seats and irresistible new-leather smell; above all so *powerful*! Was there ever in the entire history of the world so absolutely desirable an object?

Entering the thronging halls, however, I feel oddly uncomfortable – aware at every step that for devotees such as these I must seem supremely unqualified to write a book about cars. In motor show terms I am an anomaly on many counts: female; unmechanical; a driver, certainly, but of the least glamorous wheels imaginable – a seven-year-old Peugeot 205, its soft top, more or less useless in the British climate, my only concession to automobile romance: an unremarkable vehicle that I shall doubtless continue to own until one or other of us falls to pieces. In no way, professionally or as an amateur enthusiast, am I involved with automobiles. Smoke and mirrors, that's my usual field: motivation, conscious and unconscious, façade-stripping a speciality. In short, I am not, nor ever could be, a motoring correspondent. And this, perhaps, explains my discomfort. For the Motor Show purveys, *par excellence*, the motoring correspondent's view of life. It is the world's motoring columns made flesh.

But – but! The significance of the automobile extends infinitely beyond the motoring columns – pervades, on the contrary, every aspect of life. Without my car I could not live where I do, eat, shop, travel as I do, holiday where I do, perceive the world as I do. Through the automotive prism a new light falls upon the great questions of our age – class war, alienation, the destruction of the countryside, the influence of big business on politics, feminism, the power of fantasy, the death of the environment. I might have discussed the birth of the touring holiday, the car as national emblem (the Ambassador and India, the Fiat 500 and Italy), the automobile in literature, the varieties of motor racing and what they represent, the car as ultimate refuge in the dustbowl-driven flight of the Okies, the Japanese car industry as an encapsulation of post-war history, automobile architecture (drive-ins, Turin's amazing concrete Fiat factory with the raceway on top), the internal combustion engine's transformation of war . . . There's material here for a thousand books, each quite different and still utterly relevant, each reflecting its author's particular interests as this book no doubt reflects mine.

But a book must end sometime, choices must be made. And as I read and thought and discussed these seemingly infinite possibilities, a structure imposed itself. Each period seemed to bring some particular topic into focus, and with it a place, or places. So my book became a series of journeys, explorations at the same time historical and actual. I set out in France, the first country to experience serious motoring and its effects, then moved on to Henry Ford's Detroit, home of mass production and all that followed from it. Town planning and the rise of the suburb took me to Pasadena in southern California, Letchworth in Hertfordshire and Prince Charles's version of the urban idyll at Poundbury in Dorset. The problematic ideals of the 30s led to Hitler's Berlin and on into 1960 as conceived by Norman Bel Geddes in 1939. I followed the post-war auto fantasy to John DeLorean's Belfast. And finished – where else? – on the Los Angeles freeways, paradigm of the automotive future.

» » »

Though I am no automane, only a stick could leave the Motor Show unaffected by desire. Do new cars leave you cold? Then here are yesterday's dreamboats – for instance, something I'd never thought to encounter in the flesh: auto design supreme in the shape of a 1936 Cord, a huge royal blue Phaeton convertible with torpedo nose, streamlined fenders, white-wall tyres and four gleaming chrome exhaust pipes looping back from the engine: all yours for just £55,000. A wheeled madeleine that transports me back to Oklahoma *c.*1970, where, in Broken Arrow, just outside Tulsa, a man called Glenn Pray was building Cord reproductions, seven-eighths the original size. He had extended a most CORDial invitation to visit his facilities 'should you be in Oklahoma in the summer', and when we arrived was working on a special order for a sheikh: pink, as I recall, with green upholstery.

For a moment enchantment bites. I dream of driving sheikh-like through the desert with the hood down and the hot wind in my ears, through Marble Canyon and past the Coral Pink Sand Dunes, Chuck Berry playing along on the radio, movie cameras turning as the sun sets behind the red rocks of

1. Dream car: the Cord Phaeton.

Monument Valley . . . But there's the little question of finance. And more potently, on the drive home, the base reality of the M1, so far in every way from Olympia's pristine dream. Buying a Cord isn't out of the question, not entirely, merely a question of what the business schools call prioritizing (house and contents versus wheels). But only a madwoman would risk a Cord on a British motorway. A tank would be more to the point. And indeed that's what most people seem to be driving, every other vehicle one of those enormous four-wheel-drives with a rhinoceros on the spare wheel and bull-bars in front, technically known as a sports utility vehicle or SUV. Enormous trucks tower to my left, poised to swing out, while a solid stream of hundred-mile-an-hour maniacs hogs the fast lane, leaving no room for manoeuvre. In my fragile tin bubble I am reminded of lying in a khaki-coloured ridge tent in a khaki-coloured State Park on that same trip to Oklahoma, and wondering, as the Winnebagos manoeuvred alongside, whether one of them might simply fail to register us, and crush us like the molehill we strongly resembled. Am I any more visible now to these forty-tonne monsters? One day some trucker simply won't notice me: I'll be wiped out by a sideswipe from the brontosaur's tail. It actually happened to a friend of mine: she swerved to avoid collision, hit the centre barrier; the car was a write-off, but miraculously she wasn't hurt. As for the truck, it didn't even notice, but simply thundered on. Six lanes of traffic pounding along at seventy, one little lapse and – carnage.

Still, Britain, despite its huge number of vehicles, remains one of the less terrifying places to drive: three times safer than Belgium, nine times safer than Hungary,[8] and a mere nursery slope compared to that part of the world known as 'developing', which chalks up 70 per cent of all road deaths, despite possessing a minority of vehicles, and where road accidents have become the leading cause of mortality for men aged between fifteen and forty-four.[9]

And now we're past Luton and the traffic clears and I put my foot down and the little car flies forward and the fields pass in a blur, and if it went on like this in a few hours I could be in Scotland. Not that I shall do it today. Today I shall turn off at Junction 14 and follow the familiar route leading to the familiar front door. But the possibility remains, and it's the possibility that matters, beguiling, entrancing: parked outside my door, ready to roll, the stuff of dreams.

Chapter Two

Paris to Bordeaux: The Freedom of the Streets

'I used to dream of skimming over the country highways, up hill and down dale, with no effort except that of steering,' wrote Hiram Percy Maxim of the automobile's thrilling early days, when for the first time in history the prospect of effortless travel stretched ahead.[1]

The freedom of the streets – how simple it sounds; how little to ask! But freedom is not a simple issue. Freedoms clash: my freedom may threaten yours. In 1896 the Duke of Teck, who lived in Cumberland Lodge, the royal residence in Richmond Park, sent a distressed letter to his brother the Duke of Cambridge, who forwarded it to the Home Secretary:

> We had a very curious experience yesterday . . . About 2,000 to 3,000 Bicycles through the Roads of the Park, not as if guided by sensible thoughtful People, but by Maniacs, persons in a state of madness. They went about in a pace like Lightening [sic], looking neither right nor left . . . Many Groups, actually abreast, of from 10 to 20 or more, formed of Roughs and others apparently members of Bicycle Clubs . . .[2]

2. Poster for the wind yacht *L'Éolienne*, *c*.1834.

For the cyclists, the trip to Richmond Park was just another jolly day out. But for the Duke of Teck they were doom-laden presages of an unwelcome future, laying claim to a world from which they had hitherto been strictly excluded. As Lady Jeune remarked in *The Gentleman* in 1901, 'Leisure and pleasure are presently no longer confined to the better off': a circumstance the better-off found distinctly unpleasing. 'Cycling had its social side, so had boating among other amusements; but the moment they came into universal use they lost their charm,' complained the same Lady Jeune elsewhere, here using the word 'social' in that specialized sense which includes only the well-connected.

> People became frightened of the crowds which took possession of the roads and of the Thames and left both; and the social side of cycling has ceased to interest the community any longer . . . Both cycling and boating possessed a qualification, advantageous or the reverse, in that they were not expensive amusements, and by the help of both the river Thames was rendered accessible to the teachers and the workers, both male and female, of this great toiling metropolis; and what was only for a brief period the pastime of the rich became to them the means of giving them many happy hours during the week of fresh air and peace . . .[3]

What were the rich to do now? There was only one answer. A new pastime would have to be found – one costly enough to render it forever inaccessible to the toiling, threatening masses.

» » »

The idea of a horseless carriage was by no means new. Sail-powered land-yachts had been around since at least the seventeenth century. But the wind is an unsatisfactory source of direct energy. It has the merit of simplicity, but unlike a horse you can be sure of neither its speed nor its presence. The first serious possibilities were offered by steam power. In France, a steam engine which moved a short distance was built by Joseph Cugnot as early as 1769, but only ran for twenty minutes at a time. Two years later Cugnot produced a new, improved version, but it was not manoeuvrable, and overturned when attempting to turn a corner near the Madeleine in the centre of Paris, after which he and his engine were locked up in the interests of public safety.

In 1801, the action crossed the Channel: a steam road-engine built by Richard Trevithick was run in Camborne, Cornwall. Fifty-seven years later an old man recalled that momentous journey:

> In the year 1801, upon Christmas Eve, towards night, Trevithick got up steam, out on the high road, just outside the shop. When we saw Trevithick was going to turn on steam, we jumped up as many as could, maybe seven or eight of us. 'Twas a stiffish hill going up to Camborne Beacon, but she went off like a little bird. When she had gone about a quarter of a mile, there was a rough piece of road, covered with loose stones. She didn't go quite so fast, and it was a flood of rain, and as we were very much squeezed together, I jumped off. She was going faster than I could walk, and went up the hill about half a mile further, when they turned her, and came back again to the shop.[4]

Was this it, the machine that would challenge the gods? Perhaps it seemed possible. However, a few days later tragedy struck. A friend of Trevithick's recounted how the carriage broke down and was forced under some shelter, and the Parties adjourned to the Hotel, & comforted their Hearts with a Roast Goose & proper drinks, when, forgetful of the Engine, its Water boiled away, the Iron became red hot, and nothing that was combustible remained either of the Engine or the house.[5]

Trevithick set to work once more and took out a patent for a steam carriage the following March. By 1803 it was constructed and named the *London Steam Carriage*. But it was too primitive to operate reliably. So was the *Orukter Amphibolos*, an amphibious scow constructed to dredge and clean docks in Philadelphia by Oliver Evans in 1805. This worked, just, but the engine was too feeble for the heavy loads, and it was abandoned.

There was another wave of interest in steam during the 1830s, but this too came to nothing. Most road surfaces at that time were gravelled, and at their top speed of fifteen miles per hour, the heavy, iron-wheeled steamers simply tore them apart. Crippling tolls were therefore imposed on steam traction to pay for the incessant repairs. And by the time Telford opened his great London to Holyhead road in 1830, road traction had been upstaged by another transport revolution – George Stephenson's locomotive, which made its first run in 1829. This combination of heavy tolls and smooth-running railways proved fatal to British road transport. While the railways burgeoned and flourished, Britain's once-admired road network fell into disrepair. Any impetus to improvement was nullified by the 'red flag' laws, introduced in 1865. These set maximum speed limits for road locomotives of four mph in the country and two mph in built-up areas; in addition to which a man waving a red flag had to walk at least sixty yards ahead of the vehicle to warn the unwary and calm horses. In 1876 this was reduced to twenty yards for England only, but both red flag and speed limits remained in force until November 1896, when the repeal of

3. Trevithick's steam engine.

this 'obnoxious and obsolete law' was celebrated with a run from London to Brighton, won in pouring rain by the Bollée steam tricycle and commemorated every year by the famous vintage-car rally along the same course.

The early iron road steamers indubitably moved forward without the intervention of a horse. But they were huge and cumbersome; as a means of individual transportation, no replacement for a cheap, manoeuvrable animal. 'Why did so many different and widely separated persons have the same thoughts [about cars] at about the same time?' Maxim wondered.

> It has been the habit to give the gasoline engine all the credit for bringing the automobile . . . In my opinion this is a wrong explanation . . . We could have built steam vehicles in 1880, or indeed in 1870. But we did not. We waited until 1895. The reason . . . in my opinion, was because the bicycle had not yet come in numbers and had not directed men's minds to the possibilities of independent, long-distance travel over the ordinary highway.[6]

The modern safety bike, with its low wheels, pneumatic tyres, and pedals set on the frame rather than the front wheel and connected by a chain to the back hub, was invented in 1885. In terms of personal transportation it was the first serious rival to the horse, and at once caught the popular imagination. At first, bicycles were not cheap: when the League of American Wheelmen was founded in Newport, Rhode Island, in 1880, 'to ascertain, defend and protect the rights of wheelmen, to encourage and facilitate touring', American-made bicycles (then still the large-wheeled variety) cost between $150 and $200 – a significant sum for anyone of limited means; though once you had bought them bicycles, unlike horses, required minimal upkeep and storage space. But the price soon came

4. Gottlieb Daimler on his motorized bicycle, 1886.

down until it reached $30, at which point almost anyone could own a bike; and almost everyone did. By 1893, 150,000 bicycles were in use in France, and more than a million a year were selling in America. By 1896 the Birmingham Small Arms Company, better known as BSA, was turning out two thousand bicycle kits a week. For the first time in history the advantages of speed and independent locomotion were available to all. Cycling clubs became the rage, organizing weekend outings anywhere the state of the roads allowed. Road travel, hitherto a tiresome necessity, was transformed into a pleasure. As Maxim observed, it was 'a revolutionary change in transportation'.[7]

In 1892, cycling back late at night from a visit to his fiancée, Maxim realized that 'if I could build a little engine and use its power to do the propelling, and if I could use a regular carriage instead of a bicycle, there would be no limit to where I could go'.[8] And in this realization he was not alone. Many of the first automobiles were adapted bicycles or tricycles, and such automotive essentials as steel-tube framing, ball bearings, the chain drive and differential gearing were all first developed by the bicycle industry. Opel, Peugeot, Rover, Rambler are just a few of the famous car marques that began life as makes of bicycle.[9]

In France the bicycle's popularity was such that it supported a daily paper, *Le Vélo*, published by Pierre Giffard. In 1891 Giffard organized a bicycle race from Paris to the Breton port of Brest and back. And so much interest did this arouse that he was encouraged to try something similar with automobiles.

Giffard's event took place in the summer of 1894. It was a road test rather than a race: a promenade from Paris to Rouen, a distance of seventy-eight miles, prizes to be awarded for safety, simplicity and economy of operation. One hundred and two vehicles registered, though when it came to the day only twenty-one showed up. However, so much enthusiasm was kindled that it was decided to organize a race. The Comte de

Dion, who manufactured his own steam quadricycles, brought together a committee of prominent journalists and auto-mobilists, wealthy aristocrats and industrialists. This was the committee that would evolve into the Automobile Club de France, and it was they who decided upon the daring notion of a long, non-stop test. The Baron van Zuylen put up ten thousand francs prize money. He could easily afford it: he was prodigiously wealthy, a Belgian banker who had made a fortune and married a Rothschild.[10] The race would be from Paris to Bordeaux and back again, a distance of 730 miles (1,200 kilometres). The automobile was about to establish itself (should any complete the course) as serious transport.

That France should be the setting for the first automobile race was no accident. For cars need roads, and good roads were a rarity. Maxim described a trip made in 1897 from Hartford, Connecticut, where he lived, to Springfield, Massachusetts, twenty-five miles distant. He was then in the early stages of building his first automobile, and the time had come to test it out. The trip was made at night, to avoid attracting the attention of a jeering public. 'Macadam prevailed to the city line,' he wrote.

> From this point the road to Springfield was a winding country dirt road. The frost had come out and had done a wonderful job. The road was about like country back roads today immediately after the frost comes out of the ground; it was nothing less than a quagmire. We advanced about a hundred yards, wallowing and slithering sidewise in the dark . . . Happening to glance down, I saw the cylinder head of the engine glowing in the dark. It was red hot. I had never seen a gasoline engine running red hot before, and it appeared the better part of wisdom to pause a moment and look matters over . . . When I stopped the engine [his friend] Lobdell ceased pushing. It was very

dark and very cold and the prospect was far from being cheerful . . . I may have commented unfavorably upon the condition of the road and the length of time we should require to reach Springfield at the rate we were traveling. Straightening up, and raising his hand as though to shade his eyes, he peered ahead into the blackness. When I asked him what he thought he saw, he replied, 'Twenty-five miles of road like this.'[11]

Twelve years later, little had changed. A spectator of the 1907 Glidden Tour, a motor race from Cleveland, Ohio, to New York, describes a

slippery, slimy, treacherously dangerous ooze . . . The roadbed, itself, was hard, and this covering of slime, from a foot to two feet deep, made just the correct combination for fancy skidding . . . The State road was full of great holes, the depth of which could not be ascertained until the car plunged right into them . . . The car . . . continually skidded around at right angles to the road and into ditches, although the most expert driver was at the wheel . . .[12]

As late as 1913 conditions in Michigan, a state with a reputation for good roads, remained so bad that Ford could only deliver cars by road to buyers within a hundred miles of its Detroit factory.[13]

Things were little better in Britain. The British road system had once been the envy of the world, but since the triumph of the railways it had fallen into decline. This, in combination with the red flag rule, might have been – indeed, had been – designed to discourage automobilists; and it succeeded admirably. No less a person than Sir David Salomons, Mayor of Tunbridge Wells, an enthusiast who organized several motor shows and in 1902 began his own motoring magazine

5. Beautiful Ohio, 1905.

(*The Motor*), declared in 1897 that 'The best existing motor the world has yet seen, for its power, method of fuelling, suspension, springs, and travelling long distances before recharging, is one which is likely to remain in use for many a long year to come, whatever may be the future development of motor traffic. It is known and loved by all, young and old, under the name of the horse.'[14]

France and Germany, on the other hand, had excellent roads – a result of the almost continual military manoeuvres that had occupied them for the past century. In Germany, however, this did not, despite German engineering excellence, lead to an early interest in automobiles. Any industry needs customers if it is to develop, and the wealthy aristocracy which in Britain and France supplied most early motor enthusiasts, in Germany preferred its country estates and its horses.

But in France things were different. In Hilaire Belloc's words, 'The great broad, straight roads of the eighteenth century formed the model continuously applied, so that the most recent examples today are in the same tradition as those of two hundred years ago and yet amply fulfil their function.'[15] And in the nineteenth century Paris, too, received its broad, straight roads, when, following the year of the Republic, 1848, Baron Haussmann drove through his wide, asphalted boulevards, facilitating crowd control and reducing the availability of cobblestones for use as missiles and in barricades.

In 1857, when the introduction of the Bessemer process saw heavy iron give way to lighter and more durable steel, the way opened for a new generation of self-powered vehicles. Amédée Bollée built a number of successful road-steamers in Le Mans during the 1870s. He gave up when his funds ran out; but in 1881 the Comte de Dion, a wealthy man-about-town, noticed a toy steam engine in a Paris shop which suggested to him the possibility of constructing a steam tricycle and a two-seater carriage. He at once hired the toymaker, a M. Bouton.

They constructed a few vehicles, exhibiting one, alongside a similar machine made by Serpollet, at the 1889 Exposition Universelle, held in Paris to celebrate the hundredth anniversary of the Revolution. The trend caught on within twenty years Paris had become a focus of motor manufacturing, with such firms as Panhard-Levassor, Renault and Citroën all operating in or near the city centre.

This was unusual: capital cities are rarely centres of heavy industry. But Haussmann's boulevards, which made inner-city living fashionable and pleasant, were also, it turned out, perfect for cars. Substantial numbers of wealthy Parisians, eager to try out the new machines, turned to the city's numerous small carriage-making firms to supply them; and those firms evolved into auto manufacturers. By 1907 four thousand motors were registered in the city, and by 1909 it had become necessary to introduce one-way streets.

So it was from Paris, not New York or Berlin or London, that the first road-race set off. On 12 June 1895, twenty-seven competitors lined up for the start. They included 'sixteen petroleum carriages, seven steam vehicles, two electric carriages and two petroleum bicycles'.[16] The weather was perfect, and from nine in the morning (reported *Le Figaro*) the place de l'Etoile, the avenue de la Grande Armée and the avenue de Neuilly were thick with crowds come to watch the entrants as they left in procession for the starting-point, the place d'Armes at Versailles.

The place d'Armes today symbolizes the revolution set in motion by those twenty-seven assorted carriages. This huge empty space, directly fronting the château, was designed as an inspection ground for the King of France's armies, an awe-inspiring hiatus separating king and court from those they governed. After the King's removal the vast space remained, suitable for functions which required plenty of room for manoeuvre; for example, the start of motor races. And since

6. De Dion's steam quadricycle. The comte is leaning forward to avoid the steam blowing in his face.

the essential fact of the automobile was that it enabled anyone to go wherever they wished whenever they wished to do so, one might say that popular tourism was born on the day the motoring dream proved a practicable possibility: 14 June, 1895, the day the Paris–Bordeaux race ended.

Thirty thousand visitors a day now descend upon Versailles. But although they leave their inevitable mark the fabric of the town remains comparatively intact. At Stratford-upon-Avon, a similarly overrun tourist destination, the town has demolished so much of itself in order to accommodate the trade upon which it lives that it is reduced to a sea of parked cars, amid which loom Ann Hathaway's Cottage, the Shakespeare Memorial Theatre and a thousand tearooms. The Sun King's grandiosity, however, has sufficed for all exigencies, even those he could not possibly have foreseen. The place d'Armes, recycled as a car and coach park (the republican principle of universal access appropriately supplanting royal distance), swallows cars as once it swallowed regiments.

The competitors set out in brilliant sunshine – an important bonus, since they were exposed to the elements throughout: closed cars would not be introduced for another twenty-five years. 'Let's hope the wonderful weather lasts until the race is over, and that any accidents are light ones,' commented *Le Figaro*.[17] A throng of cyclists accompanied them as they set out through the forest of Rambouillet, part of the vast woodland belt that once constituted the King's hunting grounds and is now, with its rides and vistas, its stone picnic tables and unexpected statues, an unrivalled pleasure park for Parisians.

I must have driven the competitors' route twenty times or more, and even now the prospect never fails to stir the imagination. What could be more delightful than a leisurely drive in an open car through the dappled June shade of the great forests, on to the open road and the never-failing poetry of names: past Chartres and Châteaudun and the endless wheatfields of the Beauce, crossing the shifting Loire at Tours, then on through Poitou to ancient Angoulême with its hilltop market and its roadside placards advertising home-distilled cognac, Libourne on its wide river (which might as well be a river of wine), and so across the great suspension bridge into sleek Bordeaux, where the very airport has its own vineyard . . . And although the reality inevitably belies the romance (Chartres Cathedral covered in scaffolding, endless traffic jams in the rain at Tours, cliffs of horrible apartment buildings at Blois, Poitiers invisible behind hoardings advertising the Futuroscope, the dark-grey gloom of the Angoulême suburbs) the hope persists. One day all will be as it should, the cathedral uncovered, the Loire iridescent beneath early-morning mists, a vacant parking space at Amboise where Leonardo died at the King of France's château, the drunken smell of must drenching Lalande de Pomerol in October . . .

Today you can do the whole thing on autoroutes, in about five hours. And almost everyone does: all the traffic in France close-packed at ninety miles an hour. *Are we over the fold yet?* enquire ten million drivers, and ten million passengers, one eye on the map, the other on the exit signs, reply, *Almost*, or *Just*, or *Another twenty minutes*. For motorways are about speed, the arrival not the journey, crossing off numbers, turning the map to the next fold; the opposite of present pleasures, that old *sha sha sha* of plane trees along Route Nationale 7 and the wind in your hair. They are a separate country, not linked to the land through which they are driven, the places across which they pass mere names and distances. 'Villages skipped, towns and cities jumped – always somebody else's horizon!' crows Kenneth Grahame's Mr Toad, literature's best-known road-hog – a term Grahame himself used, though he did not coin it, *The Times* defining it in 1903 (five years before *The Wind in the Willows*) as a 'transient phenomenon' drawn mainly 'from a class which possesses money in excess of brains or culture, and which has not had an opportunity of learning insensibly, in the course of generations, the consideration for the rights of others which is part of the natural heritage of gentlefolk'.[18] Words that exactly describe Mr Toad, as his own encapsulate the motorway – a phenomenon, as it happened, that would not reach Britain for another fifty years.

The ironic result of this universal passion for speed is that other roads are ignored, so that France, with the same population as Britain but four times the area, and infinitely more space per car, remains one of the few countries where it is still possible to think of driving for pleasure. On the lethal holiday weekends at the beginning and end of July and August, when the whole of Europe rushes south for its month in the sun, a peek over the parapet of the jammed autoroute reveals another world in which Napoleon's die-straight roads undulate unswervingly over the hills with hardly a car in sight: the same roads, albeit wider now and smoother, as in 1895.

Early road racing, however, despite the low velocities and lack of traffic, can hardly have been wholly a pleasure trip. Writing in 1904 – nine years after the Paris–Bordeaux sortie, nine years in which cars, roads and drivers had all advanced beyond recognition – Filson Young's list of motoring essentials gives a hair-raising idea of the kind of eventualities that had to be catered for:

> If the tyres are in good condition it will be enough to carry one spare cover and two inner tubes, and the repairing outfit should be looked [sic] to see that it is complete and in proper condition. An assortment of nuts and bolts of the various sizes used in the engine should also be carried, as well as four sparking plugs and a complete set of valves and valve springs. I say a complete set of valves because, although there should be no trouble with the valves, anything which does happen – overheating or incrustation, for

example – will be more likely to affect both cylinders than only one. A set of brasses and a supply of insulated wire are useful 'spares'. Spanners to fit all the nuts should of course form part of the regular equipment . . . as well as a Stillson's wrench and a monkey wrench. A small table-vice is a very useful thing to carry, and does not take up much room; there should also be files, punches, a box of screw-drivers, a cold chisel, gas pliers, and a soldering outfit; a good roll of copper and steel wire, a little copper piping, asbestos washers, a length of asbestos cord, and a couple of yards of india-rubber tubing of the same gauge as the pipe of the water system, must also be carried. These things will not take up very much room, and as most of them will not be wanted at all, they can be stowed well out of the way. A can of paraffin should be carried with the lubricating oils, and a small reserve of carbide and wicks for the lamps should also be carried. These supplies should all be assembled together a day or two before the beginning of the journey, and arranged on the bench or floor of the motor-house, all the contents of the car being also taken out for inspection and, if necessary, replace-ment . . .[19]

And this was the minimum! It seems inconceivable that anyone should ever have driven anywhere. In H. P. Maxim's recollec-tion, 'Only the fit and young survived.'[20]

One would be inclined to believe him were it not for the fact that the first car to reach Tours that evening, a two-seater petrol-driven Panhard-Levassor No. 5, was driven by Emile Levassor, then aged fifty-three. Next morning he was still in the lead, reaching Bordeaux at 10.40 a.m.; he had taken just twenty-two and a half hours to drive 585 kilometres – 'that's to say, 24 km 400 cm an hour', as *Le Figaro* eagerly informed its readers. 'Who would have believed it possible?' And twenty-six hours after that, having held the lead from the start, he drove triumphantly across the finishing-line at the Porte Maillot in Paris, 'covered with dust and with the flowers he was given all along the route, that people threw into his car so that he shouldn't lose time'.[21] Like all the competitors he had ridden with a mechanic but, such had been the excitement of the moment, had driven the entire distance himself. Later, after a celebratory drink, he relived his triumphant journey, to all appearances quite unfatigued despite two sleepless nights, though he admitted to some bad moments during the second night, on the return leg between Angoulême and Ruffec:

> I should have left the car at Ruffec to have a bit of rest and taken over again when it came through on its way back from Bordeaux, to bring it back to Paris; but when we got there, I was so astonished at the time we'd made, I couldn't bear to give up my place to another driver, who mightn't have done as well as me. So I went right on to Bordeaux. And I still felt fine, so I stayed put and here I am. It was very dark, and the light, which my mechanic held in his hand, because the support broke along the way, hardly lit up twenty metres ahead, and what with the fatigue, I began to see a crowd of ghosts running along beside us. So I had to slow down, which meant I lost about two hours. But it gets light early now, and the ghosts left.[22]

Later, in the early morning by the Loire, he had felt very cold and sleepy. But what did all that matter? He had triumphed. Hard-working Protestantism (Levassor was of Huguenot origin) and the internal combustion engine had won the day over steam and the arrogant *boulevardier* de Dion, a right-wing Catholic nationalist and fervent anti-Dreyfusard, whose entry failed even to finish when a drive-shaft broke. The mechanical difficulties in the way of mechanical road traction seem to have been in great part overcome,' jubilantly observed *The Engineer*, adding optimistically: 'The time does not seem to be far distant when mechanical power will supersede animal traction upon the road.'[23]

Levassor's moment of triumph is immortalized in a plaque by Camille Lefebvre, erected at the Porte Maillot. But finding it requires determination. For the Porte Maillot, once a charming square with a park in the middle, has (with appropriate irony) foundered beneath the all-engulfing automobile. Here ten lanes of traffic meet in a mighty maelstrom at one of the interchanges leading to the *périphérique*, the terrifying Paris ring-road. In the midst of this endless river of steel the park is just visible, a despairing, muddy anachronism, attainable only via a network of distressingly unconvincing pedestrian crossings. But just as you are about to give up, a crossing actually leads to the garden. And *voilà* the victor, straining forward in high relief towards a respectful semicircle of garden benches between a circus tent and a strange spiked-steel sculpture resembling some monumental municipal hedgehog.

In the interests of artistry, and also no doubt in accurate reflection of social perception, Levassor is depicted alone, his mechanic's place occupied by a large bunch of flowers. Behind him a cheering crowd waves its hats in the air. His suit creased, his shabby hat jammed down over his brow, he crouches for ever at the tiller of his iron-clad car with its battleship rivets, its absurd starting-handle and its solid tyres. The lethal discomfort of that ride! But at least he was spared the endless punctures which were one of the less appealing aspects of early pneumatic tyres. The Michelin brothers, who entered the race in the first automobile to be equipped with such tyres, had to change the entire set every ninety miles. Nevertheless they completed the course, despite water in the petrol tank, broken spokes and gears and a fire; though not within the

7. Levassor's monument, Porte Maillot.

hundred-hour limit.[24] Their car was christened The Lightning, not (evidently!) because of its speed but because it zigzagged, due to the lack of a differential.

Of the nine cars which finished the race in less than a hundred hours, eight were petrol-driven. The only steamer to finish was Bollée's *Nouvelle*, built in 1880 and carrying seven passengers.[25] Three years earlier, Thomas Edison had predicted that the cars of the twentieth century would be powered by gasoline rather than steam or electricity.[26] The Paris–Bordeaux race not only established the car as a serious vehicle, but proved his proposition.

Steam's appeal had always been its simplicity. As a friend pointed out to Maxim, at that point wrestling with an internal combustion ignition that refused to spark, 'If there's water in the boiler, and a fire under the boiler and the boiler doesn't bust, then it's a cinch that the engine has got to run.'[27] The internal combustion engine, by comparison, presented endless problems. Maxim recalled his earliest efforts (in 1892) to put together a powered tricycle, a task he had imagined simple. 'I strove mightily at first to design the general layout – the chain drive, the clutch, its operating mechanism, a change-gear system, gasoline tank and support, engine mounting and engine. But every effort resulted in something that would require an express wagon to contain it. And I had to have it on a little tricycle!'[28] Nevertheless he persevered, knowing that once the problems were overcome the internal combustion engine would be superior on all counts – lighter, faster and with no danger of bursting boilers.

In fact internal combustion was almost as venerable a concept as steam. It made its first appearance in 1807, at Chalon-sur-Saône in Burgundy. Here, in a large, square house, lived the ingenious Nicéphore Niepce, a scientifically inclined aristocrat who wisely spent the turbulent years of revolution and empire keeping his head down and experimenting in his backwater.

vital device of the four-stroke mechanism. But it was not what he was searching for, so he put it to one side, concentrating instead on a different and far less efficient machine, which none the less outperformed Lenoir's and won a gold medal at the 1867 Paris Exposition. Otto and his financial backer built a factory at Deutz, on the opposite bank of the Rhine from Cologne, to manufacture these new engines, and in 1872 Gottlieb Daimler, a trained engineer where Otto was self-taught, came in to manage it.

Otto produced yet another engine, compressing the combustible mixture and operating a four-stroke cycle. Daimler improved this, and may have redesigned it: it carried off all the prizes at the 1878 Paris Exposition, following which Lenoir designed his own four-stroke engine for a Paris company, Rouart. The Deutz company sued for patent infringement, but Rouart dug up some French drawings from 1862 depicting the intake, compression, ignition and exhaust strokes of the piston in an internal combustion engine. They had never been developed, but were enough to satisfy the French courts. So the internal combustion engine entered the public domain. Levassor's winning car was powered by a Daimler engine, the Phénix, designed in Germany and modified in Paris, producing four horsepower with two vertical cylinders.

After the triumph of Paris–Bordeaux, everyone wanted to race cars. It was followed by Paris–Marseille–Paris in 1896, and Paris–Bordeaux and Paris–Amsterdam–Paris in 1897. The bug even hit America, with its undeveloped auto industry and unspeakable roads: the first auto race there was staged in Chicago on Thanksgiving Day 1895, under the auspices of the *Chicago Times-Herald*. Maxim took part, transporting his machine on the train.

The headquarters was at a large race track some miles south of the center of the city. The race track had been selected because it gave the various entrants an opportunity to run their machines and tinker with them. This opportunity for tinkering was important because every machine needed about five hours of tinkering for every hour of running.

In a heavy snowstorm there were only two finishers – the Duryea brothers, who took 'hours and hours', and a German Benz which took even longer.[30]

For professionals such as Levassor and the Duryeas, road racing provided a matchless test of the product and (should it win, or even finish) the best possible advertisement for it. Following Levassor's victory the Panhard et Levassor factory was swamped with orders. 'We receive visitors from morning to night, always English, in a never-ending stream,' wrote Hippolyte Panhard to his father shortly afterwards. 'And every day we receive at least ten letters from England.'[31]

But motor racing also offered other, less tangible attractions. Here was the ultimate answer to the plebeianized bicycle, a new and high-profile sport combining the thrills of novelty and risk with the assurance (since motor racing was, for anyone not a motor manufacturer, prohibitively expensive) of only the wealthiest and most exclusive company. There was also the pleasant certainty, bolstered by open-mouthed crowds, that one was a heroic pioneer. As *Motor* magazine put it following the furore caused by the accident-ridden Paris–Vienna road race in 1902, 'To those anti-motorists . . . who have sufficient intelligence to perceive that motoring is something more than a pastime, who can see far enough into the future to recognise it already as a great national industry . . . the death of one brave motorist today may be the means of saving you from a motorcar accident tomorrow.'[32] Would people imagine closing mines because of accidents? *Motor* wondered, a question clearly expecting the answer no. Such a sport, offering opportunities to play with the ultimate new toy while displaying oneself in a heroic and manly light, could not fail to attract gentlemen of means and leisure.

Prominent among these enthusiasts was William Kissam Vanderbilt, great-grandson of 'Commodore' Cornelius Vanderbilt, a railroad king who in 1877, the year before William K.'s birth, had left $105 million, untaxed. Now the getting was all over, and only spending required. In 1902 Vanderbilt set a record by driving from Monte Carlo to Paris in seventeen hours in his Mercedes 'The Red Devil', and a week later beat Baron Henri de Rothschild in a race on the streets of Paris. He then won auto races in Vienna, Madrid, Newport and Florida, before (in 1908) building his own road, the Long Island Parkway, as a venue for the Vanderbilt Cup Race and a drive for wealthy car enthusiasts on the North Shore of Long Island, where Jay Gatsby built his house of dreams and where Vanderbilt himself was about to build a palace beside Northport Bay (now the Vanderbilt Museum).

Activities such as this were the subject of one of the great books of the age: Thorstein Veblen's *Theory of the Leisure Class*. 'With the superior pecuniary class,' mused Veblen, 'the most imperative of [the] secondary demands of emulation, as well as the one of widest scope, is the requirement of abstention from productive work'[33] – a requirement fulfilled in every particular by William K. Vanderbilt.

There they sit, at opposite corners of some boxing ring of the mind. In the red corner, lanky, languid Veblen with his floppy brown hair and ineradicable Norwegian drawl; in the blue, chipper young William K., busily hatching schemes for the reputable expenditure of his great-grandfather's millions. Veblen dissects Gilded Age society as an entomologist his specimens, from a viewpoint so detached as to be almost extra-terrestrial. Indeed, the society in which he grew up – a Norwegian pioneer community in Wisconsin living in pre-industrial style off what

9. Escaping the masses, 1896.

it produced, pressing its own cheese, churning its own butter, milling its own flour, boiling its own soap, producing its own cloth from its own plants and animals – might as well have existed on a different planet from Manhattan's spendthrift sophistication. 'Overcoats', writes his biographer, 'were made from sections of calfskin. As for overshoes, it was a common thing to have the neighbours come and ask for a section of the hide that they might make a kind of leather foot covering.'[34] And although Veblen graduated to actual shoes, in Wisconsin, psychologically, he remained throughout his life. His ideal was a productive, craftsman-based society, his only substantial possession an old henhouse bought during his years at Stanford University – one of a number of academic jobs in which he spectacularly failed to shine. This he set up as a cabin in the hills behind Palo Alto, using it to entertain his lady friends – for the austere Veblen was twice married and constantly unfaithful: yet another nail in the coffin of his academic career.

There, too, he meditated on the leisure class. And what a godsent solution to the problems of leisure motor cars represented! The moment Levassor dismounted at the Porte Maillot, the car took its place as the ultimate consumer good. Not only did it dispose of large amounts of cash in the most public possible way, but there was, especially given the state of American roads, no danger of its being mistaken for a merely useful object. The belles of Newport, Rhode Island, staged a parade of horseless carriages covered with flowers; the family of millionaire George Jay Gould was photographed clustered around his Panhard Levassor, uniformed chauffeur at the wheel, his five children posed beside their three half-size but fully operable machines. As *Motor* magazine put it, reporting a leap year motoring ball whose favours included black ribbon fobs with a perfectly modelled little gold automobile in place of the conventional seal, matchboxes for the desk shaped like a chauffeur's cap, and little Paris dolls dressed up in long rubber coats, with their curls tucked up under rubber hoods, 'They are expensive, to be sure, but motoring and money have a way of always whisking by together.'[35]

And where, later, status would be indicated by a particular marque (Rolls-Royce = discreet wealth; Ferrari = brash wealth; pink Cadillac convertible = film-star wealth; Bugatti Royale = king), in the early days mere ownership sufficed. To be in the swim you simply had to have a car – and being in the swim was, in America, a matter of the utmost social importance.

In England the upstart cycling masses might have caused the Duke of Teck some momentary alarm; but not only did the car put them back in their place – the location of that place was never really in doubt. As Mrs Hemans' popular hymn so felicitously put it,

God made the high and lowly,
And ordered their estate.

In the United States, however, things were different. There the notion of social standing had had to be created from scratch, almost within living memory. 'How many of the swellest of the swell were anything at all twenty years ago – fifteen years even?' mused *Town Topics* in 1877. 'Where were the Vanderbilts, socially, even five years ago? The Astors had just fifteen years the social start.'[36] And what distinguished Vanderbilts and Astors from the rest? Emphatically not breeding. Money – that was what counted; possessions; *proof* of possessions. Ladies were in the habit of bringing all their jewels to dinner parties and laying those they couldn't wear beside their plates. And automobiles were even better than diamonds: a jewel you could sit inside and parade to the whole world. As one writer observed, 'A home is more visible; but it does not accompany its owner from point to point, and its costs can only be roughly appreciated by a layman.'[37]

10. The Bugatti Royale.

Automobiles, what was more, came complete with yet another highly visible mark of status – a body-servant in the shape of the chauffeur. Such employees were characterized by Veblen as 'lusty slaves'; they included footmen and valets, long part of a wealthy man's retinue. However, where waiting at table required little skill, cars were another, esoteric matter – and this made relations between employers and chauffeurs notoriously uneasy. Few rich men, and fewer rich women, could drive, let alone maintain their cars themselves; the chauffeur therefore occupied a *de facto* position of some power. As the *New York Times* put it, 'Hundreds of chauffeurs have suddenly been raised to places of responsibility from humble and inferior positions . . . Employed by men of wealth, but who are totally ignorant of the intricacies of automobiling, these chauffeurs quickly become the boss in every sense of the word.'[38] And this threat to status was not the only uncomfortable aspect of the relationship. The term 'chauffeur' is a relic of the steam age, deriving from the French *chauffer*, to heat up; it can also be applied, transitively, to a woman, as: *chauffer une femme* – a colloquialism unlikely to set husbands' minds at ease. The American Automobile Association reassured the public that its training schools 'emphasize the moral side of a chauffeur's duty', but *Motor* magazine recommended that no chances be taken. 'Good-looking chauffeurs are beginning to prove a very serious social problem in England, in France and elsewhere on the Continent,' it reported. 'Elderly, homely and married men are taken on in preference.'[39]

Nevertheless uniformed chauffeurs continued to play an important part in the early motoring experience, employed even when (as in the case of W. K. Vanderbilt) the employer was himself a skilled driver. This might seem wasteful, but waste, concluded Veblen, was the whole point. On waste, reputation depended.

No merit would accrue from the consumption of the bare necessities of life, except by comparison with the abjectly poor . . . and no standard of expenditure could result from such a comparison, except the most prosaic and unattractive level of decency.[40]

In the past few years, academic interest has focused once again upon conspicuous consumption and its cousin conspicuous waste. Evolutionary psychologists argue that conspicuous waste plays an important Darwinian role in sexual selection. Evolution, they point out, 'is driven, not just by survival of the fittest, but reproduction of the sexiest'.[41] The excessive display Veblen found so distasteful is, suggests Geoffrey Miller, the human equivalent of the peacock's tail. Both are apparently useless but each is in fact a flamboyant announcement that here is a desirable mate, effortlessly able (for physical reasons in the case of the bird, economic in the case of the human) to sustain excessive expenditure. But where the peacock's tail is all expenditure, with no return other than the possible capture of a mate, the human courtship premium, in addition to its biological function, is also economically advantageous:

> When the Porsche-buyer pays for the car, he transfers money to the seller, who transfers some to the manufacturer, and hence to the manufacturer's employees and shareholders. The only real waste in the production of the Porsche is whatever extra steel, leather, fuel, labour and human ingenuity goes into its production compared to an ordinary car.[42]

Why was Veblen, who was after all an economist, unable to see this? Partly because Darwinism was at that time deeply unfashionable but also (suggests Miller) because, like his contemporaries Wells, Huxley, Haldane and Ernst May, politics blinded him to scientific truth.

If this is the case (and certainly Veblen's position, though never stated outright, is clear from every syllable of his book, implicit in the deadpan drawling grandiloquence that throws into relief the absurdity of the pretensions he discusses while magnifying the enormity of his scorn) it is perhaps because scholarly detachment is a luxury not available to those who live in times of upheaval. And *The Theory of the Leisure Class* was published at just such a moment. It appeared in 1899, only twelve years after the notorious anarchist riots in Chicago's Haymarket and the executions that followed, less than ten years after stone-throwing mobs had swarmed down Pall Mall breaking the windows of gentlemen's clubs. In 1892 the hated anti-union employer Henry Clay Frick had summoned a private army of Pinkertons to quell a strike at the Carnegie Steel Company's Homestead works, leaving thirteen dead, and had in his turn been the object of an assassination attempt by the anarchist Alexander Berkman. 'The dread word "Revolution" is sometimes spoken aloud in jest, and more often whispered in all seriousness,' wrote H. M. Hyndman, leader of the Social Democratic Foundation, in 1884.[43]

In this volatile political climate, reviewers were understandably uncertain how to receive Veblen's book. Was he trying to be funny? What was he advocating? Marxism? The destruction of all superfluities and a return to home-made 'leather foot coverings'? It was not until William Dean Howells hailed his book as an uproarious modern classic in two consecutive issues of the *Atlantic Monthly* that Veblen achieved fame, despite himself.

From a political standpoint, however, Howells' enthusiasm is double-edged. It assumes that Veblen, unlike Marx, is harmless: mere entertainment. And this is a correct assumption. There can be no revolution without passion, no fire without a spark. And Veblen, though scornful, remained detached, both from the busy American dream and from any desire to overturn it. It is precisely this eerie passionlessness that, in combination with its highly contentious subject-matter, imparts such a singular tone to *The Theory of the Leisure Class*.

Others, however, continued to seek out the necessary spark. And it seemed for a while as though the car might provide it. For the car was a provocation, and not only at the psychological level explored by Veblen. It raised thorny questions of ownership and access, not dissimilar to those raised by the enclosures in Britain during the previous century. Then, land in common use since time immemorial had been enclosed by landowners and swallowed into their estates. Now a similar issue arose. Who owned the streets? What were they for?

Streets, when cars first appeared, were not necessarily, or even primarily, roads. Rather they were the arena of public life. New York's first stock market met under a tree on Wall Street. The London poor, Charles Booth noted in his great survey *Life and Labour of the People in London*, gathered in the streets on Sunday afternoons to drink, play cards, dance, promenade and generally enjoy themselves.[44] They were a play-space for children and an ongoing marketplace where street vendors and peddlers, selling from door to door, supplied fridgeless housewives with perishable goods. Naturally streets also accommodated transport, but this was just one of their many uses. Large, fast vehicles such as stage-coaches kept to the few post-roads. For the rest, horse-powered transport moved at a steady pace and announced itself in good time, with a clatter of hooves or rumble of cartwheels.

But cars, unlike horses, give little warning of their coming. And if you don't get out of their way you're dead. So the question they posed was fundamental. Were streets to remain what they had always been, or were they to become roadways, in which the wheel took priority and pedestrians ventured at their peril?

This quarrel was not new. The battle lines had been drawn since the mid-century, when on 12 March 1840 residents of the Kensington district of Philadelphia rioted against a steam railroad being laid down in their street, tearing up the rails and cross-ties and replacing the paving blocks.[45] The streets of Philadelphia had been laid out spaciously to ensure an ample supply of health-giving light and air for their inhabitants. Straight and wide, they offered themselves to new transport possibilities in a way that most European cities, with their tortuous and crowded lanes, did not. The citizens of Kensington, however, did not welcome the change of use. In an early display of what in our day has become known as 'nimbyism' they did what they could to turn back the clock. Public transport was a fine idea – but not in my back yard.

As it happens steam never achieved acceptance as a power source for urban transportation; even when, as sometimes occurred, the engines were disguised as pretend horses to give a more user-friendly appearance, it remained both filthy and dangerous, its unpredictable boilers apt to explode with fatal consequences. The trolley-cars that soon became a feature of nineteenth-century city life were powered first by horses, and later by electricity. But it was the arrival of the bicycle that marked the big change, prefiguring the car in this as in so many other ways. For trams and street railways were confined to their rails, but cyclists could go wherever they wished.

Draped as they are in today's mantle of eco-friendly harmlessness, it is hard to imagine how threatening cyclists must once have seemed. Socialists opposed the asphalting of city streets because this would attract them; children sprinkled glass on the road or threw stones to keep bicycles off their playgrounds. A historian of New York's Lower East Side interviewed a woman whose earliest memory was of being run down in the 1890s, at the age of four, by 'a well-dressed man on a bicycle', she assumed on his way to Wall Street. Far from helping her up, he lectured her about playing in the street – the only place available for play in that stiflingly overpopulated spot. Eighty years later, she still resented that man.[46]

The important point, though, is that despite her resentment she remained alive to tell the tale. If a bicycle knocks you down it may hurt you, but generally speaking you survive. This is emphatically not true of cars. When the first cars began to appear, however, people were unaware of this vital difference. Never having seen cars before, they had no idea of their danger. This was especially true of children, and would remain so for many years. The streets had been their playground; now they must now be shared with a homicidal monster that moved far faster than a child could run. The result was carnage. In 1901 Louis Camille, aged two, became the first child to be killed by a car in New York City. The accident took place on the Lower East Side, and the car in question (like the bicycle so resented by that earlier Lower East Side child) was conveying financiers to their offices in Wall Street. The chauffeur was set upon by the child's neighbours, and rescued by police, who exonerated him, claiming little Louis had run in front of his car.[47] Motorists killed more than a thousand New York children before 1910.[48]

Not surprisingly, non-motorists objected furiously to this new menace. The car was offensive on two counts: it presented a lethal challenge to a fundamental right, and it was not even universally accessible. Almost everyone could afford a bike, but hardly anyone could afford a car. In America early electric carriages cost $3,000, compared with $400 for a first-class horse and buggy;[49] in Britain, where at this time the average weekly wage of an adult man was less than thirty shillings and only 4 per cent of the population left property worth more than £300, a good car (before upkeep) cost £525, and the very smallest £200.[50] And now the rich, who already owned so much of the world, proposed to expropriate the poorest of the poor from the only outdoor space that allowed them some escape from the miserable holes they inhabited. It is hardly surprising, then, that motorists were often physically attacked. In the five years following Louis Camille's death in 1901, the *New York Times* reported thirty-four anti-car incidents, including stonings, firecracker-throwings, shootings and riots. In Chicago a car owner devised a 'kid eradicator' scheme which shot hot air at assailants (how, is not explained).[51] One driver who ran over a child was killed by its father, and in Hoboken, New Jersey, the police were involved in a shoot-out with neighbourhood residents after rescuing a teamster who had run over a child. In the most publicized incident a Mrs Gottschall, being driven through the Italian neighbourhood of East Harlem by her chauffeur in an open electric car, was stoned by a gang of children and knocked out, remaining unconscious for three days. The police came under tremendous pressure to make an arrest, finally hauling in a three-and-a-half year old named Joey Russo. The *New York Times* made much of this; young Russo, it declared, was a member of the fearsome 'rubber nipple' gang (none of whom had yet graduated to drinking from cups).[52]

In Britain, a parliamentary debate was held on the matter. 'A few people claim the right to drive the public off the roads,' declaimed Mr Cathcart Wason, MP for Orkney and Shetland, during a debate on the motoring question in the House of Commons. 'Harmless men, women and children, dogs and cattle, have all got to fly for their lives at the bidding of these slaughtering, stinking engines of iniquity.' In the same debate Sir Brampton Gurden, representing Norfolk North, declared fines inadequate punishment for motoring offences: 'I would almost consent in some cases to the punishment of flogging.'[53]

It sounds excessive: but motorists' behaviour invited excess. And no one seemed able or willing to curb it. For the section of society from which motorists were drawn was the very section accustomed to do the curbing. They were the ones who made the rules and set the standards of behaviour. Any attempt to regulate *them* was seen as an insult, and they used all their considerable muscle to defeat such socialistic notions. The New York based Automobile Club of America actually wrote New York State's first motoring laws, and resisted the imposition even of a minimum driving age until 1919. Most American states did not license drivers until the 1920s, which meant that licence revocation could not be used to enforce safe driving.[54] In New York City a speed limit of twelve mph was introduced, then thrown out for the much less safe state limit of twenty-five mph. In Connecticut all speed limitations were voided.[55] And in Britain drivers declared war on the police, resisting all attempts to set or enforce speed limits. The Automobile Association's secretary actually wrote to *The Times* setting out his organization's tactics:

> I have the pleasure to inform motorists that the heavily trapped part of the Portsmouth Road from Esher to the 19th milestone will henceforth be patrolled by our cyclist scouts on every day of the week. This is our first step towards that daily protection which it is the aim of our committee to establish, and funds permitting, continue on every important road until the time shall arrive when police traps cease from troubling and the stop watch is at rest.[56]

Motorists, ran the subtext, were gentlemen; and gentlemen could and should be relied on to regulate themselves: they had no need of outside help. As for those occasions when motorists undeniably misbehaved, this (asserted *The Times*) was because they were upstarts, not typical motorists. *These* people should indeed be punished: 'for people of this order the law is an educational influence of the highest value.'[57]

But the position that 'gentlefolk' never misbehaved and never told lies proved problematic.

> It is a significant fact, [wrote the perplexed Chief Constable of Huntingdonshire, himself a gentleman], that two gentlemen of education and position, who have during the past quarter been proceeded against, when exceeding 20 mph passed horses and cars . . . which they subsequently declared they never saw. It being impossible to doubt their word, the question arises as to whether great mischief may not be done, by want of attention on the part of drivers, or their inability to see what is on the road.[58]

Why could one not doubt their word? Because one had to believe members of one's own class. If not, what would become of the status quo? What, demanded Henry Norman MP, would be the effect on 'young constables learning their duties' of hearing the word of one in authority ignored while the magistrate remarked that motorists must learn to obey the law, and be obliged to pay 'forty shillings and costs'?[59]

This patrician attitude was not confined to class-ridden Britain. As late as 1911 the *New York Times* blamed a wave of accidents not on wealthy owners and their chauffeurs but on new drivers such as 'the East Side butcher who buys a used car and joy rides'.[60] Even in America, it seemed, cars were deemed a rightful perquisite of the upper classes. And if motorists wanted, as in Hempstead, Long Island, to spread oil on the main street so that, mixing with the dirt, it would improve the surface for an auto race, they did so; the public's spattered carpets and furniture and oil-covered shoes and horses were none of their concern.[61]

» » »

Nowhere were the interests of motorists more contentiously opposed to those of the general public than in road racing. For it soon became clear that these races were terribly dangerous. Too dangerous, concluded the British *Horseless Age* as early as 1897: 'If people want to take the risks and the public demands them, let them be held on race tracks, built for the purpose.'[62]

But the plea fell on deaf ears. Road races might be lethal but they were wonderful proving-grounds, garnering incomparable publicity for both future prospects and present attainments. And whatever the danger, the public adored them. The first Vanderbilt Cup in 1908 attracted an unprecedented crowd of two hundred thousand. As it happened there were no fatalities; and the *New York Times*, until then critical of cars and an upholder of pedestrians' rights, praised 'The All-Conquering Auto', urged New York mothers to accept responsibility for keeping their children off the streets, and even opposed speed limits. And what if there *had* been casualties? People only went to auto races in the hope of seeing someone killed, opined the famous racing driver Barney Oldfield.[63]

He may have been right: but there was a difference between watching drivers dice with death on a specially built course (all horse and commercial traffic was banned from the limited-access Vanderbilt Parkway) and being killed in the name of sport on the public roads. In the Paris–Berlin race in 1901, Brasier, at the wheel of a Mors car, hit and killed a small boy. The news-agency report of the accident concluded coolly: 'Brasier continued on his way, having been delayed for forty-five minutes':[64] a typical example of the organizers' attitude to lower forms of life such as bystanders and mechanics. Waldeck-Rousseau, the Minister of the Interior, stated that there would be no more racing on French roads. But he was disregarded: casualties were, it seemed, as yet insufficient to outweigh commercial advantage and special pleading. Another race, Paris–Vienna, took place in 1902, with yet more deaths. The winner,

Marcel Renault, brother of Louis, caused 'considerable astonishment . . . when he failed to stop his car in accordance with directions and flew past the officials at full speed. Our correspondent thinks he must have failed to observe the waving flag . . .'[65] – not a good omen for anyone unfortunate enough to share the road with him, though his victory brought in the customary deluge of orders. Renault died three years later in a race from Paris to Madrid: blinded by a cloud of dust raised by the car ahead, he ran into a tree.

The number of dead in the Paris–Madrid race was never admitted. The official tally was six, but that counted only the drivers. When W. K. Vanderbilt added in mechanics and bystanders, the figure rose to fifteen. Vanderbilt himself was disqualified at the start (once again the place d'Armes at Versailles) for having approached the line on the wrong side of the timer, knocking over, on his own estimation, about a hundred spectators perched on boxes and barrels. None, fortunately, was much hurt – or not badly enough for him to record it. 'There was a considerable hub-bub for a while, but gradually the officials quietened down,' was his only comment on this incident.[66] Mortality, let alone the mere possibility of mortality, paled in the pursuit of conspicuous leisure. Vanderbilt recalls chatting to his 'personal friend' Lorraine Barrow just before the latter set off. 'He was in splendid form and hoped to win. Unfortunately, in trying to avoid a dog, he ran full speed into a tree, his car being split in two, his mechanic killed, and he himself mortally injured.'[67] Unfortunate, indeed. In the worst accident of the race, at Libourne, 'a young boy, getting in the way of a machine, was seized by a soldier, who saved the boy but was killed himself, and the driver, trying to avoid both, ran off the road and upset, killing himself, his mechanic and two bystanders'.[68] After public protests, the race was stopped at Bordeaux.

As he ploughed nonchalantly through the spectators at

the place d'Armes, did echoes of nemesis resound, however remotely, in Vanderbilt's mind? Versailles of all places embodies the alarming – indeed, fatal – potential of such incidents. Vast and grandiose, it stands as a monument to certainty: specifically, the certainty of Louis XIV, the Sun King, who declared that 'L'état, c'est moi.' Over half a century, Louis transformed a pretty hunting lodge into the epic of stone and glass, topiary and water that we see today. A century later, as France careered headlong towards bankruptcy, the then monarchs Louis XVI and Marie-Antoinette turned their backs on reality and created a make-believe world inside the world that was Versailles. The Queen ordered the construction of a hamlet and little farm where she could play at dairy maids, a mockery (or so it must have seemed) of the smelly, toilsome realities of rural life. And that mockery received its crushing come-uppance when the royal dairy maid and her unhappy spouse were beheaded in the cause of liberty, equality and fraternity. Would the car-owning classes, equally oblivious to most people's realities, suffer a similar fate?

It seemed not impossible. That, certainly, was the view of Woodrow Wilson, future President of the United States. In 1906, Wilson, then president of Princeton University, looked into the future and did not like what he saw. In a widely reported speech he announced darkly that 'nothing has spread socialistic feeling in this country more than the automobile.'

It so happened that that very year W. K. Vanderbilt and his wife were the focus of just the kind of incident Wilson had in mind. Driving through Pontedera, a small Tuscan town between Florence and Pisa, they knocked down a boy of six. They were driving, says Vanderbilt, very slowly, and the car stopped before it ran the boy over. But even though (according to Vanderbilt) the child was not badly hurt, a lynch-mob quickly gathered, and set about him.

11. Mr and Mrs W. K. Vanderbilt with one of their motors, 1904. The gentleman at the back is not named. He is presumably the chauffeur, or some such mechanical unperson.

I stopped the engine, but before I could move was seized by the mob and pulled from my seat . . . the men around me kicked, punched, pushed and tried to choke me . . . I seized my gun, but someone from behind wrenched it from me . . . The mob seemed to be wilder than ever and numbered about four hundred . . . I finally beat them off and took refuge in a shop. On entering same two or three men seized me by the throat and others drew knives. I had a revolver in my pocket but did not try to draw same. I noticed two or three men fighting for me . . . I managed to beat off two attacks successfully when the crowd approached for the third time, most of them with knives drawn. Noting this I seized my gun, but someone from behind snatched it from me . . . At that moment someone pushed me into a closet and drew a curtain in front of me . . .[69]

His life was saved by the arrival of the police, who, themselves understandably nervous, arrested him, handcuffed him and locked him in the police station. There he was at least safe from the crowd, and soon after was extracted and entertained by the local mayor. He finished the journey by train, leaving his chauffeur, doubtless no less shaken than himself, to meet him in Monte Carlo with the car. We are not told whether the chauffeur experienced any difficulties driving out of Pontedera.

Perhaps Vanderbilt played down the injury to the child, perhaps (as he implies) the mob simply swelled out of control, enjoying a fight for fighting's sake. Or it may be that the injured child was merely the precipitating factor, an excuse to vent less explicit furies. As when he ploughed through the crowd at Versailles, Vanderbilt seems to have been almost bent on provoking some sort of uprising. His account uncannily echoes the incident in Dickens's *A Tale of Two Cities* in which the death of a poor child beneath the wheels of a nobleman's carriage – the symbol of aristocratic oppression – is one of the sparks leading to revolution.

Thoughts of revolution would surely not have seemed far-fetched to the citizens of Pontedera. Even now *Toscana la rossa* votes solidly communist; in Vanderbilt's day it was a land of subsistence peasants and large landowners operating the hated *mezzadria* sharecropping system. So the rich were not popular. And now came this wealthy foreigner, forcing them off their own streets and almost killing a child. No wonder Vanderbilt aroused their rage. He was lucky to escape with his life. Where would it end? While cars remained a rich man's luxury, tears seemed the only answer.

Thomas Edison was more sanguine. If everyone had a car, then no one would feel hard done by; and in his view everyone would certainly soon have a car. In December 1895 he prophesied that 'ten years from now you will be able to buy a horseless vehicle for what you would have to pay today for a wagon and a pair of horses . . . It is only a question of a short time when the carriages and trucks of every large city will be run with motors.'[70] The *Horseless Age*, reporting this interview, agreed with Edison in all but the timescale, which it thought unnecessarily pessimistic, showing 'that he is not aware of the amount of intellectual energy that is being concentrated upon the motor vehicle problem in America'.[71]

Predictably, the British took a less sanguine view of the car's egalitarian future. In 1897 the *Autocar* reported witheringly that

A New York daily recently published a ridiculous story, in which the names of Thomas A. Edison and the General Electric Co. figured, and the statement was made that the latter were preparing to flood the market with motor carriages at $100 apiece. Mr Edison himself was represented as indulging in a great deal of loose and extravagant talk about motors and motor vehicles, but the most pre-posterous part of it is that in which the Wizard is credited with saying that 'a serviceable, light vehicle to carry two or even four persons can be made at a cost of from \$100 to \$125.'

This, spluttered the *Autocar*, was 'nonsense'.[72] Two years later the *Literary Digest* considered that although the price of the horseless carriage, 'at present a luxury for the wealthy', would 'probably fall in the future, it will never, of course, come into as common use as the bicycle'.[73]

As the nineteenth century ended and the twentieth got into its stride, Edison's prophecy continued unfulfilled. The car remained an instrument of pleasure for the well-off, and of lethal oppression for many. Would ordinary people let themselves be run off the streets? Or would they unite to the call of Karl Marx and sweep the motorists and all they represented into oblivion? The Duke of Teck had stupidly misread the bicycle. Would his own class, using the car as invasively as those cyclists he had so roundly condemned, provoke the very revolution he had feared?

So began the long war of attrition between the powered wheel and other forms of street life. Its progress may be moni-tored in the habits of children. Once they were kings of the street: until the 30s, in some places even the 40s, it was their playground and their domain. With the rise of motor vehicles, specially built play areas denoted the end of this freedom; but even then children were not completely banished. I know this because in the 1950s, from the age of seven, I used to cycle to school. We lived on a main road, already heavily trafficked. Nevertheless I and my friends continued to pedal, mornings and afternoons, our heads devoid of helmets or second thoughts. And anyone who didn't cycle walked. Only one of my classmates was regularly delivered and collected by car, a circumstance so exceptional that I can still remember not only the colour of that car – a bright turquoise – but its registration letters, MRO.

When did this cease to be the norm? As recently as 1971, 80 per cent of seven- and eight-year-old children in Britain still made their way unsupervised to school.[74] No longer. Now every school gate is besieged by cars, and the solitary walk to school – once the first step along the road to self-reliance – is regarded as an aberration. When, in the 80s in a quiet country town, I dispatched my six-year-old daughter to dawdle her way alone, other mothers shook their heads and took me to task. 'Aren't you afraid?' one asked me accusingly. What of? 'That someone might attack her.' Such a thing had never crossed my mind (and never happened in all the years my daughter walked to school). That mother might more reasonably have cited the dangerous crush of cars around the school gate, though in fact statistics show that accidents involving children happen relatively rarely on the journey to school. But no statistics would have satisfied her: the fear she was stating was greater, more inchoate, than any mere reality. She was quite simply afraid of the streets. Once everyone's front yard, they have become alien spaces haunted by terrors. And this fear has become institutional-ized: British government guidelines now warn parents that it is irresponsible to allow children under the age of twelve out of the house unsupervised.[75] Are the death-dealing bogeymen real or imagined? It doesn't matter: the result is imprisonment.

In 1904 Filson Young prophesied that 'In a little while, a generation of children will grow up wary of motor cars, and trained, poor mites, in the taking of cover.'[76] This process of education took time, and exacted its toll. A Ford joke, *c.* 1915, reflected the grim reality:

Sunday schoolteacher: What little boy can tell me the difference between the 'quick' and the 'dead'?

12. The intruding motor scatters all before it:
L'Effroi (The Terror), Paul Gervais, 1904.

Willie: Please, ma'am, the 'quick' are the ones that get
out of the way of automobiles; the ones that don't
are 'dead'.

The learning curve is reflected by the children of Muncie,
Indiana. Driven from the street to the sidewalks by 1925, they
were soon forced even further into retreat: in 1935 a newspaper
editorial headlined 'Sidewalk Play is Dangerous' observed that
'It is safe to say that children under the age of eight years should
not be permitted to play upon sidewalks.'[77]

Today the grim harvest is diminished, though traffic has
increased a millionfold or more. Three times more British children died in road accidents in 1922, before they had learned to
take care, than in any one year during the 1990s.[78] No doubt this
reflects both increased road sense and improved hospitals. But
does it not also signal the final victory of the car? Pedestrianism
is still the most common mode of getting around Western cities.
But one step off the crowded pavement, and you take your life
in your hands. The car's priority is absolute, universally accepted
as a matter of practical necessity. Almost without discussion,
yesterday's freedoms have been swept away.

The once contentious nature of this state of affairs has been
so long relegated to the mists of history that it hardly now
seems a pressing question; barely, indeed, a question at all.
But surely the freedom of the streets is too important an issue
to be decided thus piecemeal, by *force majeure*? Perhaps, at
last, we are beginning to recognize what we have lost. Perhaps, too, it is no coincidence that the loose-knit association of
anarchists which, in the interests of a changed world, brought
the City of London to a halt in June 1999, undermined the
World Trade Organization in Seattle the same year, and began
the new millennium by skiing to the attack against the global-
izing bastions of Davos, has given itself the title Reclaim the
Streets.

Chapter Three

Greenfield Village to the Rouge: The Epic Journey of Henry Ford

Who would believe that Detroit was renowned for its gardens? But so it once was. How beautiful it must have been, set on the strait (*l'étroit*) from which it takes its name, between Lakes Huron and Erie – a strategic situation that soon did for the gardens, as the town swelled from a trappers' settlement into a busy port and manufacturing centre serving the rich, forested hinterland of southern Michigan.

Its first manufacturing boom occurred during the Civil War. The expanding workforce needed a transit system, and rails were laid down for horse-drawn trams, replaced in 1888 by a network of electric streetcars. You could ride the streetcar system for a flat 6¢ – half that if you bought a book of eight tickets. In 1906, Detroiters made 148 million streetcar trips. Routes ran to Port Huron, Grosse Pointe, Farmington, Ypsilanti and Ann Arbor. As in other cities they seemed a safe and profitable bet, and investors flocked to buy a piece of them.

But, as everyone knows, Detroit became Motown: a place where almost every job connects in some way to the motor industry. And the notion of mass transit for autoworkers is a contradiction in terms. Who, if not they, should buy cars? The streetcars had been useful, ensuring workforce attendance even when the weather was bad (as in Detroit it often is). But as soon as car ownership for all became a serious possibility, the industry moved to kill off the competition; not difficult, since it controlled it, as in Detroit it controlled everything. By 1913 two of the three street-railway commissioners were auto executives; in 1922 the city, led by Mayor James Couzens – Henry Ford's old friend and one-time business manager – took over the Detroit United Railway. After that it was only a matter of time.

In the city of the automobile, everyone was too entranced by cars to care. They hadn't just seen the future – they were making it. When Ransom Olds declared that 'The automobile has brought more progress than any article ever manufactured,' who in Detroit was about to disagree? The inter-urban system, in 1919 so widespread that you could ride it to Toledo or Cleveland and thence throughout the Midwest, fell into disuse. The rails were asphalted over, and the routes became today's freeways. The result is a city of over a million people, an old-style city with a downtown core surrounded by suburbs – and no mass transit system. None. The *only* way to get into or around Detroit is by car.

Driving in from the municipal airport, the auto industry spreads itself beneath your wheels. Which will you take, General Motors Boulevard, Ford Freeway, Fisher Freeway, Chrysler Freeway, Cadillac Boulevard? If you are making for the city centre you will probably choose the Detroit Industrial Freeway, Interstate 94. In that case, you will soon see signs directing you to Dearborn. And if you take the Dearborn turn-off, you will find yourself driving plumb through the split personality of Henry Ford, country boy and industrial magnate, ruthless tycoon and worker's friend, visionary idealist and bigot, quintessential American hero. On your left, the manicured lawns and mellow brick courts of Greenfield Village and the Henry Ford Museum, a monument to the rural America of Ford's boyhood. And away to your right, the instrument

13. The Detroit freeways, 1950.

of its destruction: the towering stacks of the Rouge, the great Ford industrial complex on the banks of the eponymous river. As for his handiwork, take Sir Christopher Wren's advice and look around you. Or drive, as I did, to Ford World Headquarters, where several small farms' worth of space is devoted to car-parking. Park, as I did, in some seemingly memorable spot – beside this tree, that entranceway to your left, a grassy incline just ahead – enter the building, transact your business, emerge some hours later and hopefully retrace your steps. And now try to find your car. Being a rental car, you have the haziest recollection of its make and colour. You *thought* it was dark green, but there are such an infinite number of dark green cars. You thought it was a Chrysler – yes, it was; definitely, a Chrysler. But what sort of Chrysler? And you didn't bother to note its number, as there's a number on your keyring, and you assumed that was it. But when you get to what should be your car, in what seems to be the right place, that isn't the number at all (though the car is green, and a Chrysler). Suddenly certainty falls away. Perhaps it was grey, and an Olds. Or black, and a Chevy . . .

I am not easily given to despair, but I despaired. Was I doomed to spend my life in this place, searching the ranks for I knew not quite what? I stopped a friendly-looking man and explained my predicament. I did this often during my stay in Detroit, starting with the boy at the airport car-rental lot. He showed me to my car, and before he could make his escape I already had a thousand questions for him. Where were the headlights, the windscreen wipers – the *gearshift*? Was this model so modern that it worked by telepathy? He explained pityingly: the lights were the button on the far left by the glove compartment, the gearshift that paddle on the steering-column, and a dashboard light just visible behind the steering-wheel told you what gear you were in. Unfortunately, as he also explained, the dashboard lights were constantly unreliable, warning of non-existent flat tyres, failing to indicate whether headlights were on or off; true to form the gear indicator took its leave in a crowded multi-storey car park, drive and reverse locatable only by experiment at a moment when forward led straight to a retaining wall three inches ahead. And now the damned car itself had vanished, and how was I ever to locate it? 'It happens all the time,' said my interlocutor sympathetically. 'People are always losing their cars here.' So how did they find them? 'Press your panic button,' he said. My *panic button*? I was already panicked: I needed no button. He pointed to a red horn symbol on my keyring. So that's what that was! I pressed: and as if by magic a car began braying and flashing its lights. It was the car I'd first thought of; for some reason the number on the keyring and its registration were two quite different things. Dear reader, should you ever chance to visit Ford World Headquarters, do not leave your vehicle without noting its precise make, colour, registration and location. You could perhaps take a photo. And don't forget the panic button.

Detroit was not, as it happens, the first home of American automobility. In 1899, the first year in which the United States Census of Manufacturers published separate figures for the automobile industry, most of the 2,500 motor vehicles manufactured came from New England, where there were ten firms producing electric and/or steam-powered cars. But these were soon overtaken by the gasoline car; and then the Midwest came into its own. Manufacturers here always preferred the internal combustion engine, partly because the region's awful roads were quite impassable to electrics, partly because this was a sparsely settled rural area with as yet little access to the electricity essential for recharging batteries. Gasoline, on the other hand, was a fuel universally available, and stationary gasoline engines, locally made, were widely used on farms. The region's hardwood forests had also made it a centre for carriage- and wagon-manufacturing; so that manufacturers of gasoline cars in the Midwest had ready access to suppliers of bodies, wheels and engines. And these included some quite remarkable engineers, among them the Duryea brothers in Illinois, Alexander Winton in Cleveland, and in Michigan Ransom E. Olds, William C. Durant and Henry Ford. The Dodge brothers were young machinists moving from plant to plant in Detroit, the Fisher brothers and the Studebakers were working in the carriage factories, and Henry Leland was developing his precision skills. By 1903–4, attracted by Detroit's open-shop policy and ready supply of unorganized labour, southern Michigan boasted twenty-two automobile manufacturers, whose 9,125 units accounted for 42.1 per cent of American motor vehicle production.[1]

Henry Ford was then just forty. His father, an Irish emigrant, had settled at Dearborn, just outside Detroit, because other family members were already there, and began as all pioneers did, by clearing his land. He loved farming for the independence and self-respect it gave him, and hoped and assumed that Henry, his oldest surviving son, would join him in his enterprise. When Henry married, his father's wedding present was a forested tract. But Henry already knew that farming was not for him. He cut the trees, built a cabin, and moved on. The only aspect of farm life that interested him was the machinery: everything else bored and frustrated him. He reserved particular scorn for livestock. In an interview given in 1940, when he was seventy-seven, he reiterated his doubts about farm animals. He questioned whether they would qualify for survival, and thought that 'one of these days we would probably get quit of them'. He thought the cow's chance 'particularly thin'[2] (milking had been a chore he especially loathed); one of the soybean's multifarious attractions for him was its capacity to produce synthetic milk. Leaving these unsatisfactory creatures behind him, he made for the big city.

He was therefore present when, on 6 March 1896, the

first horseless carriage Detroit had ever seen was given a demonstration run. Its builder was Charles B. King, who told the *Detroit Free Press* that these machines 'are much in vogue among the English aristocracy, and will undoubtedly soon be here'. The *Free Press* pronounced it 'a most unique machine . . . When in motion the connecting rods fly like lightning, and the machine is capable of running seven or eight miles an hour.'[3]

Ford, by then chief engineer at the Edison Illuminating Company's Detroit plant, followed its progress intently. He had seen one of these machines before – in 1893, at the World's Columbian Exposition in Chicago, where a prize had been offered for the best mechanical road vehicle. There were only four entries – two electrics, a steamer built for circus parades and an imported Daimler – but although they had received little public attention Ford had studied them with fascination.[4] Now King's wagon rekindled his interest in horseless carriages. He began to experiment in earnest with a machine of his own, working until around eleven every evening after his day at Edison was over. 'We often wondered when Henry Ford slept,' said a friend of those days, 'because he was putting in long hours working, and when he went home at night he was always experimenting or reading.'[5] But 'I cannot say that it was hard work,' Ford characteristically remarked years later. 'No work with interest is ever hard.'[6] He liked to tell a story of three men working together on a building site. Asked what they were doing, one replied, 'I am getting $2 a day,' the second, 'I am laying brick,' the third, 'I am building a church.' 'And that,' observed his interviewer, 'is about as near as anyone can ever come to explaining the success of Henry Ford.'[7]

By the end of May his machine was almost ready. He called it a 'quadricycle'; it was altogether smaller and lighter than King's test wagon had been. After several sleepless nights of final adjustments, it took to the road in the early hours of 4 June 1896.

It was raining. Clara Ford, armed with an umbrella, came out to watch; a friend, Jim Bishop, rode ahead with his bicycle to warn any horse-drawn vehicles of the imminent apparition. Ford put the clutch lever in neutral and spun the flywheel. When the motor came to life he climbed on to the bicycle seat, seized the steering rod, put the car in low, and started off. After a few hundred yards it suddenly stopped: a spring had failed. Ford and Bishop ran to the nearby Edison plant and found a new one. Some guests from the Cadillac Hotel gathered around, 'wonder[ing] what kind of an infernal machine this thing was, and who was crazy enough to spend a lot of time and money on such a contraption'. The new spring was inserted, the car restarted. Ford and Bishop, satisfied, drove back to Ford's house, where they retired 'for a few winks of sleep'. Then Clara served breakfast, and it was time to leave for work.[8]

That August, Ford was sent as a delegate to the seventeenth annual convention of the Association of Edison Illuminating Companies in New York, where for the first time he met the great inventor who would become perhaps his closest friend, though the relationship was never one of equals: Edison always called Ford 'Henry', but was never anything other than 'Mr Edison' to Ford. They were introduced by Ford's Detroit boss, Alexander Dow, a dedicated electrics man who saw no future in gasoline as a motive power and hoped Edison would support his side of the argument. However, Edison, as we know, thought differently: it was less than a year since he had made his prediction that the cars of the twentieth century would be powered by gasoline rather than electricity.[9] Far from scoffing, he called Ford over and questioned him about his machine. Ford explained its workings, sketching on the back of a menu as he talked. Finally Edison 'thumped the table so that the dishes around him jumped. "Young man," he pronounced, "that's the thing! You have it – the self-contained unit carrying its own fuel with it! Keep at it!"'[10]

Ford sold his first car for $200 and started upon another. By July 1899 he was looking for backing to start manufacturing. The previous month a wealthy lumber merchant had promised that, if Ford could drive him on a tour around the neighbouring countryside and then satisfactorily back home, he would put up some capital. Ford did so, and the manufacturer proved as good as his word. 'Reaching home without accident he was abundantly satisfied. "Well," he remarked, "now we will organize a company." '[11] And on 5 August 1899, articles for the Detroit Motor Company were filed with the county clerk.

At this point Ford had to choose. Would he remain with his secure job at Edison, or work full-time on automobiles?

The Edison Company offered me the general superintendency of the company, but only on condition that I would give up my gas engine and devote myself to something really useful. I had to choose between my job and my automobile. I chose the automobile, or rather I gave up the job – there was really nothing in the way of a choice. For already I knew the car was bound to be a success.[12]

Success, however, eluded him. A number of companies, notably Duryea, Winton and Olds, were already successfully producing gasoline vehicles; nearly one hundred other makes of car had appeared; and Ford's had no especially new or outstanding features. In 1900 the Detroit Motor Company, like so many others, failed.

Ford now turned to the idea of racing, where, as Levassor, Renault and Benz had already discovered, both reputation and orders were to be acquired. He built his first racer in 1901 and rode it to hair-raising victory over an icy track at Detroit's first motor race meeting while the town watched and Clara cheered. By 1902 he was engaged on two more cars, 999 and The Arrow – the first for racing, the second for sale. These were built with the help of a skilled young draughtsman named C. (for 'Childe') Harold Wills, in an unheated shop during the early spring of 1902. Wills, like Ford, preferred practical experience to book learning: 'If it's in a book, it's at least four years old and I don't have any use for it,' he would say.[13] When the shop got so cold that neither of them could hold a pencil or tool, they would don boxing-gloves and spar until they had warmed up.[14]

'999' had a 70 horsepower motor, a steel and wood body and four cylinders. The roar of those cylinders alone was enough to kill a man. There was only one seat. One life to a car was enough. I tried out the cars. Cooper [Ford's friend Tom Cooper, a champion racing cyclist] tried out the cars. We let them out at full speed. I cannot quite describe the sensation. Going over Niagara Falls would have been but a pastime after a ride in one of them.[15]

Who, though, was to do the actual racing? Not Ford. After his previous terrifying experience on the ice he had declared he would never race again: 'Once is Enough', as the *Detroit Evening News* headline put it.[16] Cooper, too, declined the honour of dicing with death in the 999. He suggested his erstwhile cycling partner, Barney Oldfield, and Oldfield accepted with the observation that he 'might as well be dead as dead broke'.[17] Oldfield won spectacularly: he went on to become the leading racing driver of the day, and is reported to have told Ford that each of them 'made' the other – 'But I did much the best job of it.'[18]

Ford did not stick to his non-racing resolve. In February 1904, *Motor* magazine reported 'the most recent sensation in fast motoring . . . the Henry Ford mile in 0.39 seconds, that well-known maker and driver having guided the famous "999", once the delight of Barney Oldfield, over an ice course on an inlet of Lake St. Clair . . . The "999" zig-zagged a good part of

14. Henry Ford and Barney Oldfield with a 999, 1902.

the mile, once dashing through a snow-bank, but continued to live the distance without a catastrophe.' But this was pure self-indulgence: his racing career had already done its job, attracting a backer who would enable him to put what the *Detroit Journal* called a 'family horse'[19] on the market. In 1903, the Ford Motor Company was established. It consisted, as one disillusioned but still admiring ex-employee would later put it, of 'an astonishing group of men, none of them young, none of them hitherto successful, [who] came together and fused into that unbeatable combination.'[20] There were two mechanics, the Dodge brothers; Alexander Malcomson, a coal merchant who was the firm's principal backer; James Couzens, Malcomson's chief clerk, who would go on to become Mayor of Detroit and Senator for Michigan; and Henry Ford himself. As for Detroit, it was already America's most motorized city, with eight hundred cars in use.[21] And an American motor style was being established, very different from that of Europe.

» » »

American and European (particularly British) approaches to manufacturing had been diverging since 1785. In that year the British issued an edict forbidding, under threat of heavy penalties, the export to America of any tool, machine or engine, or the emigration of any individual connected with the iron industry or manufacturing trades associated with it. The intention was to ensure that the newly independent ex-colony remained permanently dependent on British expertise and manufactured goods, so that Britain could maintain both a tame market and a permanent source of raw materials. But the effect was quite the opposite. Unable to import the machines they needed, Americans were spurred to invent their own; and these were naturally tailored to American requirements. Where Europe's weight of tradition favoured conservatism, America welcomed innovation.

Europe's skilled and organized craftsmen feared and distrusted newfangled machinery; America, with skilled labour in short supply, welcomed it. With the right machine, unskilled labour could do the job. But it would be a different job; *part* of a job. American and British machine tools reflected these divergent approaches. British machine tools were massive, built to last and to serve any number of different purposes; American, relatively small and designed with one particular job in mind. So long as they performed that job perfectly, it did not matter that they could do nothing else. And the same went for American labour.

This, of course, is the essence of the production line. It is also the secret of interchangeable parts, essential for mass production since without them quick repairs are impossible. However skilled a craftsman, the absolute accuracy needed for true interchangeability can be guaranteed only by a machine. A part, whether it be a bolt or an axle, must fit not just its particular gun, or sewing machine – or car – but any similar article or socket. Thomas Jefferson had imported this idea to America from France, where the engineer Le Blanc pioneered the system in the production of muskets (the armaments industry spearheading technological advances then as now). Muskets, of course, were vitally important for both food and defence on the American frontier, and interchangeable parts, purchasable at any store, essential for their maintenance. 'I put several [muskets] together myself taking pieces at hazard as they came to hand,' Jefferson reported, 'and they fitted in the most perfect manner. [Le Blanc] effects it by tools of his own contrivance, which at the same time abridge the work, so that he thinks he shall be able to furnish the muskets two livres cheaper than the common price.'[22]

In the automobile market, the effects of these very different approaches were soon apparent. In Europe the car was a luxury hand-built product aimed at a wealthy and discerning market. A Rolls-Royce, a Mercedes, a Daimler or Bugatti was an artwork – a connection perhaps most overt in the (admittedly extreme) case of Bugatti, each of whose cars, treasured from generation to generation, is listed along with its whereabouts and provenance in *The Bugatti Book*. Ettore Bugatti, their designer, had in fact desired above all to follow in the footsteps of his father, a well-known painter, sculptor, furniture designer and architect whose Paris house he remembered as full of musicians and painters. It was the second Bugatti boy, Rembrandt, who wanted to be a mechanic. Ettore, however, soon recognized that Rembrandt possessed the artistic gift (he went on to become a successful sculptor, exhibiting at the Louvre in 1910) while he himself was a natural mechanic. Having discovered this he abandoned brushes and palette to pursue 'a new kind of art, the mechanical',[23] his triumphant debut being welcomed with the words, 'The son of an artist, he himself is an artist to his very being.'[24]

It was products and attitudes such as these that induced scepticism in Europe when Edison prophesied mass automobility, and provoked Woodrow Wilson's despairing 1906 prognostications of imminent automobile-induced revolution. In fact, however, this outburst revealed only the narrow, East Coast patrician circles in which Wilson moved. For them cars remained a European luxury, and the notion that ordinary people might one day routinely own such things appeared absurd. Indeed, as late as 1910, when the public was flocking to automobile shows and the Model T was sweeping America, 'several brokerage houses declined to bid on offerings of municipal bonds by Western cities, explaining that these municipalities had "too many automobiles in proportion to population" and were therefore unsafe credit risks'.[25] The bankers Spencer, Trask were appalled when faced with a calculation that over $300 million would be spent on cars that year. 'Thousands are running cars who cannot afford to do so without mortgaging property,' they fretted, 'while thousands of others are now investing in motors who formerly invested in bonds.'[26]

But this was the last gasp of a vanishing world. Most American car manufacturers, seeing the future more clearly, were from the start geared to a mass market. As early as 1896, at the very outset of the automobile age and ten years before Wilson's speech, motoring pioneer Charles E. Duryea had written a letter to the editor of the *Horseless Age* setting out his populist pitch with regard to the prize offered at a New York auto race later that year:

> It seems to the writer that this is offering a premium for speed, whereas the crying need today is not speed but better construction and better operation, and possibly to suit the desires of the masses, less cost . . . We require in the horseless carriage a mechanism so simple as not to get out of order easily or give trouble to the unskilled operator, and a carriage so arranged as to be comfortable to use, viz, it should be clean, free from objectionable odor, vibration or possible danger. If it is simple in construction it will, in all probability, become cheap in cost, when the supply approximates the demand, so the item of cost is not a large one . . .[27]

The person generally credited with the realization of this dream is of course Henry Ford, whose Model T transformed America. The autobiographical *My Life and Work*, ghosted for him in 1925, places his epiphany in 1909:

> I will build a motor car for the great multitude. It will be large enough for the family but small enough for the individual to run and care for . . . But it will be so low in price that no man making a good salary will be unable to

own one – and enjoy with his family the blessings of hours of pleasure in God's great open spaces.[28]

Ford's ghostwriter, Samuel Crowthers, goes on to say that this announcement was greeted with derision.

The truth was (as so often) more complex and less dramatically satisfying. Revelation certainly did not descend like the angel Gabriel in 1909. As early as 1903 Ford had recognized the importance of mass production and interchangeable parts, telling the young attorney John W. Anderson, an investor in the Ford Motor Company, that 'The way to make automobiles is to make one automobile like another automobile, to make them all alike, to make them come through the factory just alike; just as one pin is like another pin when it comes from a pin factory, or one match is like another match when it comes from a match factory.'[29] And, talking with men in the plant where the Ford Motor Company was not yet building cars of this sort, he often said that he wished to turn out a car that working men could buy.[30] In fact the average price for Ford cars between 1903 and 1908 was $1,600: very much towards the upper end of the market, since two-thirds of the automobiles sold in the United States during 1903 cost less than $1,375.[31] But whatever the price, demand already outstripped supply. 'Now the demand for automobiles is a perfect craze,' John Anderson wrote to his father after meeting Ford. 'Every factory here . . . has its entire output sold, and cannot begin to fill orders . . . And it is all spot cash on delivery, and no guarantee or string attached of any kind.'[32]

Ford's backers, happy with their existing profits, did not share his mass-market visions. Large, expensive cars made large profits per car sold; small, cheap cars, very small profits. If you could sell enough small cars, Ford argued, then the total would be a very large profit indeed. But could you? Alexander Malcomson did not think so. He insisted that the firm stay

15. Interchangeable parts: three Cadillacs disassembled and assembled for the Denman Trophy, London, 1908.

where the profits were proven, with expensive cars; and would not budge. In order to proceed along the lines he himself favoured, Ford would have to get rid of Malcomson – something he finally achieved by the ruse of setting up a separate company, the Ford Manufacturing Company, in 1906.

A few miles away in Lansing, Ransom, E. Olds was fighting an almost identical battle with his financial backer, F. L. Smith – but with one important difference: Olds was already producing a successful cheap car. The first 'curved dash' Oldsmobiles (so called because their dashboards curved up in front like a buggy's) sold for under $400, and had been in production since 1902. Four hundred and twenty-five were sold that year; by 1905 he had sold 6,500 at $500 each, through twenty-six agencies.[33] They had even inspired a popular song, 'In My Merry Oldsmobile'.

> Come away with me, Lucille,
> In my merry Oldsmobile,
> Over the road of life we'll fly,
> Autobubbling you and I,
> To the church we'll quickly steal,
> And our wedding bells will peal,
> You can go as far as you like with me,
> In our merry Oldsmobile.

Unfortunately for Olds, Smith wanted to create a business for his two sons, and they were interested only in the rich man's market. Olds was forced to turn his attention to loss-making heavy cars, and before long they sank his business, including his light runabout.

But a trend had been set – so much so that by 1908 the *American Agriculturalist* reported at least twenty-four companies in America building cheap, simply constructed automobiles, popular with farmers because they could traverse

16. The merry Oldsmobile, 1905.

ploughed fields, snow banks and mud holes and could clear tree stumps, boulders and ridges of turf on old wagon trails.[34] However, none of these lasted, on either the road or the market. Materials and durability had been sacrificed to cheapness and lightness. The challenge was to produce something both cheap and tough. If one could remain in business long enough to develop such a product, the market (or so it seemed to Ford) would be unlimited. Rid of the obdurate Malcomson, he began to arrange the business to his liking. He was determined, he told Charles Sorensen, who would remain his faithful lieutenant for the next forty years, 'to build a car that his workers could afford to buy'.[35]

The resources and policies he developed now would stay with him to the end, and would be key elements in maintaining both his manufacturing success and his public image – so intimately associated, and such very different things. Sorensen himself exemplified one of these: his eye for men. Years later, a journalist asked him how he picked likely candidates for advancement, since it was well known that Ford never bought in men from other companies. Ford replied, 'We have no system. Such things as character analysis we have never tried. A good man reveals himself. One of the best executives we have used to be a pattern-maker. He made very good patterns . . . As the director of other pattern makers he had a chance to display his managerial ability. After that his progress was easy and fast.' The pattern maker was Sorensen. The journalist concluded that 'Ford methods can be learned only in the Ford shops. In the end what is learned is not so much a method of manufacturing as a mode of thinking – Ford's mode.'[36]

Ford carried delegation to the level of genius. Trusting, in this as in every other aspect of the business, the instincts upon which he unashamedly and absolutely relied, he picked his executives for their ability to act as proxies, carrying out his wishes in ways he could never have managed himself. For instance, physical, face-to-face violence was never Ford's style. On the contrary, his photographs project an image of unfailing calm and elegance; he is slight, neat, even gentle-looking. But he never hesitated to employ violent men. This meant that although Ford remained, to the end of his life, personal owner and autocrat of his gigantic establishment, the opprobrium resulting from the policies implemented on his behalf fell entirely upon his lieutenants. Charles Sorensen was a case in point – and well aware that blame-carrying was one of his duties: 'Ford used to pretend in all innocence not to know why I had fired a man he told me to fire,' he recalled.[37]

> [Sorensen's] the man that pours the boiling oil down that old Henry makes, [an employee told Edmund Wilson, who had heard this story more than once – it was a Detroit legend]. There's a man born a hundred years too late, a regular slave driver – the men tremble when they see Sorensen comin'. He used to be very brutal – he'd come through and slug the men. One day when they were movin' the plant he came through and found a man sittin' workin' on a box. 'Get up!' says Sorensen. 'Don't ye know ye can't sit down in here?' The man never moved and Sorensen kicked the box out from under 'im – and the man got up and bashed Sorensen one on the jaw. 'Go to hell!' he says. 'I don't work here – I'm workin' for the Edison company!'[38]

The infamous Harry Bennett, who would spearhead Ford's attempt to break the unions, was another such recruit. Both Sorensen and Bennett were detested by the workforce. But the public never seemed to make the connection between the misdeeds of Ford's proxies and Henry Ford himself.

Sorensen was in place by 1905. And that same year saw the acquisition of another of the elements that would be crucial to

Ford's success. Watching a motor-race at Palm Beach, he saw a French car wrecked in a crash. He had noticed that some foreign cars had smaller, stronger parts than American ones and, examining the wreck, picked out a light, tough valve stem. Metallurgic tests showed it to be French steel with a vanadium alloy. This was what he needed! But when he took it to American steelmakers, none could produce it for him.

> I sent to England for a man who understood how to make the steel commercially. The main thing was to get a plant to turn it out. That was another problem. Vanadium requires 3000 degrees Fahrenheit. The ordinary furnace could not go beyond 2700 degrees. I found a small steel company in Canton, Ohio. I offered to guarantee them against loss if they would run a heat for us. They agreed. The first heat was a failure. Very little vanadium remained in the steel. I had them try again, and the second time the steel came through. Until then we had been forced to be satisfied with steel running between 60,000 and 70,000 pounds tensile strength. With vanadium, the strength went up to 170,000 pounds.[39]

Vanadium became a kind of Ford talisman, a magic word for a magic material, flourishing even after other materials had superseded it for strength and lightness.

The firm tried out its cheap-car policy with the Model N. Ford's aim was to have it sell for $500, but this price could not be maintained for more than a few months after the car's introduction in 1906: six months later the list price was $600. Nevertheless the N was a success. In the year to October 1906 Ford sold 1,600 cars; the following year that figure rose to 8,243, and he was finally on the way to making real money. He had proved his point; the way forward was clear. Talking that year to Roy D. Chapin, who had been with Ransom Olds in the great Oldsmobile days and would become Secretary of Commerce in Herbert Hoover's administration, he said he intended to produce a four-cylinder automobile, that once it was produced he would stick to that standardized design without changing it, that he would reach constantly towards a growing volume because that would drastically cut his costs, and that he was going to reduce prices steadily.[40] It was a uniquely original vision in an industry where manufacturers regularly bankrupted themselves offering too great a variety of models. It is also the one for which he is universally remembered: for most people Henry Ford is the man who said two things, of which the first was *You can have any colour you want as long as it's black.* (The other, of course, was *History is bunk*: to which we shall return.)

He now also began to formulate some of the policy attitudes which would become familiar over the years, and which would prove, both now and later, that brutality need not be physical, and was by no means Sorensen's exclusive preserve. One such policy had to do with the dealer network. This was one of the Ford company's most important assets, and one which it kept under tight control. 1907 saw one of America's periodic financial panics, which bankrupted five Detroit motor companies; and although Ford was in a good position, he was building a new factory and had cash-flow problems. So he and Couzens conceived a plan whereby the dealers and suppliers would carry the company. Dealers were eager not to lose the reliable income offered by a product everyone wanted, and Ford made the most of this leverage.

> In order to get the cash to continue during that little time of depression, Mr Ford kept building these cars and shipping them out on what they called sight-draft bills of lading, so the dealers had to pay for those cars. They kept sending the cars, and the shipments were pro-rated. Oh,

boy, what a squeal! These dealers – what a time they had to get money! They didn't want to lose the dealership, so they did everything, begged, borrowed, stole, to pay for those machines as they were delivered to them . . .[41]

So the dealers kept the company in cash, as they would again when times got hard, while suppliers were fended off with notes.

Everything Ford had done until now had been mere means to an end. Finally, however, the end was in sight. In March 1908, all Ford dealers received the first circulars describing the company's new model: the T. It would not be available for some months, but it was important that all stocks should be cleared beforehand. For, once the Model T appeared, nobody would want anything else.

Ford had begun preparations for this new and revolutionary vehicle in 1905, the year he realized the possibilities offered by vanadium. On his return from the successful tests at Canton he called Sorensen over to an unused space on the third floor of the firm's then factory, and announced, 'We're going to start in on a completely new job.' The space was walled off into a little experimental room twelve feet by fifteen, just large enough to contain a model and some power tools. A rocking chair was installed in which Ford would sit for hours at a time, working, as always when he was excited by a project, until ten or eleven at night. The chief designer was a Hungarian called Galamb, but Ford took an active part in the process. Although he had no formal engineering training he knew intuitively, though without being able to explain it precisely or mathematically, why this thickness of metal, that distribution of weight or tensile strength, would work. '[Ford] brought the ideas to us,' remembered one of his team. 'First, he would think the thing up, then he would have [the draughtsmen] draw it up, and then we would make it up.'[42] 'Charlie, we're on the right track here now,' he told Sorensen. 'We're going to get a car now that we can make in great volume and get the price away down.'[43]

The Model T, with its front-mounted engine and simple, easily replaced controls, represented a true leap of the imagination. It was, despite the pony-trap canopy of the earlier models, recognizably a car of the modern world. The 1903 Oldsmobile, by contrast, had still been a horseless carriage: attach traces and a horse, and, lo! you have a buggy. Such functionless reminiscences of older forms – the half-timbering sometimes stuck on to the façades of modern houses is another example – are known as skeuomorphs (from the Greek *skeua*, meaning material or kit, and *morph*, meaning form, taking the form imposed by the original material) and attest to the fact that old modes are not easily abandoned. Their influence is, on the contrary, extraordinarily persistent. Think for example, of the US standard railroad gauge: four feet eight and a half inches. Why this apparently arbitrary measure? Because that was the English gauge, and the US railroads were built by English expatriates. Why did the English choose this measure? Because the first rail lines were built by the same people who built the pre-railroad tramways, and this was the gauge they used. Why? Because the people building the trams used the same jigs and tools that they used for building wagons, whose wheel spacing this was. Why? Because with any other spacing the wagon wheels would break on some of the old long-distance roads, because that was the spacing of the wheel ruts. And those roads had been built by the Romans, and their ruts first formed by Roman war chariots, which were all built alike, to be drawn by two war horses. And four feet eight and a half inches is the width of two horses' rumps. 'So,' concludes the teller of this (true) tale, 'the next time you are handed a specification and wonder what horse's ass came up with it you may be exactly right'. (The tale does not stop there. The Space Shuttle's two big booster rockets – solid rocket boosters, or SRBs – are made by Thiokol in Utah.

17. Model T Ford.

The engineers who designed them would have preferred to make them a bit fatter, but they had to be shipped by train from the factory to the launch site; and the train had to run through a tunnel in the mountains. The SRBs had to fit through the tunnel; the tunnel is slightly wider than the railroad track; and the railroad track is the width of two horses' behinds. 'So, the major design feature of what is arguably the world's most advanced transportation system was determined over two thousand years ago by the width of a Horse's Ass!')[44]

The Model T was not, at $825, especially cheap, though its price would come down steadily with the years. But that it represented outstanding value was at once apparent. Its advertising slogan, 'No car under $2000 offers more, and no car over $2000 offers more except in trimmings,' was, for once, nothing but the simple truth. Ford, with his personal experience of what the farmer needed, had produced a car uniquely suited to the conditions of the American backwoods. Where other offerings disintegrated, the Model T, tough, light, slung high above the ground, coped inexhaustibly with ruts, holes and open fields. Its stout wheels and springs would stand any amount of battering, it was powerful, with a twenty horsepower engine, and its large tank held plenty of gasoline – sixteen gallons for the touring model, ten for the runabout. A magneto built into the motor replaced the dry batteries of earlier models, and the entire power plant and transmission were completely enclosed. And if it would do in the country it would certainly do in town, just like Henry Ford himself – who had got where he was without benefit of bankers' wiles or city sophisticates. As Edmund Wilson put it, '[his] game [was] the direct expression of Henry Ford's personal character: to make cars which, though as homely as he is, shall be at once the cheapest, the most energetic and the most indestructible possible'.[45] And, like Ford, the car, for all its power, was not bulky. The wheelbase was only eight feet four inches, and it weighed only 1,200 pounds. The face of motoring was about to be definitively changed.

And so the dealers realized, on that momentous day in March 1908, when they first saw the leaflets describing the new arrival. They literally could not believe what they read. Ford was an exacting taskmaster, but the promise held out by the Model T made everything worthwhile. It would not be available for delivery until October, and until then (since who would buy the current model once they realized something so much better was in the offing?) 'We have carefully hidden the sheets away, and locked the drawer.'[46] 'It is without doubt the greatest creation in automobiles ever placed before a people, and it means that this circular alone will flood your factory with orders.' 'We have rubbed our eyes several times to make sure we were not dreaming.'[47]

In *Farewell, My Lovely*, his immortal ode to the Model T, E. B. White rhapsodized that it was 'obviously conceived in madness' since 'any car which was capable of going from forward into reverse without any perceptible mechanical hiatus was bound to be a mighty challenging thing to the human imagination' (and a source of unending inspiration to the Keystone Kops).

It was the miracle God had wrought. And it was patently the sort of thing that could only happen once. Mechanically uncanny, it was like nothing that had ever come to the world before . . . As a vehicle it was hard-working, commonplace, heroic; and it often seemed to transmit those qualities to the persons who rode in it . . . The Model T was distinguished from all other makes of cars by the fact that its transmission was of a type known as planetary – which was half metaphysics, half sheer friction. Engineers accepted the word 'planetary' in its epicyclic sense, but I was always conscious that it also meant 'wandering', 'erratic'. Because of the peculiar nature of this planetary element, there was always, in Model T, a certain dull rapport between engine and wheels, and even when the car was in a state known as neutral, it trembled with a deep imperative and tended to inch forward. There was never a moment when the bands were not faintly egging the machine on. In this respect it was like a horse, rolling the bit on its tongue, and country people brought to it the same technique they used with draft animals.

Its most remarkable quality was its rate of acceleration. In its palmy days the Model T could take off faster than anything on the road. The reason was simple. To get under way, you simply hooked the third finger of the right hand around a lever on the steering column, pulled down hard, and shoved your left foot forcibly against the low-speed pedal. These were simple, positive motions; the car responded by lunging forward with a roar . . . the human leg was (and still is) incapable of letting in a clutch with anything like the forthright abandon that used to send Model T on its way. . .

I have never been really planetary since.[48]

The Model T's driver was 'a man enthroned': the car, with its top up, stood seven feet high. And it seemed that all America (with the possible exception of a few East Coast bankers) wanted to climb into this particular throne. 'Many farmers now own, and are immensely proud of, their "benzine buggies",' noted *Printer's Ink* in 1908, and the *Ford Times*, quoting this, added that 'the company has found some of its most aggressive agents . . . through selling to farmers and then giving the farmer the exclusive right in his town or village'.[49] On 1 May 1909, the Ford executives announced that they had enough orders for the Model T to consume the entire factory output until August, and would temporarily accept no more.[50]

» » »

It was clear from the moment Model T was conceived that a new and more efficient method of production was going to be needed; and as Henry Ford conceived the car, so too he is credited with originating the assembly line, which would enable him to build it fast enough to satisfy his ever-growing multitude of clamouring customers. He thought of it, the story goes, in Chicago's meat-packing district, where on a *dis*-assembly line whole hogs, moving on an overhead conveyor system, were systematically stripped of their component parts. But as Charles Sorensen put it, 'This is a rationalization long after the event.'

Sorensen himself places the assembly line's origin in July 1908, during the last months of Model N production. Working out the most rational and economical way of putting the car together, he and an assistant simplified the existing system as far as they were able, but were still not satisfied. 'It was then', writes Sorensen, 'that the idea occurred to me that assembly would be easier, simpler and faster if we moved the chassis along, beginning at one end of the plant with a frame and adding the axles and the wheels; then moving it past the stock-room, instead of moving the stockroom to the chassis.'[51] He rigged up a rough assembly one Sunday and showed it to Ford and two assistants, Harold Wills and Ed Martin. According to Sorensen, Ford was sceptical but willing to go along with the experiment; Wills and Martin 'doubted that an automobile could be built properly on the move'. Wills in particular was against it: 'That way of building cars, he said, would ruin the company.'[52]

In fact, like the notion of the small car, the idea of the

mechanized assembly line had been taking shape for some time. In 1784 Oliver Evans had devised a grain mill in which the process was propelled by gravity: the grain was elevated to the top, was cleaned, ground and bolted without human intervention and emerged as flour at the bottom. On a horizontal plane, the Royal Naval Arsenal at Deptford, in London, had created in 1804 a large-scale biscuit bakery with one kneading machine and an assembly line of skilled workers, turning out seventy ship's biscuits a minute. The original Olds factory had been built along these rationally planned lines, and in 1903 the Kahn brothers, Albert and Julius, had developed the idea further in a plant designed for another auto manufacturer, J. W. Packard. Now they were commissioned to do the same thing for Ford. As the Model T's popularity grew, and existing plant became increasingly inadequate, Ford's scepticism, if any, vanished. The Kahns' new Ford factory in Highland Park would incorporate the assembly-line system. 'Before the end of [1913] a power-driven assembly-line was in operation, and New Year's saw three more installed.'[53]

As Ford himself described the process,

> Every piece of work in the shop moves; it may move on hooks on overhead chains going to assembly in the exact order in which the parts are required; it may travel on a moving platform, or it may go by gravity, but the point is that there is no lifting or trucking of anything other than materials.[54]

The assembly line alone, however, did not guarantee efficiency. What made the difference was timing.

The pioneer in this field was Frederick Winslow Taylor, a clever Quaker two years younger than Ford. The controlled and high-minded Taylor, after breaking down in school from overwork, had gone into a machine shop instead of to Harvard,

18. The world's first assembly-line, 1914.

learning the pattern maker's trade while at the same time working for an engineering degree and becoming a lawn-tennis champion. Moving to the Midvale Iron Works at the age of twenty-two, he persuaded the management to let him handle a lathe rather than confine him to the clerical work he hated, and within six years had risen from machinist's assistant to chief engineer. And as he rose through the ranks, 'from machinist's helper to keeper of toolcribs to gangboss to foreman to master-mechanic in charge of repairs to chief draftsman and director of research to chief engineer',[55] so (at least in the perception of his former workmates) he changed sides.

Taylor's god was efficiency. He wanted to ram as much productivity into the workshop as he had into his own life; and the secret, as he saw it, was the opposite of that painstaking craftsmanship which until then had formed the bedrock of manufacture. The craftsman identifies with what he is making, staying with it until he has got it right; and this combination of skills and perfectionism is what he passes on to his apprentices. This sense of pride in a good job well done is, as John Ruskin observed, the key to pleasure at work. It is not, unfortunately, the key to maximum industrial efficiency. If the process can be broken up into its component parts, and precision supplied by machine tools instead of long practice, then both skill and time can be reduced. This was Taylor's great *aperçu*, and with this in mind he set about 'gathering in on the part of those on the management's side all the great mass of traditional knowledge which in the past has been in the heads of the workmen and in the physical skill and knack of the workmen'.[56] Once he had done that he could break each process down into its component parts, and no man need perform more than a single action. Long and elaborate training would be a thing of the past, super-seded, as the industrial age superseded that of the craftsman.

The workmen, not unnaturally, resented Taylor's activities, which they saw as a betrayal on the part of a man they had treated as one of their own. 'I was a young man in years but I give you my word I was a great deal older than I am now, what with the worry, meanness and contemptibleness of the whole damn thing. It's a horrid life for any man to live not being able to look any workman in the face without seeing hostility there, and a feeling that every man around you is your virtual enemy.'[57]

Nevertheless, he continued upon his upright and inflexible way. At Midvale he used time studies to set daily production quotas. Those who made their quotas would receive incentive payments; those who did not would receive only the basic 'differential' rate. Using time study, systematic controls and tools, functional foremanship and the new wage scheme, he doubled productivity at the plant. It was possible for diligent workers to make much better money than before. But workplace morale suffered. For once skill became irrelevant, it was no longer possible to take a personal pride in your job.

Even management was at first suspicious of Taylor's innovations. When he read his first paper to the American Society of Mechanical Engineers they dismissed his ideas contemptuously. 'I have found,' he wrote, 'that any improvement is not only opposed but aggressively and bitterly opposed by the majority of men.'[58] But in Detroit he found himself, for once, preaching to the converted. His first visit there was in 1909, when he spoke for four hours to the Packard management. Packard at once instituted scientific job analyses, and by 1913 'the plant had been largely Taylorized'.[59] In 1914 he visited the town again, addressing more than six hundred superintendents, foremen and others drawn from all over the city. Told that several manufacturers in the city had already anticipated his ideas, he commented: 'This is most interesting, as being almost the first instance in which a group of manufacturers had undertaken to install the principles of scientific management without the aid of experts.'[60]

It is of course not surprising that Taylorism found such ready acceptance among the auto manufacturers.

> For the chassis alone [writes Allan Nevins of the Model T], from 1000 to 4000 pieces of each component had to be furnished every day at just the right point and right minute; a single failure, and the whole mechanism would come to a jarring standstill . . . Superintendents had to know every hour just how many components were being produced and how many were in stock . . . Every stocked part cost space, money, and time. To make a thousand automobiles a day, the company had to buy monthly about $8,000,000 worth of materials, drawn from a thousand different localities, and to unload a hundred freight cars every twenty-four hours.[61]

The assembly line, the inevitable consequence of the demands imposed by mass manufacture of such a large and complex machine, had developed by sheer force of logic in the automobile factories; Taylorism, implicit in the timings essential to the line's efficient functioning, followed naturally in its wake.

And the price came down. From the initial $850 the runabouts were soon reduced to $550, then $500. In July 1914, with the new Highland Park plant in full and frenzied flow, the company announced that a further $60 would be shaved off on 1 August, bringing the runabout to $440, the touring car to $490 and the town car to $690. All this meant that a gap of about $450 existed between the Model T runabout and the next really good car. A good-looking car at around $750 might have offered some competition; but although this was as clear to Ford's competitors as to everyone else, execution was a far cry from realization. For the moment, and into the foreseeable future, Ford reigned supreme. Thirty-four thousand cars were produced in 1910–11; in 1911–12, seventy-eight thousand.

The prospect for 1912–13 was 168,000, and by 1920 it would, if the figures continued to mount at the same rate, top 1 million – beyond the capacity of Highland Park, so that the company had hardly made its move before the next step in expansion was being planned.[62] As early as 1917 the first blueprint was ready for a new plant on the River Rouge near Ford's old home in Dearborn, where the concept of flow, already demonstrated on the assembly line, would be extended to the supply of materials. Once this move was achieved, Ford would no longer depend on the vagaries of suppliers for transport and raw materials, because he would own or control the entire process himself.

To step into the clangorous River Rouge complex was (and still is) to experience the dizzying power then concentrated in the hands of Henry Ford. Inconceivably in these days of pension-fund power and impersonal management, he owned the entire vast place personally. In July 1919, he bought out his minority shareholders; and from then on the Rouge, from ore bins to blast furnaces, from docks to assembly lines and metallurgical laboratories, was his, all his, to do with as he wished.

1913, the year the moving assembly lines were finally and fully installed, is the moment singled out by Lewis Mumford as signalling the death of the environment, the moment when pecuniary interests unleashed mass pollution.[63] This position is, in some ways, as unrealistic and patrician as Woodrow Wilson's: for this was a popular revolution, not a marketing trick. If America was flooded with Model Ts, it was hardly by *diktat*. That it was an environmental turning-point, however, is indisputable: this was the moment when the private car became indispensable to everyday life. And the person responsible for this revolution was Henry Ford. For him, 1913 marked the break between ordinary riches and legendary millions. From $4 million during 1910, the company's net income had risen to more than $27 million in 1913; declared

19. The Rouge.

dividends for that year were aggregated at $5 million.[64] It was raining money, and the market seemed quenchless.

» » »

When the Model T first appeared in 1908, morale at the factory was high, even though wages had fallen since 1905 and the working day, at one time cut to eight hours, had moved back up to ten. But the men were happy to be associated with such a dazzling success as the Model T, and Ford's own elation was contagious as he moved about the factory.

> He'd be out there in the factory, watching them and kidding them and telling stories. God! He could get anything out of the men because he just talked and would tell them stories. He'd never say, 'I want this done!' He'd say, 'I wonder if we can do it. I wonder.' Well, the men would just break their necks to see if they could do it. They knew what he wanted. They figured it was a coming thing, and they'd do their best.[66]

By 1913, however, this family spirit had vanished. For one thing the workforce was vastly expanded. In 1910 it had numbered only 2,595, fewer than at General Motors, Buick, Cadillac, Studebaker or Packard. But by 1913 it had risen to 13,198: a very large family indeed.[66] Contact with Ford himself was a thing of the past, day-to-day control being largely in the hands of departmental foremen, who wielded all but absolute authority, controlling the size of the worker's wage-cheque, the severity of production standards exacted, the time allowed to learn the job, chances of promotion or transfer: foremen even had rights of hire and fire, and used their powers arbitrarily and often oppressively. And this bullying atmosphere emanated from the very top, where Ford had delegated workforce management to Charles Sorensen and 'Pete' Martin, who were feared and hated by the men.

All this naturally undermined self-respect and loyalty – qualities already under attack. Repetitive labour, Ford admitted, 'is . . . terrifying to me. I could not possibly do the same thing day in, day out, but to other minds, perhaps I might say to the majority of minds, repetitive operations hold no terrors.' And rejecting 'the terror of the machine', he asserted that 'I have not been able to discover that repetitive labour injures a man in any way.'[67] Most, however, agreed that Ford, in his horror of monotony, was less exceptional than he chose to assume. Taylorism and the assembly line, reducing craftsmen to mere 'hands', had removed men's self-respect along with any sense they might have had that the organization in some way depended on their expertise. On the contrary, too much skill now rendered a man *less* desirable, as Horace Arnold and Fay Faurote noted in their 1915 study of production routines at the Highland Park plant. 'The Ford Motor Company has no use for experience, in the working ranks anyway. It desires and prefers machine tool operators who have nothing to unlearn, who have no theories of correct speeds for metal finishing, and will simply do what they are told to do, over and over again from bell-time to bell-time.'[68] At a stroke the industry had become what it has remained ever since, one in which workers 'matter less than machines or tools' and where 'almost anyone, once trained, can perform the tasks of other employees throughout the facility'.[69]

Experience brought with it other undesirable qualities. It took years to acquire, which meant that it was associated with middle-age; and on the assembly line, where youth and quickness were at a premium, this was an absolute disadvantage. In *Middletown*, their 1929 study of Muncie, Indiana, Robert and Helen Lynd found men in young middle-age resigned to the fast-approaching end of their working lives. 'Male members of the working class start to work from fourteen to eighteen, reach their prime in the twenties, and begin to fail in their late forties,' they reported.[70] 'You had to know how to use the old carbon steel to keep it from getting' hot and spoilin' the edge. But this "high speed steel" and this new "stelite" don't absorb the heat and are harder than carbon steel. You can take a boy fresh from the farm and in three days he can manage a machine as well as I can, and I've been at it twenty-seven years,' one skilled worker told them.[71] 'In production work,' reported the personnel manager of a machine shop, 'forty to forty-five is the age limit because of the speed needed in the work. Men over forty are hired as sweepers and for similar jobs.'[72] The Lynds found that although that section of population earning its living by working for money was becoming larger, as more women joined the paid labour force, the age limits of that employment, especially for working-class men, were narrowing. And the job itself had become deathly dull. If you concentrated on it you would go mad; but if you did not, 'the steady hum of the lathe, the incessant tapping of the hammers, the dull thud of the presses, the click-clack of the shapers, the whirr of the drills, the groaning and clicking of the drilling machines and reamers' led to 'a semi-hypnotic state from which the workman's mind emerges only at intervals'.[73]

Charlie Chaplin's film *Modern Times* said more about this comatose state than any words ever could. And as in the film, such a state, on the machinery-packed factory floor, could, and often did, lead to accidents. Edmund Wilson spoke to a girl who worked making 'interior parts – ash-receivers and dome-light rims and escutcheons – those are the little brass plates behind the doorknob that holds it in'.

You have a strip of brass and run it through the press – you step on a pedal, and the die comes down and cuts it out. We were working with small No. 4 presses and we were supposed to turn out 1,624 pieces an hour. Most of the girls couldn't make it, and if they couldn't enough times, they'd get their base rate lowered. For instance, if you were a dome-rim maker, say, and couldn't do 512 pieces an hour, you'd be cut from thirty-two to twenty-eight cents. If you made a misstep on the pedal you were liable to lose a finger – I always had some kind of a cut. When an accident happens nobody ever tells about it, and sometimes you don't know definitely till a week later – but I could always tell if something had happened as soon as I came into the room: the place always seems very clean and everybody's very quiet . . . One day a girl got two fingers cut off, and they sent everybody home. A man in the hinge department lost three fingers once the same week. People often don't make use of the safety devices because they can work faster without them.[74]

In France conditions like these resulted in strikes. Like Ford, whose factories he visited in 1911, Renault had introduced some aspects of Taylorism as early as 1908; and in 1912 he extended the time study system in an attempt to establish the piecework rate on a scientific basis. A strike alleging favouritism was settled after a day, when management agreed to modify its time-study procedure to bring it more in line with actual working conditions; but another broke out, this time lasting three weeks and known as the time-study strike. The men did not win: after ten days Renault opened his factory gates and the workers, of whom few were unionized, drifted back.[75] But memories of the strike persisted: at least they had asserted their independence.

In Detroit, on the other hand, where working conditions were (to say the least) no better, there were no strikes. They would have been useless: the Employers' Association of Detroit, determined to resist unionization, had established a

Labor Bureau which would simply pour reserves of eager immigrant labour into a strike-hit factory. By 1906 the Bureau listed about forty thousand workers, half the entire Detroit workforce.[76] And although the EAD urged its members not to brutalize the men, as this would simply create union-friendly conditions, the combination of Taylorization, insecurity and the piecework system was enough to reduce most to despair.

In fact Ford disliked piecework, which he thought made for shoddiness as people rushed to fulfil their quotas: he always paid by the day. Even so, his jobs were as soul-destroying as anyone else's. And as Detroit boomed and demand for labour grew, he, like everyone else, suffered from this absence of job satisfaction in the shape of an unnervingly rapid labour turnover: 370 per cent in Highland Park during 1913. Seventy-one per cent of employees lasted less than five days there. These absurd turnovers not only demoralized the workforce, they threatened to undermine both quality and production. Clearly something had to be done about them.

And then Ford, apparently out of the blue, proposed a new solution to the problem.

On the morning of Sunday 4 January 1914, he summoned his chief lieutenants, Sorensen, Martin and John R. Lee, and announced, to their surprise, that he wanted new wage scales that would more fairly reflect the company's position. 1913's extraordinary profits had come about because the assembly line had lowered production costs; and these costs promised to be even lower in 1914. Customers and shareholders were all benefiting. Now Ford felt the workforce should share in the prosperity it had helped bring about.

The company already had a tradition of profit sharing, albeit limited. Employees who had been with the company three years or more received end-of-year bonuses of 10 per cent of their annual pay, and executives and branch managers received efficiency bonus cheques. But, given the high turnover of labour, this still left most of the workforce out in the cold. Ford now asked Sorensen to find some figures that had been prepared on volume and cost.

> Then I caught his idea and saw how those estimates of gains and earnings fitted into his plan. Mr Ford had a blackboard in his office. On it I chalked up figures for materials, overhead, and labour based on expanding production and lowered car prices. As expected, production rose, costs fell, and up went figures for profits. Mr Ford then had me transfer figures from profits column to labour costs – two million, three million, four million dollars. With that, daily wage figures rose from minimums of $2 to $2.50 and $3. Ed Martin protested. I began to see how the increases would give greater incentive to our workers and that savings from lower costs and resulting higher production might be sufficient to take care of the major part of the increases. I could envisage more efficient production facilities that would reduce cost, and that there would be further economies from satisfied, willing workers.
>
> While I stood at the blackboard, John Lee commented upon every entry and soon became pretty nasty. It was plain he wasn't trying to understand the idea and thought he might sabotage it by ridiculing it. This didn't sit well with Mr Ford, who kept telling me to put more figures down – $3.50, $3.75, $4.00, $4.25, and a quarter of a dollar more, then another quarter. At the end of about four hours Mr Ford stepped up to the blackboard. 'Stop!' he said. 'Stop it, Charlie; it's all settled. Five dollars a day minimum pay and at once.'[77]

So it was fixed; and even the famously penny-pinching Couzens agreed without a murmur, because 'I want to be governor of Michigan and this will help elect me.'[78] (In another version Sorensen has Couzens at the original meeting, and snapping, 'Well, so it's up to $4.75. I dare you to make it $5!' At which Ford did just that.)[79] Next day a directors' meeting was held and the $5 wage approved to take force from 12 January, 'Which plan, it was distinctly understood, would approximate an additional expenditure for the same volume of business of Ten Million ($10,000,000) dollars, for the year 1914.' Later that day Ford and Couzens announced to the press that the company was reducing the working day to eight hours, converting the factory to three shifts instead of two, and instituting a $5 daily wage, 'a share in the profits of the house'. Nine-tenths of employees would receive this money at once; young men under twenty-two would receive it if they had dependants. 'This,' said Ford to reporters, 'is neither charity nor wages, but profit sharing and efficiency engineering.'[80]

The $5 day caused a sensation. Its effects on public opinion were still apparent more than twenty years later, Ford's image as a model employer surviving brutality, depression, unemployment and a real devaluation of workers' wages. The *Cleveland Plain Dealer* reported that the announcement 'shot like a blinding rocket through the clouds of the present industrial depression'; the *New York Sun* called it 'a bolt out of the blue sky flashing its way across the continent and far beyond'; the *New York Herald* thought it 'an epoch in the world's industrial history'. The *Toledo Blade* reported that most newspapers felt this was 'a lordly gift' to the Ford workers; and in a more personal vein, the *New York World* called Ford 'an inspired millionaire', while the Algonac (Michigan) *Courier* ran the headline, 'God Bless Henry Ford of the Ford Motor Company'.[81]

By no means all the comment was favourable. The conservative press was appalled. The *Wall Street Journal* warned that the scheme would lead to 'material, financial and factory disorganization' and declared that Ford 'has in his social endeavour committed economic blunders, if not crimes' which 'may return to plague him and the industry he represents, as well as organized society'. The *New York Times* predicted 'serious disturbances' would follow from a policy 'distinctly Utopian and dead against all experience'; the *Pittsburgh Gazette-Times* thought it 'a demoralizing scheme'. And industrial leaders were predictably unenthusiastic. The president of the Pittsburgh Plate Glass Company declared that if employers were to follow Ford's lead 'it would mean the ruin of all business in the country . . . Ford himself will surely find he cannot afford to pay $5.'[82] Ford's peers in the automotive industry were particularly displeased. None paid even $2.50 a day, and all anticipated labour unrest in the wake of Ford's announcement. Alvin Macauley, president of Packard, telephoned Sorensen at home on the night of the announcement, wanting to know how he could 'avoid paying these wages once you start paying them here in Detroit? We are not running a philanthropic business like you,' he pointed out ruefully. But Sorensen denied, with all the authority of a supremely unphilanthropic nature, that philanthropy had anything to do with it. On the contrary,

The facts that appeared as we went along with the $5 day were startling. There was little social significance in the fact that the buying power of the Ford wage earner was increased. But raising the buying power of Ford workers increased in turn the buying power of other people and so on as a sort of chain reaction. The real significance was that the Ford high-wage policy was just the forerunner and then the example throughout American industry. As a result of it, workers' pay throughout the country increased. Also increased was their purchasing power, and this bore out Mr Ford's idea that every man working for him should be able to afford one of his motorcars . . . The most progressive period of Ford Motor Company was between 1914 and 1919. The only things we did not do were those we could not think of . . . Higher wages, higher production: that was the formula. And by applying it, the cost of producing an automobile fell before our very eyes.[83]

The coup, it seemed, was complete – increased efficiency, enhanced reputation, uncountable column inches of free publicity whose value was set by the *Everett Tribune*, in Washington, at $5 million, by the *New York Times*, *Boston News Bureau* and *Printers' Ink* at $10 million, the *Syracuse Journal* at $20 million.[84] When, on 8 January, word got out that Ford had arrived in New York for the auto show and was staying at the Hotel Belmont, the management had to employ extra house detectives to protect him from being mobbed by adoring bell boys, doormen, waiters, and hundreds of others no doubt subsisting on considerably less than the fortunate employees at Ford's.

Here, it seemed, was the simplicity of genius; whose genius, however, was another matter. In fact the $5 day was not Ford's idea, nor untested. The principle had been tried already – in England, where an exceedingly bright young man called Percival Perry managed the factory that Ford's had recently opened in Manchester. There he had found the going rate for unskilled labour to be sixpence halfpenny an hour for a fifty-six-hour week – starvation wages, on which no family could possibly live. A systematic investigation revealed that £3 a week was the minimum required; and this Perry now offered. To his delight it worked admirably: as the men's spirits rose, so did production. When Ford visited Britain in 1912, Perry spent a day with him explaining his 'high wages and straight wages' plan in great detail.[85] So that when, the following year, Ford himself came to implement a similar policy (though taking it much further), this was by no means such a risk as his American publicity implied. Indeed, if Sorensen approved the move (which he did) there can have been no doubting its hard-headedness.

But if the $5 day more than justified itself in business terms, this did not mean Ford had no interest in its humanitarian implications. There were more sides to Ford than to Sorensen: that was one reason Ford employed Sorensen and not vice versa. Sorensen acted out one aspect of Ford. Others, of very different character, were employed to implement other aspirations, and they, predictably, saw the Ford they reflected. Thus, when the Rev. Dr Samuel S. Marquis, an Episcopalian clergyman soon to take charge of the company's social policy, 'asked [Ford] why he had fixed upon $5' he received a reply heavy with philanthropy – doubtless reflecting Ford's position when dealing with the Marquis side of himself: 'I believe I can do the world no greater service than to create more work for more men at larger pay . . . and I want the whole organization dominated by a just, generous and humane policy.'[86] And as the millions poured in that would soon make him the richest man in America, he embarked upon a new crusade, one that seemed to indicate that (for the moment at least) the Marquis rather than the Sorensen aspect was in the ascendant: 'While the Company has specialized in methods, material and machinery, and a single model of car, it is also, through its Educational Department, and the Ford Profit-Sharing Plan, specializing in MEN.'[87]

For the $5 day was not to be the simple wage implied by the publicity. Only part of it was fixed; the rest was a share of profits. In the case of a man at the top end of the scale, earning 61¢ per hour, the hourly profits available were 17¢, making the possible hourly total 78¢, the possible daily total $6.25. And at the bottom end, with the wage per hour fixed at 34¢, the hourly profits share was 28½¢, the total possible income per hour 62½¢, bringing the total for an 8-hour day to the magic $5.[88] But the profit part of the payment was not automatically granted. And it was this extra, potential but not assured, that persuaded Ford's employees it was worth becoming the sort of person the company preferred.

Some of these preferences reflected Ford's own idio-syncrasies. For example, he neither drank nor smoked, and discouraged his employees from doing either. His first crusade, against cigarettes, put 'The Case Against the Little White Slaver', and the introduction, signed by Ford himself, began: 'If you will study the history of almost any criminal, you will find he is an inveterate cigarette smoker.'[59] That might be crazy, but it was clear enough. Other requirements were broader and more subjective. The 'Sociological Department' now set up under Lee and Marquis was there to establish employees' eligibility for their share of profits. If they were not at once eligible, the Sociological Department would help them become so. And in this way as mixed a bag of immi-grants as could well be imagined would be transformed, as efficiently as possible, into acceptable Americans.

> At the outset a corps of about 200 men . . . picked out for their peculiar fitness as judges of human nature – men who had made a success of running their departments – was organized and put to work gathering facts and figures with reference to every employé of the company. They consulted every available source of information – churches, fraternal organizations, the Government, family Bibles, passports – everything that would give the truth about the men was scrutinized. They also gave advice to the employés as to their living conditions, and the method of handling their money.
>
> No man was urged to change his mode of living if he did not willingly so elect. [But if he did not then of course he might not receive his full wage.]
>
> . . . We find there is only a small percentage of our men that need such help and constant reminding, for just as soon as a man understands our work, and the life worth-while, he needs no help . . . As a matter of fact, there is not

one solitary thing that an employé 'MUST DO' or 'MUST HAVE' to entitle him to a share in the profits. Manhood and thrift are the only requisites . . .

In visiting the homes of foreigners, the Advisors explain to the people, through an interpreter if necessary, the joy and healthful advantage of cleanliness and order, and . . . try to impress this fact especially upon the housewife. Books of photographs showing the desirable home conditions are very often used to great advantage . . .

THRIFT has played an important part in the Profit-Sharing Plan since the beginning. It is expected that employés without dependents will save or invest practically all the profits received by them . . . Young men and women who live up to and beyond their means are revealing traits of character which prevent their being given places of responsibility . . .[90]

Such practices could of course be taken amiss. 'The Welfare Department,' wrote Edmund Wilson severely, 'went in for checking up on the home-life of the workers . . . and this was strongly resented by them.'[91] And John Dos Passos jeered at

That five dollars a day
Paid to good, clean American workmen
Who didn't drink or smoke cigarettes or read or think,
And who didn't commit adultery
And whose wives didn't take in boarders . . .[92]

But Wilson and Dos Passos were sophisticated, educated men; exactly what the Sociological Department's clients were not. And the 30s, when these passages were written, were different and more cynical times. The Sociological Department, as it appeared at its inception, might have been narrowminded, but it was a remarkable enterprise. Under such men as Marquis the Ford Motor Company maintained an employment strategy that could only be described as socially conscious. When Ford boasted that 'A man . . . is equally acceptable whether he has been in Sing-Sing or Harvard,'[93] this was a literal description of company policy. By 1919 hundreds of ex-convicts were working at Highland Park, along with 9,563 'substandard men', a group including amputees, epileptics, the blind, the tubercular and deaf-mutes. Otherwise, however, there were few native-born Americans. A survey in November 1914, revealed that only 29 per cent of Ford employees were American-born; the rest were immigrants from southern and eastern Europe, Poles (21 per cent) and Russians (16 per cent) being the largest groups.[94]

It could reasonably be argued – and was – that this preference for the apparently unemployable was a matter of necessity rather than choice. If few able-bodied Americans were to be found at Ford's, this was because the working conditions there were so intolerable that anyone with a choice preferred to work elsewhere. Only immigrants, fleeing conditions so abjectly frightful that even the assembly line was preferable, would take the kind of work Ford offered. How reliably they would perform it was (at least in the company's view) another matter. So the Sociological Department, like the $5 day, was in the company's interest as much as the workers'. As long as immigrants still retained the tribal loyalties they had arrived with, the shop floor would remain a Babel: foremen had to know how to say 'Hurry up' in several different languages. Worse, impromptu days off might be taken for any number of outlandish festivals: a group of Greeks and Russians was sacked wholesale for absenteeism on the occasion of the Orthodox Easter. The sooner these people could be turned into proper, English-speaking, toilet-trained Americans, the sooner they would produce the standard of work Ford required.

Nevertheless, as in Manchester, genuine enlightenment was

also part of the mix. Impartial observers were impressed by the changes in living conditions among Ford employees between 1914 and 1920. The chief housing inspector of the Detroit Board of Health found them 'greatly improved', especially in congested areas. Homes once filthy had been brought up to a high standard. A Hungarian pastor in Detroit spoke approvingly of the adoption of neat, cleanly ways. A Detroit probation officer considered the good that had been done 'inestimable'. The rector of a church in the Polish district noted the decline in heavy drinking, and the Highland Park police chief thought the change wrought by the Ford plan 'indescribable'. 'Previous to the inauguration of the Plan there were from thirty to forty Ford employees in the cell block each morning . . . but now Ford employees are rarely seen in the Police Station.'[95] There was even a company English school, with lessons taken in company time.

In this almost neurotic desire to iron out national differences, to transform the diverse nationalities with their various languages, customs and religions into acceptably socialized Americans, Ford – as in so much else – reflected his time. As Peter Hall points out, unsocialized immigrants occupied the same threatening niche in the bad dreams of the American middle class as had the urban underclass in Victorian Europe. But where the European reaction 'took the form of a secular Last Judgment: the virtuous poor would be assisted to go directly via the settlement house or the municipal housing project to the garden-city heaven', this did not at all fit the American view, in which 'God helped those who helped themselves, Horatio Alger-fashion, out of the slum and into the ranks of the entrepreneurs.'[96] Whether this wholesale dismantling of the immigrants' own forms of social organization actually improved public order is, of course, another question. But that was not Ford's problem. If suitable ready-made Americans would not come and work for him, he would grow his own.

20. Henry Ford, schemer and idealist.

This golden age of public-spirited social responsibility (Ford even set up a model hospital and trade school) lasted only a few years. By 1919 its impetus was dying away, and Marquis left the company two years later when Ford, during another depression, once again forced his dealers to carry the company by buying unwanted stock for cash. But by then the public image of Henry Ford had taken on a life of its own, bearing little relation to that elusive entity people like to call 'reality' – a connection made more tenuous by the protean and ungraspable nature of Ford's 'real' character. Everyone who knew him remarked on his contradictory nature and unpredictable changeability.

> Take any recent front-view picture or photograph of Henry Ford, and lay a sheet of paper on top of it in such a manner as to cover one eye and one half of the face. You will find that the left half is the face of the idealist, the dreamer, the humanitarian. Kindliness and goodwill beam forth . . . Then take the other half. It is the shrewd face of a sharp business man, alert, somewhat suspicious, full of cunning . . .[97]

Was he, as some thought, a highly complex man who wore a misleading mask of simplicity, or a fundamentally simple man who 'made a good car but . . .wanted to instruct the cosmos'?[98] A man of real social conscience or, in the words of E. G. Pipp, a newspaperman who knew him well, 'as selfish a man as God permitted to breathe'?[99] Some refused to credit him even with making his own good car: according to Peter F. Drucker he 'invented nothing, no new machine, not even a gadget'; J. K. Galbraith discounts his business abilities and attributes the company's success mainly to James Couzens.[100]

Up to a point both Drucker and Galbraith are right: Ford was not an original inventor, like Edison, nor a brilliant businessman like Couzens. But success such as his does not come to the merely lucky. It was founded, above all, on a series of astonishing and original insights. The coups – the concept of the Model T and a marque devoted to a single model, the recognition of the assembly line's revolutionary import, the crucial realization that the factory hand must become a consumer and that welfare provision could benefit the employer as well as the employee – were both stunning and disparate: all they had in common was vision, the ability to follow a hunch in the certainty – borne out time after time – that this was the way to go. He was happy – as with Taylorism or the $5 day – to use other people's good ideas; but W. J. Cameron, an astute journalist and close associate for many years, considered that 'most of what Ford came up [with] was his own. He was a thinker; he wasn't a repeater.'[101] And as Ford himself liked to say, 'Thinking is the hardest work that anyone can do.'[102] Unlike the variety practised by Drucker and Galbraith, however, his thinking was not logical. 'I don't like to read books,' he said. 'They muss up my mind.'[103] Rather, he was intuitive: 'Well, I can't prove it, but I can smell it,' as he once said to Cameron.[104] It was this sense of what both men and engineering required that set Ford apart. Otherwise he remained what he had always been: a country boy fascinated by machines. And in what may have been the greatest coup of all, the public sensed this. For them Ford was and would remain a personal friend and benefactor.

It is true that timing was on his side. Ford became famous too late to attract the attention of the great muckrakers and populist campaigners against big business such as Ida M. Tarbell, Upton Sinclair and William Jennings Bryan, whose heyday straddled the turn of the century. Tarbell had successfully demonized John D. Rockefeller, Sinclair's *The Jungle* had exposed the brutal meat-packing business, and Bryan liked to quote J. P. Morgan as saying, 'America is good enough for me,' before adding, 'Whenever he doesn't like it, he can give it back to us.'[105] The vicious business practices they exposed led to a generation of American tycoons being dubbed 'robber barons'. But by the time Ford reached the zenith of his fame in the 1920s the climate of opinion had changed, and industrial leaders, far from being publicly vilified, were held up as models to be emulated. This was the era summed up by Calvin Coolidge when he said, 'The business of America is business.'

Even so, the public is not naturally attracted to rich men. On the contrary, it welcomes their humiliation. But the machine affectionately known as the 'flivver' or 'Tin Lizzie' was a member of the family; and so, by extension, was her begetter. Countless Model T jokes echoed this affection.

The Ford owner stopped to get his breath after spinning his motor furiously in three unsuccessful attempts to start it. A little girl standing on the curbstone watched him intently for awhile, then timidly inquired, 'Don't you think it would play if you put on a new needle, mister?'

A successful home-made washing-machine can be constructed by putting clothes, water and soap into a barrel and keeping it revolving on the wheels of an inverted Ford.

Gatekeeper: A dollar for the car.
Ford owner: Sold!

Just as Hiram P. Maxim mourned, in a sense, the birth of the auto industry proper, because it marked the end of the daring, footloose 'horseless carriage days' when automobility was a thrill rather than a business,[106] so those countless drivers who knew every wheeze and foible of their Model T, who coaxed it into life on frigid mornings and ministered tenderly to its ailments, never felt the same about later cars. You couldn't have an emotional relationship with them, as so many did with their flivver, and, at least in their own heads, with its maker.

The Ford archives bulge with letters from Model T owners – most of them farmers. Almost all had some improvement to suggest. Some hoped their invention might help pay hospital bills or stave off imminent foreclosure: Mr Ford would understand. Others offered suggestions simply because their car was not perfect and they thought it could be improved – for instance, by a headlight-dipping mechanism or the provision of an adjustable padded headrest: both suggestions taken up by auto companies much, much later. For the basic Model T lent itself to adaptation and modification on a scale unheard of before or since. 'The great days have faded, the end is in sight,' wrote E. B. White in 1936. 'Only one page in the current [Sears Roebuck] catalogue is devoted to parts and accessories for the Model T; yet everyone remembers springtimes when the Ford gadget section was larger than men's clothing, almost as large as household furnishings.'[107] Just as significant, however, is the intimate, joshing, man-to-man tone of this one-sided correspondence:

You know, Mr Ford, when I drive through blizzards on the way home from town, my hands are all bundled up with three pairs of mittens, but they still freeze. Why don't you run the exhaust-pipe up the steering column so I can warm my goll-darn hands?[108]

Would the best transmission in the world interest you? Listen Baby, I've got the Deluxe Baby. Now listen boy. I'm no scientist or automotive engineer or yet a master of machines, but listen here, man, I want some pay for all this. If I come to Detroit, will you promise to give me a square deal? I don't know what anything is worth, but I will trust you. I will have to. If I prove to be a blank, I can work off what I owe you in your shops.[109]

Writing in this way, as thousands did, these people showed their certainty that Henry Ford was one of them. Like them, he distrusted city slickers. 'The modern city has been prodigal, it is today bankrupt and tomorrow it will cease to be,' he wrote.[110] They could not have put it better themselves. And now he had produced the machine they would have produced had they had his application and inspiration. They could rely on him as they might rely on a neighbour or on the Tin Lizzie parked outside in the yard: he knew how they felt, and they knew how he felt. Nothing would or could undo this certainty.

The Model T revolutionized the farmer's life. But for his wife the change was even greater: quite simply, earth-shaking. 'You know, Henry,' wrote a farmer's wife in Rome, Georgia, 'your car lifted us out of the mud. It brought joy into our lives. We loved every rattle in its bones.'[111] Suddenly, into those overworked, isolated existences burst the prospect of freedom. And more than one freedom: for the Model T's engine was not confined to merely automobile uses. It could be hooked up to power anything from a saw to a washing machine.

> Mary [a servant] put the soap in the washing-machine, and the hot water, and the clothes, and I started the engine. It was all that I hoped. Never, never indeed, had I seen clothes washed so rapidly. Luckily, I had thought to nail the legs of the washing-machine to the floor of the back porch . . . Of course some vibration was conveyed along the belt from the automobile, and Mary had to hasten to and fro, bringing more hot water to refill the washing-machine. It was like a storm at sea, or a geyser, or a large fountain. When at good speed the water hardly entered the washing-machine before it dashed madly out again and Isobel [the

21. Customizing the Model T – on the farm and in the snow.

writer's wife] had to help out by putting in more clothes continuously. It used up clothes as rapidly as Rolf's friend's fodder-cutter used up fodder, but I think it cut the clothes into smaller pieces. We discovered this when we hunted up the clothes afterward. We did not know it at the time. All was excitement at the time.[112]

The world of women like these had been limited to the radius of the 'team haul': five miles. As one writer commented in pre-car 1912, 'These farm women find themselves in a new civilization, but not of it.'[113] But with the growth of car ownership (fastest in rural states) their isolated homesteads were knitted into the community, becoming part of a township, a county, a state, ultimately America itself. Ford saw his car, rightly, as more than just a machine: it was 'an educational invention' for 'breaking down sectionalism'.[114] By 1919, 62 per cent of farms owned cars, with the midwest leading at 73 per cent, followed by the west (62 per cent) and the more closely packed east (48 per cent). By 1920, 8 per cent of farms had more than one car.[115]

Predictably, this rush of unprecedented freedom raised eyebrows. 'Women of the central Illinois farms emphatically denounce the libel that the egg industry has gone to pot because they are spending most of their time scudding across the countryside in motor cars and neglecting the poultry yards which have been the foundation of egg production from time immemorial,' scolded *Motor Age* in 1916, its tongue not entirely in its cheek.[116] But the women didn't care: never again would they consent to the loneliness and monotony which had been their lot until Henry Ford released them from it. The automobile was no longer a luxury but an essential: it offered possibilities that, once tasted, could never be given up. 'No one has a right to one [a car] if he can't afford it. I haven't the slightest sympathy for anyone who is out of work if he owns a car,' one businessman told the Lynds. And another virtuous citizen crisply informed them that 'No, sir, we've *not* got a car. That's why we've got a home.' But plenty of Muncie families unhesitatingly mortgaged their homes in order to buy wheels. 'We'd rather do without clothes than give up the car,' said one mother of nine children, and 'I'll go without food before I'll see us give up the car,' said another woman.[117] And as the 1930s wore on and the Depression bit, these women were proved right. As long as you had a car, you had both a home and the mobility to look for work. While there were wheels, there was hope.

The family car opened horizons hitherto closed to all but a privileged few. 'Vacations in 1890? Why, the word wasn't in the dictionary!' exclaimed one 'substantial citizen' of Muncie.[118] But the whole world was open to the automobilist, even if he couldn't afford a hotel. A Canadian wrote to Ford describing how he had travelled two thousand miles, sleeping in the car at night, rising every morning fresh in spirit, listening to singing birds and 'breathing the Lord's free air'.[119] Some were happy to sleep in or beside their machine, wrapped in a blanket, others applied their ingenuity to the holiday problem. Among the most popular of the Model T's myriad adaptations (animal carrier, travelling chapel, snowmobile, police wagon) were those which transformed it into a camper. You could hinge the front seat so that it folded back to form a bed, or the back seat so that it flattened into something like the end-gate in a covered wagon. Or heavy rods might be run from the top of the back seat to the front seat, with a mattress placed on the rods, keeping the sleepers well away from snakes. The *Ford News*, always eager to report new ways with the T, described

One ingenious solution to 'where shall we spend the night' consist[ing] of a canvas cot, extending from the hinges of the front windshield to the back of the rear seat . . . the coiled steel springs, whose tension can be changed by adjusting the ropes, put a comfortable amount of tension on the canvas cot, and it can be adjusted for light or heavy persons. In order to prevent strain on the windshield brackets, the ropes, supporting the front end of the cot, are carried over the windshield posts and are fastened to the headlight brackets, or other convenient part of the car.'

This arrangement would accommodate 'even the tallest men.'[120]

Ford himself did not disdain the simple pleasures of the camping life. With his friends Thomas Edison, Harvey Firestone the rubber magnate and John Burroughs the naturalist, he took two heavily publicized camping trips, in 1918 and 1919, during which the campers were photographed sleeping and eating *al fresco*, chopping wood, and otherwise enjoying themselves, alone but for the photographer, two Packards, two Model Ts, two Ford trucks, tents, cots, stoves, ovens, electric lights, a table large enough for twenty, and a seven-man crew (the supporting cast, needless to say, not evident in the pictures). Stupendously wealthy as Rockefeller, Vanderbilt or Morgan, sole owner of a vast industrial empire, Ford nevertheless remained imaginable: an ordinary fellow who happened to have struck it rich.

» » »

Thomas Jefferson saw cities as 'a tumor on the body politic'; Jane Addams thought the city 'a unit whose organic character had been destroyed'. And Henry Ford followed in this great tradition. 'There is no city now existing that would be rebuilt as it is if it were destroyed,' he said – a sentiment certainly true of

Detroit. He thought cities 'places where social impurities break out in a festering sore'.[121]

Yet, unlike Jefferson or Addams, Henry Ford, always contradictory, designed, built and still owned his very own and personal city: the vast and deafening Rouge with its innumerable buildings, its pipes and chimneys, docks and railroads, ore into automobile in twenty-eight minutes flat. By 1924 forty-two thousand people worked there, by 1929, more than 103,000; as late as 1937–8 it was still expanding. At first he loved it, knew all its corners, spent his happiest hours visiting its far-flung outposts and chatting to his employees, so that his frantic secretary never knew where to find him. But as time went on it palled, until one day he confessed that 'the Rouge is no fun any more'.

At that point, as if in reaction to all that the Rouge represented, he set about building a second complex, one that would express the other Henry Ford, farmer's son and advocate of the simple life, the Henry Ford who liked country dancing and entertained startled visitors to sandwiches filled with a concoction of weeds mashed, ground, seasoned with bergamot, salt and lemon juice and mixed with soybeans. (Purslane he found excellent, including the stems, buckhorn somewhat fibrous, chicory bitter, curly dock good, with a mild flavour, grass fibrous, lambs' quarters tender and good.)[122] This was the Ford who experimented with rural industry, decentralizing light engineering processes so that they could be carried out in village workshops; the Ford who thought the future of car manufacturing lay in materials derived from the infinitely adaptable soybean – a vision of the plastic future, just as his use of soy fibres for suiting looked forward to a world of artificial fibres then undreamed-of. And this was the Ford who built Greenfield Village, recreating the past as avidly and energetically as once he had envisioned, and fashioned, the future.

Greenfield Village is a lovingly assembled memorial to the rural culture that produced Ford and his friends Edison, Burroughs and Firestone. Walk the mellow brick pavement past the replica of Independence Hall that houses the Henry Ford Museum, and you step back into another age. Here, with a hundred antique plant varieties, are merino sheep 'back bred' to be as wrinkly as during the late 1800s on Harvey Firestone's family farm in Ohio. Here is the railroad station from which the young Thomas Edison set out on the momentous journey which ended when he was thrown off the train for conducting experiments in the rear car; and a meticulous recreation of his Menlo Park laboratory. Here is Henry Ford's birthplace, the church at which his family worshipped, the Edison Illuminating Company shop where he had his first job. Here are Edgar Allan Poe's cottage from Fordham, New York, Walt Whitman's house from Melville, New York, Barbara Frietchie's house from Frederick, Maryland, and Patrick Henry's house from Red Hill, Virginia; here is the courthouse where Lincoln practised law, here Luther Burbank's office from Santa Rosa, California. Here are a gristmill, a Michigan sawmill, a cider mill, a carding mill, a tinsmith's, a covered bridge . . . As you or I might buy a table or chair that caught our fancy, so Ford would stop at an antique shop and buy the entire store with the words, 'Pack it up and ship it to Dearborn.' In yet another Fordian contradiction, Greenfield Village's horse and carriage clops round to the rhythm of a gentler life, one which Ford regretted, and which, thanks largely to himself – and despite his best efforts – was dead as the dodo.

When he bought the Wayside Inn near Sudbury, Massachusetts, he had the new highway where the newmodel cars roared and slithered and hissed oilily past (*the new noise of the automobile*)

Moved away from the door,
put back the old bad road,
so that everything might be
the way it used to be
in the days of horses and buggies.[123]

Such an enterprise sits oddly as the work of a man who
so famously proclaimed that 'History is bunk.' In fact, as Ford
himself explained, 'I did not say [history] was bunk. It was
bunk to me . . . but I did not need it very bad.'[124] What he hated
was the paraphernalia of dates and names, the whole mind-
mussing bookish thing. Greenfield Village, though, was another
kind of history – a Fordian history, history as object, tangible
and concrete.

But Greenfield Village is more than a history lesson. As
with everything Henry Ford did or made, it is a journey to
the interior of his head. And like his soybean experiments, or
his encapsulation of the ideal life as 'a city wage and a country
house' – that is, suburbia – Greenfield Village is a vision of
the future as well as the past. Unlike the zoos of artworks put
together by such well-known aesthetes as Henry Clay Frick
the brutal steel baron, or Henry Huntington the land specula-
tor, Ford's collection is intimately connected to its begetter's
imagination. Once again he had demonstrated his direct line to
what made Americans tick, sensed the coming thing: history as
theme park, open to anyone able to drive there. His way into
history was America's own way:, as early as 1938, Greenfield
Village had half a million visitors.

'In 1898 there was one car in operation for every eighteen
thousand people . . . Today,' reported *National Geographic* in
1923, recording Ford's revolution, 'there is one motor-car to
every eight people . . . thirteen million motor cars! Who can
visualize them! . . . the Lincoln Highway, from the banks of the
Hudson to the Golden Gate, is 3,305 miles long. To put them all

on that highway, even in traffic-jam formation, would require that it be widened so that fifteen cars could stand abreast!'[125]

'Why on earth do you need to study what's changing this country?' one of their respondents demanded of the Lynds. 'I can tell you what's happening in just four letters: A-U-T-O!'[126]

Chapter Four

Letchworth, Pasadena, Poundbury: The Suburban Idyll

In 1957, economist Colin Clark published a seminal paper entitled 'Transport: Maker and Breaker of Cities'. This shows that transport, or the lack of it, is the main constraint on the size and growth of cities. And as for almost the whole of history transport has consisted chiefly of boats, horses and wagons, these were the needs most of the world's cities reflected. No citizen of ancient Athens or Rome, Peking or Persepolis, would have been overwhelmed by either the scale or the pace of eighteenth-century London, Paris or Amsterdam.

By contrast, it is impossible to imagine such a person surviving five minutes in any modern city. Where do people live, where do they buy food, what are these hurtling vehicles lacking all visible means of propulsion? Where does the city begin, where does it end? Within fifty years of its introduction the car transformed a coherent way of life that had survived virtually unchanged since the beginning of civilization.

Before the arrival of mechanically propelled transport, city boundaries were limited by the distance a person could walk in an hour, which was as far as a person living at the city's edge could be expected to travel to work in the centre. This is known to planners as 'the walking city'. Another big constraint on growth was the high cost of city living, food in particular being expensive to transport and keep fresh, so that urban life was only possible for those earning relatively good wages in specialist, high-value work. But then came the railways; and for the first time in history this economic barrier to urban growth could be overthrown. Trains brought food and raw materials quickly and cheaply into the city centre, and took finished goods out. The result was an explosion in nineteenth-century city populations. The number of people living in Paris quadrupled, from 547,756 in 1801 to 2,269,023 by 1881. And London swelled from 864,845 in 1801 to 3,834,354 by 1881 and 4,232,118 ten years later.[1]

But this vast increase in population was not accompanied by any change in the physical size of the city envelope. For, although the railroads meant that large cities could now employ and feed many more people, there was no equivalent modernization of transport within the city itself. You might travel from Manchester to London in three or four hours, but once you arrived there you were back with muscle power – chiefly your own. As the century progressed, a few horse-drawn omnibus services were introduced. But fares were expensive, and wages low. So most people still had to live within the walking city.

The results were both predictable and horrific. City centre population densities rocketed to unheard-of levels. In Paris they reached, by 1856, 120,000 per square mile; in London, by 1841, 110,000 per square mile; in New York, by 1900, 100,000 per square mile.[2] And these figures by no means told the whole story. For the better-off still lived comparatively spaciously, while the poor were crammed ever tighter into rotting tenements. In London and Paris the top densities were probably around 150,000 per square mile, while in Manhattan's Lower East Side this figure was more than doubled.[3] By 1893, New York's 10th Ward, populated mainly by Russian and Polish Jewish immigrants, was 'more crowded than the most congested

European city; part of the 11th Ward, with nearly 1,000 to the acre [that is, 640,000 per square mile], was even more congested than the worst district of Bombay . . . almost certainly the most crowded urban neighbourhood in the world'.[4] The notorious 'dumb-bell' tenement design, the result of a competition held in 1879 – an *improvement*, be it noted, on what had gone before – 'allowed twenty-four families to be crowded on to a lot twenty-five feet wide and 100 feet deep, with ten out of fourteen rooms on each floor having access only to an almost lightless (and airless) airwell'.[5] Thirty-nine of these tenement houses were squeezed on to one two-hundred-by-four-hundred-foot block; they contained 605 separate units housing 2,781 people, who shared 264 water-closets, with not one bath between them; 441 rooms were entirely unventilated, and another 635 gave only on to airshafts.[6]

This was the 'City of Dreadful Night' that inspired, if that is the word, Edward Bellamy's utopian fantasy *Looking Backwards*, published in 1887 and set in a transformed Boston of the year 2000 – a Boston of spacious, airy streets and houses, congenial working arrangements, social equality and gentle shopping trips. 'Do you not know', demands its hero, Julian West, on his return from the future to the Boston of 1887, 'that close to your doors a great multitude of men and women, flesh of your flesh, live lives that are one agony from birth to death?' *Looking Backwards* was an instant bestseller, propelling Bellamy to the forefront of radical politics; and the fact that this rather mild and colourless blueprint for hygienic socialism, devoid of either characterization or excitement, should speak so directly to so many, shows (among other things) the extent to which people felt trapped within the terrible and, it seemed, inescapably overcrowded late-nineteenth-century industrial city.

The tenement houses of these cities were notoriously filthy; but the streets were even filthier. For as economic activity increased, so did the number of horses needed to service it. The railway age extended no further than the freight depot: within the city, there was still no alternative to the horse and cart. As the century went on, electric streetcars carried increasing numbers of passengers, but they were useless for delivering loads door to door; and bicycles, which could move door to door, could not carry heavy loads. Between 1870 and 1900 the human population of America's ten largest cities doubled, but the number of heavy-horse teams more than quadrupled. By 1900, Manhattan contained over 130,000 horses.[7]

This system was unsatisfactory on many counts. It was expensive: moving freight by horse and wagon for short distances within cities cost far more than moving it far greater distances between cities by steam railroad. It used up scarce space: horses that worked in the city had to be stabled there. And urban herds could not go on growing indefinitely. Five acres of land were needed to feed each horse,[8] and suitable agricultural land, even in America, was a commodity in finite supply. In addition, horse traffic was slow, leading to congestion; and if a horse dropped dead in the street – which often happened: working horses did not have long life expectancies – the carcass could take hours to remove. During the 1880s, the New York Sanitation Department was removing fifteen thousand dead horses every year.[9] And not just horses but their by-products, solid and liquid. Each horse dropped between ten and twenty pounds of manure daily. In New York, this meant a minimum of 1,300,000 pounds of manure a day: the manure pile next to the Central Park stables measured thirty thousand cubic feet.[10]

> The mud! And the noise! And the smell! [wrote H. B. Creswell, remembering London in the 1890s].
> . . . Meredith refers to the 'anticipatory stench of its cab-stands' on railway approaches to London: but the

characteristic aroma – for the nose recognized London with gay excitement – was of stables, which were commonly of three or four storeys with inclined ways zigzagging up the faces of them; [their] middens kept the castiron filigree chandeliers, that glorified the reception rooms of upper and lower middle class homes throughout London, encrusted with dead flies and, in late summer, veiled with jiving clouds of them.

A more assertive mark of the horse was the mud that, despite the activities of a numerous corps of red-jacketed boys who dodged among the wheels and hooves with pan and brush in service to iron bins at the pavement edge, either flooded the streets with churnings of 'pea-soup' that at times collected in pools overbrimming the kerbs, and at others covered the road-surfaces with axle-grease or bran-laden dust . . . The pea-soup condition was met by wheeled 'mud-carts' each attended by two ladlers clothed as for Icelandic seas in thigh boots, oilskins collared to the chin, and sou-westers sealing in the back of the neck . . .[11]

This carpet of horse shit was not just unpleasant, but dangerous to health. Tuberculosis was the leading cause of death in the 1890s, but although no pharmaceutical cure was discovered until the 1940s, death rates fell significantly as soon as city horse populations began to decline.[12] It is ironic now to reflect that clean city air was perceived as one the car's first great gifts.

It was the electric streetcar that first loosened the tight boundaries of the walking city, which now typically took the form of a star or wheel of tramcar and rail lines whose spokes converged on a central hub. Given a (slow) average travel speed of two mph on foot, a walking town had encompassed only seven square miles of land, slightly more if faster walking was previsioned. The horse omnibus, travelling at four mph, opened up fifteen square miles. The horsecar, where friction was diminished by metal rails, travelled at six mph and opened up thirty square miles. And the electric trolley, travelling at twelve mph, opened up a hundred square miles.[13]

But the real agent of transformation was the car. Its advent meant that the spokes of the transit-line star no longer dictated the pattern of housing. Now it was possible to live anywhere. For the first time in human history the city envelope was, finally and absolutely, burst apart.

» » »

As the twentieth century began, a generation of idealists and experimenters turned their attention to the question of the good city life. Some, such as Edward Bellamy, envisaged a transformation of the city itself. Others, such as Henry Ford, pursued a different ideal, in which the pleasures of country living would be combined with urban opportunities. On both sides of the Atlantic, routes were mapped out to this town/country paradise. But although they started out in similar ways, they took very different directions – dictated, as always, by the dominant transport modes.

Letchworth, in Hertfordshire, and Pasadena, California, were two such communities. Both were founded at the same time, early in the twentieth century. And although in some ways the contrast could not be greater (Pasadena, nestling beneath the the spectacular backdrop of the San Gabriel Mountains, the epitome of gleaming, sunsoaked California prosperity; Letchworth, set in modest, mildly picturesque Hertfordshire with its old market towns and terrifically restored villages, redolent of unassuming vegetarianism, wooden armchairs with adjustable backs, and George Orwell's pink-kneed socialists boarding the bus to summer school) they still retain a surprising amount in common. The diamond-paned, picturesque Arts and Crafts architecture that characterizes Letchworth is scattered –

albeit on a much larger and grander scale – throughout Pasadena. In both, trees line the streets and shade the gardens. Both retain the sense of a place laid out for pleasure and amenity rather than mere profit or utility. But as the twentieth century progressed they developed into different worlds.

In Europe, which still travelled by train, and would continue to do so until well after World War II, the notion of the good life remained urban. H. B. Creswell, remembering horse-ridden London, recalled too the city's enchantments – its infinity of curious shops, its wonderful foods and restaurants: attractions so potent that, despite the squalor, the centre city still remained the centre of fashion. For European idealists, the aim was not to abandon the city but to create new and better forms of urban life, tight-knit communities which would offer city amenities but avoid the drawbacks of overcrowding.

The first and most famous of these experiments took place in England, in the new 'garden city' of Letchworth. Thirty miles north-west of London, with excellent train connections to both London and its sister-settlement Welwyn Garden City, Letchworth was built firmly around the railway station. Not only were cars unnecessary to life in Letchworth, they were, even as late as 1930, virtually non-existent there.

Letchworth was the creation of an apparently modest but deceptively forceful shorthand writer called Ebenezer Howard. Born in London in 1850, Howard had emigrated as a young man to America, where he unsuccessfully tried farming in Nebraska before moving to Chicago and taking up stenography. These travels gave him a sight of the technology-led, self-sufficient communities of the American west; and his interest in town planning may well have been aroused by his experience of the great Chicago fire of 1872, in which much of the city was razed to the ground, to be rebuilt from scratch. In 1898, having returned to England and become involved in Fabian socialist politics, he produced his own blueprint for an ideal community

22. Letchworth High Street, *c.*1930.

under the title *To-morrow: A Peaceful Path to Real Reform*, reissued four years later as *Garden Cities of To-morrow*.

Howard summarized his aims in a famous diagram, The Three Magnets. In the centre are The People. Where will they be pulled? Magnet number one is the town, with its high chances of employment but its foul air and murky sky. Magnet number two is the country, with its abundance of water and bright sunshine but its lack of jobs, amusement and public spirit. And combining the best of both is a new concept: the third magnet, the town-country, combining beauty of nature with social opportunity in an atmosphere of Freedom and Co-operation. Garden cities would offer jobs as well as houses: easily accessible work was an essential part of the mix. Garden cities would be walking (or bicycling) cities, set in the countryside and linked by electric railways.

Letchworth was conceived as a business enterprise, albeit a non-profit one. It took delicate and secret negotiations with fifteen owners to buy the original site in 1903 – if word had got out the land price would have risen, and Howard was not a rich man: raising money for his Garden City Pioneer Company was always a headache. A diagram entitled 'The Vanishing Point of Landlord's Rent' showed how the scheme would work financially. As rentals paid off the loan taken out (by Howard personally) to establish the city in the first place, they would be used, not for private profit, but to provide funds for amenities and also 'to found pensions with liberty for our aged poor, now imprisoned in workhouses; to banish despair and awaken hope in the breasts of those that have fallen; to silence the harsh voice of anger, and awaken the soft notes of brotherliness and goodwill'.[14] As urban land values built up, accrued profits would flow not into the landlord's purse but back into the community. For Howard, as for Edward Bellamy, socialist and co-operative values were an essential part of his project.

With his architectural associates, Barry Parker and Raymond

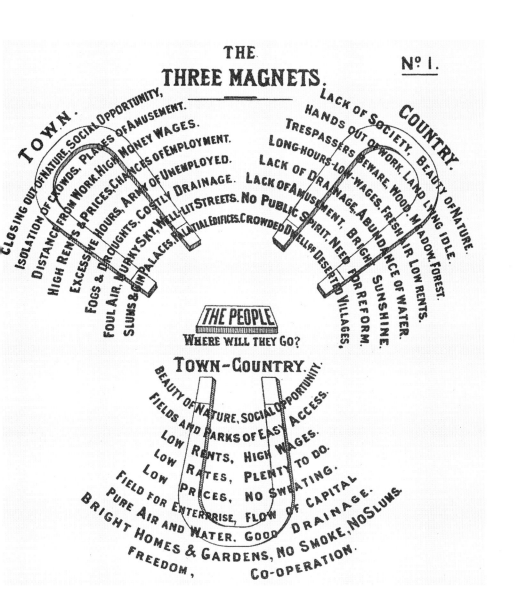

23. The Three Magnets.

Unwin, Howard now set about funding and designing the first stage of his new project: a Co-operative Quadrangle where housing and domestic work would be shared by co-operating tenants. He produced a prospectus for potential investors, emphasizing Letchworth's convenient rail links to London and its salubrious climate. Unfortunately, though not unexpectedly, such financiers as were prepared to support Howard preferred to put their money into something less *outré* than co-operatives, and the early years of construction produced only conventional dwellings. This occasioned a brisk argument between Howard and his fellow-Fabian H. G. Wells, like Howard an enthusiast for both progressive social engineering and the Arts and Crafts movement – he was then living in a splendid house commissioned from the young Charles Voysey. Wells was very impatient at Howard's failure to build his co-operative flats, characteristically arguing that 'in a few short years all ordinary houses will be out of date and not saleable at any price'. But Howard told Wells that he must wait: the Letchworth experiment would make people 'green with envy' rather than 'red with laughing' at it.[15]

Wells was, of course, himself a prolific creator of social and scientific utopias (though when he tried to put his ideals into practice in real life, the results were, to say the least, mixed).[16] His *Modern Utopia*, published in 1905, set out the parameters for a supremely Wellsian dwelling – one that might have come straight from a Parker and Unwin brochure, though the notion of the brilliant and social Wells inhabiting Letchworth is so unthinkable as to be comic:

A pleasant boudoir, a private library and study, a private garden plot . . . There are sometimes little cooking corners in these flats – as one would call them on earth – but the ordinary Utopian would no more think of a special private kitchen for his dinners than he would think of a private flour mill and dairy farm.[17]

The co-operative flats, which would turn out very much as Wells had described, were finally begun in 1909, and in 1913 Howard and his wife moved into Homesgarth, the first quadrangle. Nothing could have been less revolutionary-looking. Parker and Unwin were part of the Arts and Crafts movement inspired by William Morris, preferring steeply pitched roofs and small-paned casement windows that give little indication of the airy spaces within. The charge for a three bedroom flat with two sitting rooms was £6. 3s. 4d. per week for two persons, 'including rent, rates, water rates, central heating during winter months, full attendance in Central Dining Room, outside window cleaning, boot cleaning and removal of house refuse daily, together with table d'hote breakfast, luncheon and dinner, plus 28s a week for each additional person'.[18]

Letchworth embodied the progressive spirit of the time, in which physical improvements were bound up with social ideals such as the freeing of women from such traditional bonds as childcare and housework. Wells, always looking for ways to liberate higher natures from the inhibiting demands of compulsory family life, had proposed a scheme for the 'endowment of motherhood', by which those who did not wish to spend their lives looking after children could hand over their babies to those who did. But Howard's experiment, unlike Wells's or Bellamy's, was now actually under way. And it extended beyond mere housing. People had to have employment, and much of Howard's effort was directed towards attracting suitable industries to Letchworth. This was not easy, but eventually J. M. Dent, a big publishing house, agreed to establish its printing and binding works there. And soon after came the huge Spirella factory, 'to make corsets which Letchworth women obviously never wear, but which their husbands sell at great profit to the less enlightened women in other towns'.[19]

The magnificent Spirella building, Letchworth's nearest approximation to a cathedral, stands as a secular monument to Ebenezer Howard's view of the good life. Designed by an otherwise obscure Arts and Crafts architect called Cecil Hignet and built in three stages between 1912 and 1920, it employed, in its heyday, two thousand people. Then the bottom (so to speak) fell out of the corset market, and by the time the factory finally closed its doors in 1987 the building was falling into disrepair. Refurbished as offices, little now remains of the original interior spaces, once loud with the buzz of extra-heavy sewing machines inserting bones and eyelets into firmly controlling undergarments. But the visitor may still get some sense of the original Spirella spirit when she emerges into the great ballroom, its sprung floor and imposing stage loud with the ghosts of big bands and foxtrotters.

A ballroom, in a factory? But this was no ordinary factory. Spirella, like Letchworth itself, catered for every aspect of life. Like Ford in Dearborn, though starting from an almost diametrically opposite political position, Ebenezer Howard had created a kind of welfare state *avant la lettre*, within which a benign management, industrial but also social, smoothed your path from the moment you were born until it was time to take up your co-operatively husbanded pension.

The experimental urban spirit was not confined to Britain. In particular, there was a long-standing American tradition of experimental communities in which domestic work, childcare and, occasionally, husbands and wives were shared. The Owenites of New Harmony, the Oneida community, the Fourierites, the Shakers, the Rappists, all lived variants of this communal life. Most, though not all, of these communities sooner or later faded away, either through fallings-out or (in the case of the celibate though longer-lasting Shakers) natural inanition. And in

24. The Spirella Building.

1910, a year after building work began at Homesgarth, another pair of Arts and Crafts architects, the Heineman brothers, decided to try something similarly co-operative, if on a smaller and less ambitious scale, in Pasadena, California.

Pasadena was a winter resort town built, like Letchworth, around the railroad station, whence it connected to downtown Los Angeles and so, via the Santa Fe Railroad, to Chicago and the east. A little later a trolley-car line opened another route, to Santa Monica and the beach. There was also a tourist railroad up Mount Lowe, with restaurants and a funicular. For Pasadena revolved around tourism and was famous for its great hotels, the Hotel Green beside the railroad tracks, the Royal Raymond across the road, the huge Huntington, designed by an architect specializing in railroad stations, and the luxurious Vista del Arroyo overlooking the Arroyo Seco. These, like the Spirella factory in Letchworth, provided not just a living but a focus for Pasadena life. Both tourists and residents enjoyed concerts, outings to the mountains and the beach, and balls throughout the winter season. And although a hotel is very different from a factory, however enlightened, the comparison is not entirely far-fetched. In both places a small, permanent community was making a model life for itself away from the big city – a life that included both work and pleasure, and with a sense of public spirit that was given concrete expression in Pasadena's elaborate town hall.

The Heineman brothers' vision echoed this social spirit. It was embodied in the bungalow court, a new form of low-cost housing consisting of a number of small attached houses or separate bungalows grouped around a central garden. Like Howard's quadrangles, these combined the amenities of a single-family residence – privacy, gardens – with the community and security of an apartment. Unlike the quadrangles, these were not service apartments: each bungalow had its own kitchen. But they did incorporate some advanced ideas. Double

25. Horse-tram leaving the Royal Raymond Hotel,
Pasadena, late 1880s.

26. Bowen Court, one of the Heineman brothers'
bungalow courts, Pasadena.

bungalows were designed as two self-contained units connected by a sliding door, so that the inhabitants – whether married couples or friends – could live separate lives should they so wish. And a communal sewing room and laundry overlooked a play area, facilitating easy and pleasant childcare. (Howard dealt with the childcare question by the peculiarly British expedient of banning children under ten from his schemes: 'Families with children cannot go to central dining-rooms.' Another scheme was proposed which would 'be unique in that the promoters desire children to live there instead of repelling them', but this was never built).[20]

Letchworth today remains much as it was when Ebenezer Howard built it. You can still negotiate it on foot; the rail station remains at the centre of the town. By contrast, Pasadena is

transformed, its rail station long closed, its old core a mere pinprick amid the spreading avenues of today's city. Even as the Heineman brothers were building their co-operative courts, the United States was passing from one transport age to another. And California, whose abundance of oil and sunshine ensured cheap motoring on continuously passable roads, was at the forefront of this transformation. By the end of the 1920s there was already one car for every two Californians.[21] Wealthy Pasadena probably reached this figure even sooner. As a result, the small town planted around the great hotels lasted, as a commercially viable entity, less than twenty years, its centre already in decline by the mid-1920s, outdated almost as soon as built. In automobile terms it was an anachronism, lacking space, parking or indeed any *raison d'être*. The separated, self-sufficient automobile way of life was diametrically opposed to that habit of shared amusements which had grown up around the railroads and hotels. The rail line up Mount Lowe closed down, no longer needed now that people could drive there; the hotels faded away as people discovered the pleasures of family holidays in the car. In 1929 the decision was taken to widen Pasadena's main

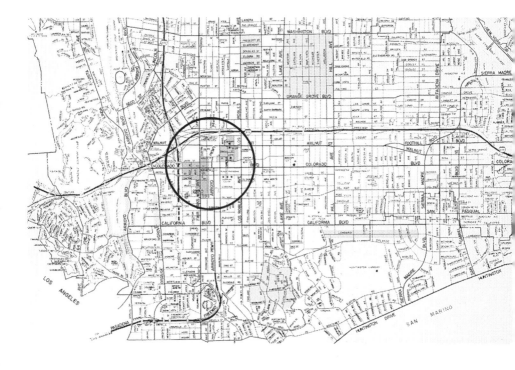

27. Pasadena. The tiny pre-car city occupied the shaded blocks around Fair Oaks Avenue and Colorado Boulevard.

avenue, Colorado Boulevard, by fourteen feet on each side so that automobiles could make a U-turn there. The town took on wholly new proportions, both physical and psychological.

This second great building phase, of long avenues and wide, wide streets across which you peer as a traveller might survey the further reaches of the Amazon, stands as a monument to the automobile's great gift: the freedom to do exactly what you want. Shaded by huge magnolias, Pasadena's boulevards display a zoo of dreams – Arts and Crafts, Mission Revival, Spanish Colonial Revival, Monterey Revival, Mediterranean Revival, Moorish Revival, and countless others that defy categorization, their luxuriantly tree-thick plots kept verdant by built-in sprinklers, so that a walk across a Pasadena lawn resembles some Renaissance *jeu d'eau*, fountains breaking out beneath your feet just when you least expect them. But then, feet are not the required mode in this post-pedestrian city of the machine age. Plots, buildings, trees – everything combines to dwarf the merely human. Only wheels can provide the scale and speed necessary to negotiate the new Pasadena.

This – individualism crystallized around the automobile – was the dream that swept America.

» » »

The American response to the overcrowded city was simple. Anyone who could, moved out.

The 'rise of the suburbs' [wrote Adna Ferrin Weber in the *North American Review* in May 1898] is by far the most cheering movement of modern times. It means an essential modification of the process of concentration of population that has been taking place during the last hundred years and brought with it many of the most difficult political and social problems of the day. To the

Anglo-Saxon race life in the great cities cannot be made to seem a healthy and natural mode of existence. The fresh air and clear sunlight, the green foliage and God's clear blue sky are dear to the heart of this people, who cannot be reconciled to bringing up their children in hot, dusty, germ-producing city tenements and streets.[22]

'Respectable families', the 'Anglo-Saxon race' – these were the ones whose tolerance for the vicissitudes of city life was, apparently, lowest. And since travelling to work by public transport was expensive, costing roughly 20 per cent of the average daily wage,[23] these, by great good fortune, were also the ones who could afford the new suburban houses, and the transit fares and automobiles to go with them. By the 1880s about 10 per cent of residents in major American cities owned their own home and employed at least one domestic servant,[24] and it was this prosperous WASP group – lawyers, doctors, successful businessmen – that led the move to the suburbs. Wealthy and prominent New York families began to colonize the North Shore of Long Island as early as the 1870s; fashionable settlements followed the railway lines up from New York into Westchester County and out from Philadelphia along the Reading Railroad's main line. The burden of fares for the daily journey into the city was eased by 'commutation' – a cheaper deal for regular customers. 'The electric railway', declared its inventor Frank Sprague in 1904, 'has transformed American life.'[25]

But the railways' contribution was insignificant compared to that of the car. Within a decade of its introduction, the automobile had become – for those who could afford it – the key to the ideal life. For the first time in human history you could live almost anywhere you liked with no sacrifice of amenity. 'I doubt if today there is not in the heart of every young man and woman an ambition and hope to someday own a little home out in a subdivision of some charming wooded hillside,' wrote one suburban booster in 1920.[26] Work, shops, schools remained necessary parts of life. But so long as you had a car, their location need have only the most minimal bearing on where you lived. 'When I sold a car,' said Roy Chapin of Oldsmobile, 'I sold it with the honest conviction that I was doing the buyer a favour in helping him to take his place in a big forward movement.'[27] By 1922, 135,000 suburban homes in sixty American cities were wholly dependent upon the automobile for transportation; by 1940, 13 million Americans lived in suburban communities unreached by public transport.[28] It was a solution to urban problems the author of *Looking Backwards* had never envisaged – one so successful that by 1980, a century after Edward Bellamy sprang to fame and with the date at which he had set his utopia fast approaching, 83.7 per cent of the population of metropolitan Boston lived in the suburbs.[29]

As early as 1901 this future was visible to those with the eyes to see it. 'Automobiles, motor bicycles and flying machines . . . will make it easy to travel fifty or sixty miles an hour in your own conveyance,' proclaimed an optimistic, or prescient, urban reformer that year. 'No respectable family will be without its automobile or flying machine, and motor bicycles will be thick as mosquitoes on the Jersey coast. The country will be covered with a network of magnificent highways.'[30] And so it was. For Europeans the adjective 'suburban' has somewhat pejorative associations of unadventurous dullness. But in America the suburbs soon became the place to be.

As a result, city life swiftly declined. Once the fashionable streets had been located near town centres; now they lost their cachet as the money moved out – frequently to see the automobile trade, first brought in to service the cars of wealthy residents, take over. 'Probably never before has a popular mechanical invention had such a potent influence in diverting a prominent street from its original purpose . . . as has the automobile industry in transmuting Michigan Boulevard in Chicago from a residence to a business street,' observed the *Architectural Record* in 1910; and the same might have been said of almost any city in America.[31]

The mechanics of this transformation may be observed in the metamorphosis of Peachtree Street, Atlanta. Before 1910, this was the city's smartest residential street. It therefore contained many early automobile owners; and they needed places that would garage their cars in winter and provide general mechanical repairs all year round. As a result, a number of automobile-related businesses established themselves on Peachtree Street. In 1910, six firms had set up in business there. By 1915 there were twenty, and by 1920, forty. There were also tyre dealers, electric battery companies and shops selling general auto accessories. By 1920 automobile-related businesses outnumbered single family residences. 'At the present time,' reported the *Atlanta Constitution* in 1921, 'all but a few of the handsome homes . . . have been dismantled and removed.' Between 1920 and 1930 other businesses moved in, and by 1930 only two single-family residences remained. All the rest of Peachtree Street's one-time residents had relocated to newly fashionable neighbourhoods on the north edge of the city, growth to the east being blocked by the city of Decatur, to the south by a number of small townships, and to the west by the Chattahoochee River and the black population of Atlanta's 1st Ward.[32] In time middle-class African-Americans established their own suburbs; for those who could afford cars this was a double freedom, both in the sense that cars brought freedom to everyone, and also because they no longer had to cope with segregated public transport. Those who could not afford cars remained in the city, caught in the downward spiral, unable to travel to work in new industries located in the suburbs, their old neighbourhoods destroyed as new roads sought the cheapest land.

Even where cities possessed natural amenities these slipped into disuse as attention was redirected outwards. Writing in 1947, Paul and Percival Goodman pointed out the 'ludicrous anomaly of New York's bathing-places'. Robert Moses, the city's Parks Commissioner, legislated himself powers to drive parkways through Long Island's carefully secluded private estates, at the end of which he created wonderful bathing-beaches for New Yorkers. These, however, were accessible only by car – and specifically *in*accessible to public transport: the parkway bridges were too low for trucks, and also, not coincidentally, for buses. Non-car-owners rode the subway to Coney Island. Meanwhile swimming on the city's doorstep in the Hudson and East Rivers was forbidden because of pollution. Why did the Parks Commissioner not make some effort to clean the rivers up and create bathing places along the city frontage? Because the parkways, including their leisure benefits, reflected the shifting tax-base and the desirability of suburbanization. The commuter population of Westchester and Nassau Counties, served by Moses' new roads, increased by 350,000 during the 1920s. And when Levittown, the apotheosis of the suburb, was built in the post-World War II boom, it was located just off an interchange on Moses' Wantagh State Parkway, built nearly twenty years earlier as one of the approaches to Jones Beach State Park.[33] Meanwhile the 'venturesome poor boys of the city' made do, as they always had, with what the city offered for free: fire-hydrant fountains in the ever more dangerous streets, swimming under the 'sidelong surveillance of usually reasonable police' in the polluted river at the end of their street.[34]

Recreation was not the only amenity to vanish from city centres. Shops, too, began to move out. The car had changed living patterns: now it began to revolutionize shopping habits.

California, with its early and widespread car ownership, naturally led the way in car-related innovations, and the seeds of this new way of shopping may be traced to a new type of automobile service station that appeared in Los Angeles just before World War I. These 'super-service stations' offered a variety of services previously available only under an array of different roofs: not only gas and oil but lubrication and cleaning, general repairs and sales of tyres and other accessories.

The difference between filling-stations and other shops was situation. Where shops were traditionally tied to a local customer base in a particular village or town, filling-stations could be anywhere, so long as plenty of cars passed by. So filling-stations (and then super-service stations) located out of town, where land was cheaper. Meantime, as the number of cars increased, shopping in the traditional manner became increasingly problematic. Downtown business districts became choked with traffic and short of parking; stopping was often specifically forbidden on the busy corners that had formerly been the best trading sites. And retailers realized that the car and refrigerator between them made all this agony unnecessary. If customers could buy petrol out of town, why should those same customers be tied to the high street when it came to buying food? As the head of an advertising agency specializing in food accounts put it, 'distance is a negligible consideration [and] the automobile is a convenient shopping basket'.[35] The result was the drive-in market, in which many different food retailers shared a single space, located, like the super-service station, not in a town or suburb but alongside a busy road. Customers drove in and parked facing the storefront, giving their orders directly from the car. Even if they got out, they still did not have to face the hurly-burly of the street but could shop in a semi-private controlled environment. From the customers' point of view the advantages were convenience and informality (if you didn't leave the car there was no need even to take out your curlers or change your slippers). For

28. Drive-in market, *c*.1929.

the retailers, there were savings on shared rental and utilities, a larger customer base (since patrons were not tied to any particular locality but stopped off as they drove by) and, as a result, faster turnover.

Soon even the drive-in market began to seem dowdy and old-fashioned. In 1931 the number of new such projects planned for Los Angeles amounted to only one-third of those undertaken the previous year; in 1932 only three were built.[36] Of course, these were depression years. At the beginning of 1931 business activity in the region was 30 per cent below 'normal' and declined a further 20 per cent the following year.[37] This, however, was not the direct reason for the drive-in market's decline. The customer base was still there and still eating. But it had to be competed for (something car manufacturers would also find at this period). People had less money, and it had to go further. So low prices became an ever more important factor in attracting custom; and if a merchant was to lower prices he had to increase turnover, by drawing in more customers and selling more goods. The result was the supermarket.

In the supermarket, shopping became entertainment. In 1938 the *Saturday Evening Post* followed a fictional family – the New Jersey Muzaks – as they took in the new shopping experience:

[The Muzaks] discovered their first supermarket one Saturday night when a traffic jam slowed up their fourth-hand automobile. The three Muzak children saw a glare of light down the street and simultaneously shouted 'Fire!' Poppa Muzak maneuvered the car out of traffic and parked. They elbowed through the sidewalk crowds, to stand finally with mouths agape. The glare came from red and white floodlights illuminating a square one-story white building of modernistic design. Its seventy-five foot plate-glass front was covered with banners announcing: 'Supermarket Grand Opening.' Strings of pennants fluttered on the streamlined roof; and multicolored signs flamed from the triangular tower. The interior was a blaze of brilliant white light. Down one side of the building glittered the sparkling glass and enamel of the longest meat case Momma Muzak had ever seen. Across the front of the store spread a monster display of fresh fruits and vegetables . . . The huge building was completely filled with pile after pile of foods – acres of it, it seemed to momma . . . The store was jammed with a thousand customers.

Big-eyed, the little Muzaks led the way through clicking green metal turnstiles, and things began happening to them – free chocolate-coated ice-cream bars for the children, cigarettes for Poppa Muzak, a cut flower for momma . . .

'Look, poppa,' [Mrs Muzak] cried. 'My coffee! Only thirteen cents! Never did I buy it cheaper than nineteen cents at Schmaltz's. Maybe I should get a pound.'

Poppa waved his cigarette expansively. 'Maybe two pounds you should get. Or three.'[38]

So the supermarket embarked upon its all-conquering career. By 1953 over a third of American food chains were estimated to have switched to self-service, which had become the rule for all new units.[39] Frank Lloyd Wright's Broadacre City, envisioned in 1931, had arrived:

. . . the great architectural highway with its roadside markets, super-service stations, fine schools and playgrounds, small, integrated, intensive farming units, great automobile objectives and fine homes winding up the beautiful natural features of the landscape'.[40]

Within the cities, meanwhile, a cycle of decline set in that would soon become familiar, creating problems that remain unsolved.

As . . . taxpayers left, the demand for middle- to upper-income dwelling units in older neighborhoods declined. At the same time, population increase among low-income minorities, coupled with the demolitions of inner-city housing for new expressways, produced an increase in the demand for low-income housing. The new residents required more health care and social-welfare services from the city government than did the old, but they were less able to pay for them. To increase expenditures, municipal authorities levied higher property taxes, thus encouraging middle-class homeowners to leave, causing the cycle to repeat. In contrast, suburbs were often able to keep tax burdens low by having private trash collection, volunteer fire departments, and unpaid ambulance services. In particular, they benefited from having a small percentage of population living at the poverty level and so requiring government assistance.[41]

The effect was such, writes urban historian Kenneth Jackson, as had previously been experienced only after plague or whole-sale imperial decline. And once begun, it was hard to reverse. By 1990, 14 per cent of city census tracts were classified as high-poverty, more than twice the figure of twenty years earlier.[42] Jackson quotes a federal official: 'There are some parts of these cities so empty they look as if someone had dropped nerve-gas.'[43]

Auto historian Clay McShane writes that 'In their head-long search for modernity through mobility, American urbanites made a decision to destroy the living environments of nineteenth-century neighborhoods by converting their gathering-places into traffic jams, their playgrounds into motorways, and their shopping-places into elongated parking lots.'[44] But the people who owned the cars lived in the suburbs, not the cities. These were not *their* neighbourhoods or playgrounds; they drove into the city to work or shop and out again at night, occasionally remaining to enjoy such non-participatory urban attractions as theatres. For them, parking-space was the overwhelming city requirement. Amenity was a matter for the 'dormitories' – as they significantly became known – where the better-off now lived.

The new suburbanites were naturally eager to avoid a repetition of the cycle of property devaluation that had destroyed their old neighbourhoods, and the method they chose was 'zoning', first tried out in Germany. This policy, introduced to New York in 1911 by Edward M. Bassett, enabled cities to regulate land use and building heights in their various districts, keeping industry and commerce separate from housing. Zoning's stated aim was (in Bassett's words) to guarantee 'the health, safety, morals, comfort, convenience and welfare of the community'.[45] But this left unspoken the most important guarantee of all. Zoning ensured that suburban properties could never be devalued by encroaching industrial development. And it worked: a standard text of the late 1920s was able happily to report that, in every city with well-established zoning, 'property values are reported stabilized and in many instances substantially increased'.[46]

» » »

The essence of a town, whatever its size, is multifariousness. Letchworth, no larger than many suburbs, has its more and less prosperous sections, its residential streets and its shopping areas, its factories and workshops, all part of the same whole and easily accessible. But this mix was the very thing zoning was designed to avoid. When you stepped outside your front door in the zoned suburb, you saw only houses like your own, inhabited by your exact social, economic and racial peers. You could spend your whole life segregated in this way, beginning in a development aimed at young married couples with small children, ending in a retirement community. And in this unvarying homogeneity, zoning encapsulated the distinction between the suburb and the town. In the suburb, life was irrevocably split into its component parts. Every activity involved a journey – which was to say, a drive.

To be free in the suburbs, then, you had to have a car. And this adds particular poignancy to a surprising statistic: while more than 70 per cent of American men aged over seventy in 1987 held driving licences, this was true of only 30 per cent of women the same age.[47] Presumably this thirty per cent comprised the better-off, including many suburbanites. But it still meant that many women of the first suburban generation did not drive. And in the absence of public transport, the consequence was *de facto* imprisonment.

It would clearly be nonsensical to suggest that the suburbs were designed with female segregation in mind.[48] But that they marked the victory of a particular view of women's lives is unarguable. Cities teemed with opportunity, for women as well as men; by retiring to the suburbs, and confining their lives within a purely domestic setting, women turned away from those opportunities.

In 1870, Frederick Law Olmsted, the great American landscape architect and city planner, set out what he saw as the incomparable advantages of the modern city:

> Consider what is done . . . by the butcher, baker, fishmonger, grocer, by the provision vendors of all sorts, by the iceman, dust-man, scavenger, by the postman, carrier, expressmen, and messengers, all serving you at your

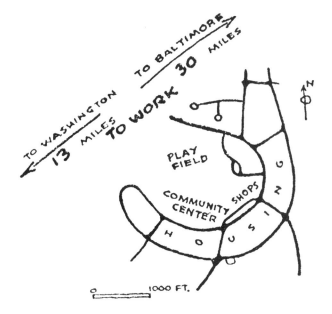

29. Zoning in action: the Goodmans'
sketchmap of Greenbelt, Maryland.

house when required; by the sewers, gutters, pavements, crossings, sidewalks, public conveyances and gas and water-works . . . There is every reason to suppose that what we see is but a foretaste of what is to come.

Olmsted went on to speculate about the possibility of providing municipal steam heat to every home. He thought tradesmen might use the electric telegraph and the pneumatic tube for orders and deliveries. He also suggested that public laundries, bakeries and kitchens might promote 'the economy which comes by systematizing and concentrating, by the application of a large apparatus, of procedures which are otherwise conducted in a desultory way, wasteful of human strength'.[49]

The effect of this approach was to free women from the tyranny of domestic chores; and shortly afterwards a vogue for 'apartment hotels' carried the trend even further. Plans for ninety such hotels – run much along the lines of Homesgarth, but for profit – were filed with city officials in New York between 1901 and 1903. The *Architectural Record* noted that 'thousands of steady New Yorkers have been moving into them – people who are neither business nor social Bohemians'.[50] Feminists welcomed this development: Charlotte Perkins Gilman observed that 'This is the true line of advance; making a legitimate human business of housework; having it done by experts instead of by amateurs . . . is good business. It is one of the greatest business opportunities the world has ever known.'[51] But the *Architectural Record* was outraged.

The consummate flower of domestic irresponsibility . . . the most dangerous enemy American domesticity has yet to encounter . . . A woman who lives in [a boarding house or an apartment hotel] has nothing to do. She cannot have food cooked as she likes; she has no control over her servants; she cannot create that atmosphere of manners and things around her own personality, which is the chief source of her effectiveness and power. If she makes anything out of her life at all, she is obliged to do it through outside activities.[52]

The implication is that woman's chief interests are *ipso facto* domestic: hardly a startling piece of news. But this notion of 'separate spheres', seemingly so immemorial, is in fact very much an effect of industrialization.[53]

In pre-industrial households, both sexes and all members had to labour to keep the household afloat. Elaborate or simple, this was for all but the very richest a full-time joint enterprise. Only with the arrival of industrialization did this domestic balance begin to change. Bought-in coal took the place of home-cut and hauled wood as chief domestic fuel. Piped water and bought flour meant that water-hauling and corn-grinding no longer consumed time and energy. Refrigeration, canning and large-scale meat-packing eliminated home butchery. Factories began to supply hitherto home-made footwear, and manufactured cloth supplanted home weaving. These were the heavy tasks, which had fallen to men for the usual peasant reason of brute strength. Meanwhile the women's tasks of laundry, cooking, sewing and childcare continued unabated. As a result, women's lives became separated from men's. Women stayed home and taught their daughters housework. And boys, instead of being taught by their fathers to chop wood, build fireplaces, tan hides, mend pots and butcher pigs, learned that the man's role was to leave the house and earn a wage in order to provide the household with necessary cash to buy in what had once been the fruits of male labour.

With men's traditional role thus undermined (for where at home he had been in charge, this was rarely the case at work), a culture of exclusive masculinity began to develop. This was the great age of gentlemen's clubs, saloons, Elks, Masons and

Rotarians. It was also a time when the advance of scientific and mathematical knowledge was establishing new middle-class professions in science, medicine and accounting. These were kept tightly closed to women. How could such responsibilities be combined with child-raising, or women's (supposedly) more delicate and nervous constitutions? In poorer households, meanwhile, only a woman's constant presence and unremitting care could, in the absence of her wage-earning husband, hold dirt at bay, get the meals cooked and fend off the ever-present spectre of infant mortality. If she had to work for cash (in a factory, or doing the heavy housework for another woman) then her own household inevitably suffered.

A stigma was thus attached to the notion of married women working outside the home – the very situation co-operative arrangements were designed to support. And this stigma persisted even after technological advances had made house-hold jobs easier. For by then the pattern was ineradicably established. The presence of a woman at home, supported by her husband's wages, had become deeply bound up with family pride and expectations. And in the automobile suburb this way of life was, quite literally, built in.

Of course women, just like men, could escape if they could drive. And they could not be kept out of automobiles altogether. But they might be (and were) guided towards more suitable varieties: in particular, electrics. By 1908, a survey in *Motor* magazine recorded 4,290 of these operating in 'selected cities' throughout the States – undoubtedly an underestimate since the selection for some reason excluded New York City and Washington, D.C.

Sedately paced, clean, silent and simple to operate, and often (unlike gasoline cars) designed as closed vehicles, electrics reinforced the most traditional and (to men) comfort-ing notion of woman's role. Even Henry Ford's wife drove one, thus confirming her unchallenging femininity. 'Has there ever been an invention of more solid comfort to the feminine half of humanity than the electric carriage?' wondered C. H. Claudy in 1907. 'What a delight it is to have a machine which she can run herself, with no loss of dignity, for making calls, for shopping, for a pleasurable ride, for the paying back of some small social debt.'[54] Electrics were also ideal for taking the baby for an airing – 'It would not be amiss to call the electric the modern baby carriage.'[55] Indeed, the baby might almost drive itself – the electric was 'strong, durable, light, refined, and safe for a gentleman or lady, and we may say even for a child to drive'.[56]

Electrics also possessed another, far more substantial virtue: the freedom they conferred was strictly limited. As C. H. Claudy put it, 'A practical electric vehicle cannot be built so that it can go fast *and* far *and* climb hills. *Speed* you can have, or great *radius* you can have – but not both at once and still keep down weight and cost.' But what did this matter? 'It can be roundly stated without fear of contradiction that the times a woman wants to run an electric 30 miles an hour, are few and far between . . . It is an unnecessarily fast speed for pleasure driving . . . If the car you select has a maximum speed of 25 miles on the level it goes quite fast enough.' A radius of sixty to eighty miles (probably an overestimate) was, he suggested, 'ample for any electric car'.[57]

Gasoline cars of course went much faster and further than this. But such excitement was pictured as dangerous, explicitly male and unnervingly sexual:

> To think of 'The Monster,' as she called it, was to long for it. That great living, wonderful thing with its passion for motion seemed to call and claim her as a kindred spirit. She wanted to feel the throb of its quickening pulses; to lay her hand on lever and handle and thrill with the sense of mastery; to claim its power as her own – and feel its sullen-yielded obedience answer her will.[58]

How could a mere woman be expected to control such a thing?

Men liked to imagine she could not, though some intrepid ladies showed this to be demonstrably untrue. In 1907, for example, Mrs Joan Newton Cuneo famously and single-handedly drove her six-cylinder Rainier on the Glidden Tour from Cleveland, Ohio, via Chicago to Central Park, New York, braving clouds of dust, hub-deep mud, flash floods, a bent axle, a broken spring, defunct headlights that meant driving across the Alleghenies by the light of a kerosene lantern, and countless dead tyres, while her husband, mother-in-law and a family friend rode along as passengers. The only woman driver on this event, she received a special trophy, and reported only kindness from beginning to end despite being prepared for 'a showing of ill-feeling on the part of at least some of the drivers'.[59] And in 1913 the *New York Times* reported that a Mrs Schultz was running a taxi-cab in the city 'equipped with all the comforts of home', including a warming device 'that will do anything but fry an egg'; she also carried a wardrobe of fur coats and woollen mittens to fortify passengers against the rigours of the New York winter.[60] But this was a specifically feminist enterprise – the headline identified Mrs Schultz as a 'suffragette' – and the very fact that such exploits were recorded in this way shows their comparative rarity. Meanwhile, in Cincinnati in 1908, when a woman ran over the City Treasurer, Mayor Markbreit at once proposed a ban on women drivers. 'The only proper machine for a woman to run is a sewing machine,' he observed, seizing his opportunity to reinsert the genie into the bottle.[61]

It is certainly true that gasoline cars *were* for a long time dirtier and more awkward than electrics. In particular, where with electrics you turned a key or flicked a switch to start the machine, gasoline models were started by a hand crank, a procedure both cumbersome and even, at times, dangerous.

Your car came equipped with a serviceable crank [wrote E. B. White in *Farewell My Lovely*], and the first thing you learned was how to Get Results. It was a special trick, and until you learned it (usually from another Ford owner, but sometimes by a period of appalling experimentation) you might as well have been winding up an awning. The trick was to leave the ignition switch off, proceed to the animal's head, pull the choke (which was a little wire protruding through the radiator) and give the crank two or three nonchalant upward lifts. Then, whistling as though thinking about something else, you would saunter back to the driver's cabin, turn the ignition on, return to the crank, and this time, catching it on the down stroke, give it a quick spin with plenty of that. If this procedure was followed, the engine almost always responded – first with a few scattered explosions, then with a tumultuous gunfire, which you checked by racing round to the driver's seat and retarding the throttle. Often, if the emergency brake hadn't been pulled all the way back, the car advanced on you the instant the first explosion occurred and you would hold it back by leaning your weight against it. I can still feel my old Ford nuzzling me at the curb, as though looking for an apple in my pocket.[62]

Not all cranking memories were so benign. The hand crank was not forgiving. There was a proper way to do it, with the four fingers around the handle and the thumb tucked in against the index finger: it was important never to put the thumb around the crank 'because when it kicked back, as it often did if the spark was not properly adjusted, the result might be a broken thumb or wrist'.[63]

It was one such accident which finally led to the invention of the electric self-starter by Henry F. Leland and Charles F. Kettering. A friend of Leland's, Byron Carter, 'went to the assistance of a lady whose car had stalled; he suffered a broken jaw when the crank handle kicked back, and gangrene subsequently caused his death'.[64] Kettering had for some time been considering the possibility of using an electric storage battery to start a gasoline engine, but the other engineers at Cadillac, where he and Leland worked, were unenthusiastic – possibly because electricity was associated with 'feminine frailty'. After Carter's accident, however, he began thinking in earnest how such a thing might be achieved, and by 1912 he and Leland had a starter that worked. It was installed on all Cadillac models; within a year electric self-starters had replaced cranks on one third of the models in the Madison Square Garden Auto Show.[65] They were (and still, unintentionally, are) portrayed as decadent gadgets that pandered to feminine weakness. Thus, auto historian John Rae declares the electric starter 'a major factor in promoting the widespread use of the automobile, particularly because it made the operation of gasoline cars more attractive to women'.[66] Which of course it did; it is also possible that men, too, found self-starters useful.

Of course many women were not taken in. As Mrs A. Sherman Hitchcock acidly noted in 1913, 'His real reason [for disapproval of wives driving] is without doubt a wholly selfish one – he fears her proficiency and doesn't want her to use the car as often as she would were she capable of its operation.'[67] But even the dangerous freedoms of gasoline need not prove too threatening if correctly directed. Far from opening up the world, the car turned out simply to extend the boundaries of home, as in this 1929 Chrysler ad:

'When I was a child it was easy for mothers to keep in touch with their children,' says a woman in Illinois. 'Today the members of the family must make a real effort to keep united. I thought a great deal about this as my children began to grow up. I decided that the most important thing

Any Woman Can Start your Car

"Crank From the Seat Not From the Street"

Send today for our illustrated booklet describing the Star Starter—a device which cranks your engine from the seat and one which is now largely doing away with the old-fashioned and dangerous methods of cranking.

30. Self-starters: a gadget for wimps and women.

I could possibly do would be to plan ways in which they and I could have good times together. My husband agreed, and for that reason we bought a second automobile, since he had to use his car in getting back and forth to business. I can't begin to tell you of the happiness it has given us – picnics together, expeditions for wildflowers in the spring, and exploration parties to spots of historic interest. It's our very best investment. It has helped my children and me to keep on being pals.'[68]

The compensation for this home-bound lifestyle had been the cosy women's world of gossip and shared chores on the porch. But the automobile was not conducive to this sociable and semi-public way of life. Traditionally, American houses had been built with covered verandahs facing on to the street – the 'piazzas' and 'stoops' within which the action of so many nineteenth-century novels takes place. In the early days of motoring the garage (if any) was a hut in the back yard. But cars soon became too important to be relegated to a hut. The garage moved forward and increased in size, while the front porch disappeared – an enactment in bricks and mortar of the automobile's revolutionary effect on social life. The porch had been part of a pedestrian lifestyle of casual callers and passers-by, but the car made all that irrelevant. Less walking meant fewer passers-by, while many of the activities (such as courting) that had traditionally taken place on the porch could now be conducted in the privacy of the car.

As the house-plan changed, so too did the wider architecture of the streets. In Pasadena, few of those roadside strips known in Britain as pavements, in America as sidewalks, exist outside the original town centre. Where they do, their makers' signatures, imprinted in the now crumbling concrete, show that they were put down when the neighbourhoods were laid out in the 1920s – a time when residential streets were still

31. Mother discovers the pleasures of driving.

automatically assumed to require such amenities. But this soon came to seem an anachronistic use of valuable space. Where school is reached by bus or car, offices and shops are situated elsewhere and the commuter railroad station, if any, is several miles away, where would you walk? And why, in that case, build sidewalks? Of course this is a self-fulfilling prophecy: once sidewalks are absent, pedestrianism becomes perilous. I once, in a misguided moment, attempted to push a stroller through the streets of Bedford, New York – the most banal of everyday pastimes: when all else fails, strap in the toddler and wheel. But not in Bedford: there are no sidewalks. After five minutes we fled back to the house in fear of our lives.

In the English town where I live the pavement is a social space, a place where you walk the baby to the shops in the hope of meeting other baby walkers, run into friends and spend a while chatting: where you get out of the house. These are the moments that keep mothers sane and retrieve the elderly from terminal solitude – a need so fundamental that one would imagine it hard-wired: the reason why people live in social groups. But these casual encounters are not possible in auto-mobile suburbs. The only people now to be seen on Pasadena's sidewalks are service personnel, the gardeners, plumbers and builders who arrive, in a sort of reverse rush-hour, as the residents leave for their day at the office. Only once, in my peram-bulations through the avenues, did I encounter residents: a mother and two young children trying to raise a little pocket money by selling home-made lemonade outside their house. It was a hot, hot day, and the lemonade was delicious; in my town they would have done a roaring trade. In fact I was (at 4 p.m.) their first customer, and almost certainly their last.

So the facts of automobile life separated women's lives from the wider world. Cut off by zoning from the male universe of work, with the supermarket replacing the corner shop, the streets increasingly perilous and the public and semi-public spaces of porch and sidewalk banished from modern life, they were thrown back into the privacy of their dream homes. Home-making became a full-time occupation, and as millions of women turned their energies to the perfection of domesticity, a new industry emerged to service the 85 per cent of American non-farm dwellings that by 1930 could boast electricity. Now that all you need do was to switch on the relevant appliance, a plethora of electric servants appeared, ready to take the drudgery out of every aspect of housework and energetically promoted by manufacturers eager to capitalize on the new and infinitely expanding suburban market. Home-making, once an endless succession of arduous battles against grime, wear and recalcitrant foodstuffs, was increasingly presented as a fulfilling pleasure.

There can be no question that electrical appliances were a genuine boon. Before they appeared, household chores, especially home laundry – the whole ghastly business of soaking, washing, drying, ironing – were so exhausting and time-consuming that the first thing any woman did, as soon as she could possibly afford to, was buy in the services of some other, poorer woman as a laundress. Communal laundries, able to take advantage of steam power to operate commercial-scale machinery (hence the 'steam laundry'), offered the first and for many years the only real alternative to hand-skivvying, providing, in the pre-suburban years, a logical focus for the feminist anti-housework movement.

For the first generation of houseproud city escapees, however, the great attraction of suburban life was that it promised a refuge from from everything communality represented. They had spent their lives confined in cramped city quarters, inexorably surrounded by other people's noises, smells and demands. Now the prospect of a detached house standing in its own lot spoke louder than any amount of cloudy idealism. Co-operation, in the words of Letchworth's Raymond Unwin,

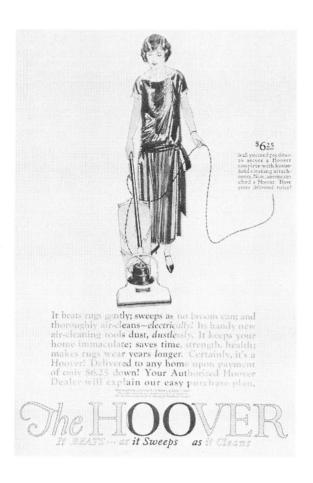

32. The vacuum cleaner – every woman's dream.

enabled everyone to 'share . . . the convenience of the rich . . . if we can overcome the excessive prejudice which shuts up each family and all its domestic activities within the precincts of its own cottages'.[69] But electrical appliances meant that such convenience was now available to individual housewives within those very precincts. There was, it is true, a great American tradition of experimental living. But the internal combustion engine opened up hitherto unimaginable prospects of realizing another equally time-honoured tradition: that of individualism, Americans' deeply prized right to live their own lives in their own way unmolested by their neighbours.

As World War II drew to an end, this tradition increasingly chimed with the political mood. Men, back from the war, wanted to reclaim the jobs women had successfully filled; a woman's place, briefly, might have been in the union, but now separate spheres reasserted themselves. A wave of anti-communist hysteria swept the country, in which such notions as feminism, communality and co-operation could seem dangerously un-American. In 1953, during the most extreme phase of the McCarthy witch hunts, students at the University of Michigan's Ann Arbor campus avoided renting rooms in houses run by the housing co-operative for fear of being labelled communists.[70]

By 1970 there were 50 million small houses and over 100 million cars in the United States. Seven out of ten households lived in single-family, suburban homes. These were no longer just middle-class families: over three-quarters of union members owned their homes on long mortgages. America had moved to the suburbs.[71]

» » »

The problem lay buried, unspoken, for many years in the minds of American women. It was a strange stirring, a sense of dissatisfaction, a yearning that women suffered in the middle of the twentieth century in the United States. Each suburban wife struggled with it alone. As she made the beds, shopped for groceries, matched slipcover material, ate peanut butter sandwiches with her children, chauffeured Cub Scouts and Brownies, lay beside her husband at night – she was afraid to ask even of herself the silent question – 'Is this all?'[72]

So begins *The Feminine Mystique*, the book in which Betty Friedan analysed the mysterious, unexplained depression that seemed to consume so many of the women she met. Better educated than any previous generation of women, their lives and interests were nevertheless curiously narrow. Friedan talked to publishers of women's magazines who never ran stories on politics, public affairs, satire or travel, because their readers were full-time housewives and not interested in these things. She described how a meeting of magazine writers and editors 'spent an hour listening to Thurgood Marshall on the inside story of the desegregation battle, and its possible effect on the presidential election. "Too bad I can't run that story," one editor said. "But you just can't link it to a woman's world."'[73]

It was true: removed in her suburb from the arenas of industry, culture and politics, the housewife's world had by now become as entirely separated from the 'real' world as a child's. Writing in 1963, Betty Friedan remembered that in 1939

the majority of heroines in the four major women's magazines . . . were career women – happily, proudly, adventurously, attractively career women – who loved and were loved by men. And . . . the strength of character they showed in their work as nurses, teachers, artists, actresses, copywriters, saleswomen – was part of their charm. There was a definite aura . . . that men were drawn to them as much for their spirit and character as their looks . . . And then suddenly the image blurs. The New Woman, soaring free, hesitates in midflight, shivers . . . and rushes back to the cozy walls of home . . . In [1949] the *Ladies Home Journal* printed the prototype of the innumerable paeans to 'Occupation Housewife' that started to appear in the women's magazines, paeans that resounded throughout the fifties. They usually begin with a woman complaining that when she has to write 'housewife' on the census blank, she gets an inferiority complex . . . Then the author of the paean, who somehow never is a housewife . . . roars with laughter. The trouble with you, she scolds, is you don't realize you are an expert in a dozen careers, simultaneously. 'You might write: business manager, cook, nurse, chauffeur, dressmaker, interior decorator, accountant, caterer, teacher, private secretary – or just put down philanthropist . . .'[74]

This loss of a woman's own identity to become a mere adjunct of her family – *caterer, teacher, private secretary, philanthropist* – lasted well into the bra-burning 70s. Long after the usage had become obsolete in Britain, married women in America were (as I discovered to my horror and astonishment) invariably introduced as 'Mrs John Smith'. Locked away from the world in their separate houses, living within the physical confines of another generation's failed dream, the ironic consequence of individualism and separate spheres had been to deprive America's housewives of all autonomy. What had once been seen as the solution had become the problem.

The effect of Friedan's book was electric. Throughout the world women began to look at their lives and take action to change them. No longer would they allow themselves to be gentled into padded oblivion. They wanted to be taken seriously, to be treated as equals; to use rather than lose their minds. By

1985, over half of all American married women with children under six and almost half those with children under one had salaried employment, most of it full-time.[75] But they were living, for the most part, in a setting designed for a quite other way of life. The suburb was predicated on the nuclear, two-parent, one-earner family – a vanishing commodity. Of the approximately 17 million new households formed in America during the 1980s, only 27 per cent were married couples, with or without children. Thirty-eight per cent were singles and single-parent families.[76] Lone women headed almost 20 per cent of all American families with children, and most were in full-time employment.[77] Fifty years earlier, the career-woman was the exception; young men grew up assuming that they would end up taking sole financial responsibility for several other people; if women did earn, it was 'pin-money'. But by the end of the twentieth century 54 per cent of all American families were double-income households[78] – and in almost all cases the second income represented necessity, not luxury. And this pattern was reflected throughout the developed world. British government policy now takes it for granted that, given the choice, young mothers will *prefer* to work outside the house rather than stay home with the baby.

The result, for many, is life on wheels. Three US National Personal Transportation Studies, conducted in 1969, 1977 and 1983, showed that the number of vehicle trips per household increased by 45 per cent over this fourteen-year period.[79] (The corresponding rise in Europe was even steeper, but this partly reflected a much lower base of car ownership: many Europeans were then buying their *first* cars.) By the mid-90s, Americans travelled on average 50 per cent more miles per year than in the mid-70s.[80]

Naturally not all these trips are work-related. Food must be bought, children need chauffeuring. And time-budget studies show that the burden of housework – now including those aspects of car use, such as ferrying children, that fall within the traditional maternal sphere – is still everywhere carried by women. In one American survey, although 54 per cent of male respondents routinely chauffeured children under six, 75 per cent did so less than once a week. Ninety per cent of the women, however, reported such chauffeuring duties once a week or more, 16 per cent more than three times per week per child.[81] And this imbalance is not confined to America. In Holland, land of the bicycle and cheap, reliable public transport, cars are used far less overall. But where children do need chauffeuring, this duty falls almost entirely upon the mother. Ten per cent of couples share it equally; the father is reported as 'most frequent [chauffeur]' by 12 per cent of unmarried mothers (cohabitees being, perhaps, more modern-minded) but less than 5 per cent of married couples. Otherwise, Mother does the driving.[82]

And while she does so (unloading more carbon dioxide into the atmosphere every minute), the daytime suburb remains eerily empty. It was designed around the culture, in Paul Goodman's words, 'of afternoon clubs':[83] the committees for this and that which occupied so much of my mother's time. But the committeewomen have vanished into their cars, and the empty suburban streets bristle with burglar alarms. The automobile suburb, spacious, removed from the grime of commerce, free from inner-city congestion, has spawned its own problems: of sprawl, separation, and incessant driving.

Faced with these problems, many see the garden city as an ideal solution. And indeed, a place like Letchworth has a great deal going for it. Above all it has kept what Pasadena has lost (and what all town planners now crave): a sense of ongoing street life. It has not escaped the car, but it has survived it more or less intact. Indeed, as late as the 1960s only 30 per cent of British households owned a car.[84] So Letchworth, not having changed its transport mode, never underwent a Pasadena-type transmogrification. Instead it remained as Ebenezer Howard planned it, densely built and offering a good number of local jobs and shops. As a result, even on a rainy afternoon, and even though out-of-town supermarkets have drawn away much high-street custom and here as everywhere most adults are at work, you feel relaxed walking the streets. There are people around – children, old people; dispossessed by the suburban car culture, here they retain their freedom. Everything is within reach, a short walk along pleasant streets.

But does this in itself make Letchworth more desirable? If we conflate street life with communal life, what are we to make of those clubs, sports, museums, restaurants, parks, beaches, so readily accessible to Pasadenans with access to a car (as though it were possible to imagine any other variety)? Are they in some way less valid simply because they must be driven to?

This discussion, simmering throughout the mid-century in the works of Lewis Mumford, was brought to a head in 1961 when Jane Jacobs published *The Death and Life of Great American Cities*. Seeking to define what made cities work, she found herself strolling, with unexpected pleasure, around Boston's North End. This was a poor district on the waterfront whose old warehouses were being converted into dwelling- and work-spaces, which in their turn generated numbers of small shops and cafés: a familiar scenario now, but at that time unusual. So impressed was she by the atmosphere of the place that she mentioned it to a friend, a city planner in Boston. To her horror, he confirmed that North End was due for demolition. It was, as everyone knew, a slum: a definition reflecting, as so often, not what was true but what *had been* true.

Here was a curious thing. My friend's instincts told him the North End was a good place, and his social statistics confirmed it. But everything he had learned as a physical planner about what is good for people and good for city neighborhoods, everything that made him an expert, told him the North End had to be a bad place.[55]

What Jacobs was describing is what (largely thanks to her work) every city planner now desires. Diversity and walkability are once more accepted as essential to the amenities of city life; Boston's North End, preserved by the skin of its teeth, is now one of the city's most sought-after historic neighbour-hoods, part of the 'walking city' that these days constitutes the nub of Boston's tourist pitch. The pendulum has swung, the fashion changed. What we want, now that remote country-side is increasingly scarce and precious and even America is filling up, now that commutes are ever longer and more con-gested and the sheer number of vehicles defeats even the most draconian pollution controls, is the traditional high street: a place where people live near their work, everyone is on first-name terms, young mothers meet to chat while shopping, and cheery artisans ply their crafts. 'Most of us actually know what we want in a neighborhood – we just don't know how to get it, because developers have been building the wrong thing for 50 years,' as *Newsweek* put it in a cover story.[56]

Many planners are trying, in their different ways, to recre-ate such places. But this is no easy matter. Functioning high streets need a complex mix of factors if they are to survive. In my own town these include the absence of immediately neighbouring supermarkets; plenty of local employment, so that trade can be maintained throughout the day; easy parking (this street once had a cattle market down the centre, so that it is very wide, and the two kerbside lanes are now *de facto* car parks serving residents and shops); a local population large and wealthy enough to support a full range of desirable shops and services, but small enough to focus upon a single main street and to know each other, if not by name, at least by sight; a hinterland of villages willing to trade the supermarket's range and cheapness for the pleasures of personal service and acquaintance; a range of activities that foster a genuine sense of civic identity – schools, a football club, a tennis club, a weekly market . . .

A number of widely publicized attempts have been made to recreate this ambience. I looked at three, each representing a very different approach and philosophy.

Laguna West, on the edge of Sacramento, California, is an attempt to coax suburbanites out of their cars by starting, like Ebenezer Howard, from first principles: everything from the placement of shops to the provision of jobs. Built in the early 1990s, it was designed by Peter Calthorpe of the Congress for the New Urbanism, a group influenced by both Jane Jacobs and Ebenezer Howard, which includes designers, sociologists, economists, developers and politicians and whose 'comprehensive new vision of the American community . . . emphasizes the principles of connectedness, walkability, diversity and ecological sustainability'.[57] They also, in Calthorpe's words, try 'to make conscious the forces and the policies that are shaping the region'[58] in the hope that (as happened with Betty Friedan and her depressed housewives) consciousness will enable control – in this case, of the urban system as a whole. For example, the exodus of wealth from the city to the suburbs means that poverty is seen as a city phenomenon 'and we live in the suburbs so it's not our problem'.[59] But if lower-income families are distributed more equitably throughout a region, their chances of success dramatically increase, while at the same time city centres recover their desirability. Physical planning, social and psychological factors are, the New Urbanists recognize, inextricably intertwined.

Ebenezer Howard would certainly have approved the notion of alleviating poverty in this way – an approach put into practice in post-World War II Britain, with its programme of building public housing in hitherto middle-class neighbourhoods. But then he was a social philosopher, not a planner, and Letchworth a physical means to social ends – release from the squalor of the walking city while avoiding the boredom and unemployment of the country. And although everyone now recognizes that, as Friedan demonstrated – physical decisions have social effects, often quite unanticipated, it is no surprise, given the hands-off American tradition, to find critics accusing the New Urbanists of 'social engineering and physical determinism'.[90] Nevertheless a number of New Urbanist projects have been or are being built – places where, in the small-town or centre-city tradition, 'one is less inclined to drive and more likely to walk or bicycle to a nearby video store or delicatessen', and which therefore allow 'people of all ages and walks of life to come into daily contact'.[91]

Peter Calthorpe, writing in 1993, described Laguna West as 'the first "on the ground" test of the idea that elements of growth can be modified and integrated in new ways . . . designed as a traditional town in which streets are convenient and comfortable to walk, parks form a public focus, and the real life and vitality of a small town life may be rediscovered for all age groups'.[92] Unfortunately, it did not work out that way. However craftily you may build a way of life into your design, and however desirable that way of life may seem, people will not necessarily adopt it. Angeleno David Brodsly observes that 'In LA, most people think little of driving for every purpose: to see a friend, to buy cigarettes or an icecream cone, to watch the sunset.'[93] And it will clearly take more than mere design to break them and their fellow-Californians of this habit. Pedestrians and cyclists are few and far between on Laguna West's specially designed lakeside paths; people persist in driving to the shops, even when they are near at hand. As in Letchworth, a major employer – in this case Apple Computer – has been attracted to the site. But the existence of the car means that – unlike pre-car Letchworth – proximity is no longer a major factor in employment. Apple employees are no likelier to live in Laguna West than anywhere else in the region. Separated by a busy highway, there is in fact little interaction between Apple and Laguna West.

Calthorpe adduces various reasons for this apparent failure. If people are to live out on the city fringes the *quid pro quo* is space, so that Laguna West's site was not, as it turned out, ideal for the densities needed to create 'a healthy pedestrian environment'. A promised rail transit stop failed to materialize; a major recession meant that 'the only way they could sell houses was to actually down-zone areas [i.e. allow more space per house] so areas in Laguna West even from a starting-point that was too low a density were actually down-zoned to even lower densities because of the recession'.[94]

Laguna West has convinced Calthorpe that the future for New Urbanism is suburban and urban infill, where the market will tolerate 'the kind of intensity that really does support pedestrian environments'.[95] But the astonishing commercial success of another New Urbanist project, Celebration, sited next to Walt Disney World in Orlando, Florida, suggests that other factors may also be at work here.

If Letchworth differed from Laguna West in density, local employment and public transport opportunities, that was largely because these things were out of Peter Calthorpe's control. He did not own the land. Ebenezer Howard, on the other hand, did. Not without some difficulty, he ensured that he personally (through the Garden City Pioneer Company) owned the site of his new town: an effort made not because he wanted to make money but because with ownership comes control. It meant that he was able to stick to his original plan regardless of commercial pressures. And for Disney, too, this was a vital consideration. Like Howard, though for very different reasons, he wanted total control. Indeed, Celebration may be seen as Letchworth stood on its head. In Letchworth

Howard's sole concern was the good of the community: in Celebration Disney's commercial considerations are the only considerations that apply.[96]

Disney selected the site that would become Walt Disney World from an aeroplane on the day President Kennedy was shot, and immediately set about ensuring the control he required. Above all he wanted to avoid replicating in Florida the tacky and piecemeal development surrounding the original California Disneyland, a product of fragmented land ownership and a weak public sector. And he was clear from the start that the key lay in land ownership. Like Howard sixty years earlier, he embarked upon a secret buying spree – in this case 27,500 acres south-west of Orlando, acquired for about $200 an acre. Only then did he approach the Florida authorities. And they accorded him everything he had hoped and more. The bait of the Mouse's tourist millions ensured not only total landowner control over planning and development, but public funding for many of Disney's own projects, particularly road-building. During early discussions of his new scheme, one company executive told Disney that he seemed to want 'an absolute experimental monarchy'. 'Can I have one?' Disney replied. 'The answer was supposedly no,' comments Disney watcher Richard Foglesong, 'but the Disney company came close to getting what its chief executive wanted.'[97]

In the promotional film Disney prepared for the Florida legislature in 1963, the company set out plans for an Experimental Prototype Community of Tomorrow (Epcot) with an initial population of twenty thousand. In fact, however, the promised new town of Celebration was not begun until 1991. It at once became 'the hottest real estate development in the metropolitan Orlando marketplace',[98] its properties fetching up to 35 per cent more than similar properties elsewhere in the region. By March 1997, the apartments in phase one were (in stark contrast to Laguna West) completely rented, and you had to pay to get on the waiting-list. Visitors 'were offered a $100 opportunity to put ourselves on a waiting list for a two-bedroom apartment in the next phase; $75 for a one-bedroom unit'.[99]

Celebration, although owned by Disney, was conceived as an urban whole in New Urbanist style, with public buildings by well-known architects such as Cesar Pelli, Charles Moore and Philip Johnson. But the language owes more to set-dressing than to Peter Calthorpe's bottom-up earnestness. This is an attempt to recreate the feel and thence the habits of small-town life, a 'pedestrian-oriented, mixed-use development . . . designed to offer a blend of nostalgia and futurism, with front porches for rocking chairs and fiber-optic cabling for online communication between the community's eight thousand homes, all designed by top-name architects'.[100] It is, reads the brochure, 'a traditional American town, built anew', founded on five principles: Health, Education, Technology, Community and Place. The promotional film with which all visitors are greeted stars 'a cross section of Celebration's residents' who 'exclaim, amongst other things, on the foresight of designing houses with porches and low fences, so that one can observe one's neighbors. They praise the fact that Celebration is safe and comfortable, and that the people who live there have the same ideals and goals. It is, as one resident observes, a "dream town"'[101] – an image strongly promoted in its advertising campaign, which combines New Urbanist ideals (back yards are small in the hopes that this will encourage residents to make use of the town's public parks and spaces) with Disneyland atmospherics:

> There once was a place where neighbours greeted neighbours in the quiet of summer twilight. Where children chased fireflies. And porch swings provided easy refuge from the care of the day. The moviehouse showed cartoons on Saturday. The grocery store delivered. And there was

one teacher who always knew you who had that 'special something'. Remember that place? Perhaps from your childhood. Or maybe just from stories. It held a magic all its own. The special magic of an American home town. Now, the people at Disney – itself an American family tradition – are creating a place that celebrates this legacy. A place that recalls the timeless traditions and boundless spirit that are the best parts of who we are.[102]

This cocoon of fairy-tale invincibility constitutes no small part of Celebration's potent appeal. People pay over the odds because they feel they are buying not just a house but a whole somehow magical way of life in which twenty-first century bogeys will be off-limits, just as they are in Disney's movies and theme parks. Indeed, at one time Disney even contemplated providing Celebration with a fictional history, what in movie terms is known as a 'back story', thus even further entwining illusion and reality. One commentator, observing that some residents entirely cover their back yards with black screen, remarks: 'While this is intended to keep out bugs and animals, it serves . . . as a mediator with nature, keeping its unpleasant aspects at a distance.'[103]

But of course real life does not always obey the rules. And when the magic fails there is one vital difference between Celebration and traditional American small towns: the question of governance. Traditionally, American communities are democratic, with every office up for election. But democracy, as Disney realized from the start, is incompatible with total control. So Celebration is provided with Disney democracy. The form is there, but the function is anodyne.

While Celebration claims that it has a dedication to Community unusual in the modern age, the very institutions that form the bedrock of American community are lacking in it. There is no representative government, no churches, and residents have little control over the policies of the Celebration School, although it is public . . . The Town Hall, a building representative of the small town tradition of rigorous self-governance and democratic principles, functions in Celebration as the office of the Town Manager, an unelected position that is filled by an appointee from Celebration's governing board, which is run by Disney. When you enter the building, the hall does not branch off into a series of municipal offices, such as the Registrar of Voters office, as is the case in most other city office buildings. It merely contains a receptionist, a bulletin board, stacks of Celebration promotional literature, and an unmarked elevator.[104]

A homeowner's agreement, called the Declaration of Covenants, is signed by everyone buying property in Celebration, and lists the rules by which residents must abide. It dictates the length of time that you can display political signs during an election period, and limits their size and number – one. Yard sales are limited to one per year, and cars cannot be parked in an individual's driveway for more than twenty-four consecutive hours, but must be kept in the garage, so that they cannot be seen from the street. If the Celebration Board, which is made up of unelected officials, receives complaints from other homeowners about a resident's pet, they can remove the pet from the community without the owner's permission. The agreement bars more than two people from occupying a single bedroom . . . How do they find out? Because once the Board has arraigned residents for some transgression (incorrectly Victorian windows, forbidden engravings on the front door, a car misparked and towed without notice) they become, it seems, paranoically hyper-aware of others getting away with it – and report them.

Despite all this, however, Celebration continues to draw in the customers. What people want these days, it seems, is the *feel* of yesterday rather than its way of life. Atmosphere is more important than anything else: demonstrably more important than autonomy, or democracy.

A comparable development in Britain is Poundbury, the village built on the outskirts of Dorchester by Leon Krier for the Prince of Wales. Charles, who famously detests modern architecture, wanted 'to produce something of real beauty in the English countryside'.[105] He owns the site and chose the architect, and his go-ahead is necessary before anything may be built.

Poundbury is Charles's fantasy town, just as Celebration is Disney's. You know you're there when you see an unmistakably new medieval castle looming on the horizon. (It contains offices for a computer firm.) Disney conjured up a New England dream in a Florida swamp; Charles has created a twenty-first century cross between a Georgian village and an Italian hill town, with a few mock-medieval trimmings like the castle and an ornate, pillared market hall. Residents' political rights are not in question, but environmental control is strict: no altering the outside of buildings, no gaudy shopfronts, no ball games in public spaces. Poundbury is close-packed, with narrow, deliberately car-unfriendly streets and gravelled pavements the residents hate because stones and dust get walked into all the houses.

What struck me was its complete absence of life. On a sunny afternoon in mid-August, with school holidays in full swing, not a resident was visible; only construction workers disturbed the stage-set perfection. The temptation to commit some terminally tasteless act was almost irresistible – I longed to rev an unsilenced motor bike or paint a front door Day-Glo orange. 'We've reclaimed the streets from cars,' says the prince's development manager.[106] But of course this doesn't

33. Poundbury.

mean Poundbury's residents don't own cars (discreetly hidden round the back of the houses). They do – indeed, they must. Like Celebration, which has no grocery store, drugstore or dry cleaner's, Poundbury – created by one of the most environmentally evangelistic figures in British public life – is entirely devoid of basic shopping within walking distance. When I visited it I found only a café, a hairdresser's, an upmarket interior designer's and an art gallery: the high street as amusement – if that's the kind of amusement you like. Clearly all the real shopping went on elsewhere – at the supermarket. Poundbury, like Celebration, is presented as a town but lacks the town's first qualification: the possibility of living a reasonably complete life within it. And although, as in Celebration, cars are hidden away behind the houses to preserve the olde-worlde pretence, they remain vital to the residents' lives.

Predictably, most architects don't like Poundbury: at the end of 1999 a London *Evening Standard* panel selected it as one of 'The 99 Worst Things This Century'. But the residents do. Although it got off to a slow start, coming onstream just as the 1991 recession bit, Poundbury, like Celebration, is a commercial success – according to the prince's development manager, 'the most profitable development per acre in Dorchester'.[107] Indeed, as Richard Foglesong remarks:

For advocates of public planning, the disturbing message is that, outwardly, privatization seems to work better. However illiberal and undemocratic, centralized land ownership offers an effective antidote to the chaos of uncoordinated private interests. Likewise, the Disney company's central administration . . . represents an antidote to the tendency of democracy to produce division and deadlock. It may indeed be easier to plan for the future, as the Disney company said in its 1966 grant application, without 'the impediment to change of political officials.'[108]

The success of Poundbury and Celebration is founded upon a deep ambivalence. We are wedded to our cars but don't like their side-effects: so instead of changing our habits we choose to live in a stage set while the dirty secret of our real, car-borne lives goes on behind the scenes. And this raises the question of whether, were the high street to be generally revived, shoppers would return to it in serious numbers. Planning fashions may have changed; but so, too, has life. My mother, a full-time, non-driving housewife, thought nothing of walking to our not-yet-supermarket Sainsbury's, spending an hour queuing at the cheese counter, the butter counter, the tea counter, the biscuit counter, and lugging her purchases home. I myself, working from home, welcome the odd twenty-minute break at the butcher's or greengrocer's; I also welcome (though he does not) the fact that the grocer two doors down must stay open until seven-thirty if he is to compete with the supermarkets. But most women now spend their days working outside the home, and for them daily shopping is not a practical option. They may spend hours driving, but at least at the supermarket they may gather the week's household needs, pay for them and transport them home within the hour: an unmitigated blessing. Why, given this possibility, would such a woman spend her exiguous free time toiling from shop to shop in the traditional manner? We may want what the high street has to offer socially, but we are not prepared to inconvenience ourselves to obtain it. If the high street survives it will be as entertainment, a place to find antiques, crafts and luxury items (all conspicuous components of the street I inhabit).

Ironically, the Prince of Wales is known not merely for his views on architecture but also for his espousal of organic farming methods. 'Organic' is a plus-word in planning, too: the form that arises naturally from patterns of use – for instance, the alterations forbidden to homeowners in Poundbury and

Celebration. The imposed can never, by definition, be organic. Such urban paradigms as Italian hill-towns and New England settlements – and Letchworth – were pedestrian because life was pedestrian. But it is not pedestrian now – as any visitor to a genuine Italian hill town will know. Can a twenty-first-century medieval village ever be other than anomalous? Poundbury is 'organic' only in that aspect of itself its creator tries so hard to deny – the fact that it is an automobile suburb.

For this, surely, is the organic settlement form of our time. In 1998, American suburbs contained 75 per cent more families than the cities, compared with 25 per cent more in 1970 (seven years post-Friedan). For every American who moved to a city during this period, four moved to a suburb.[109] And this trend is not confined to America. In a recent study of twelve metropolitan areas around the world, all – Bangkok, Manila, Tokyo, São Paulo, even the Netherlands – were suburbanizing in the same way, at 'American-looking densities'.[110] Up to 4 million new dwellings are slated to be built in southeast England over the next decade: most will be suburban. This is the form that expresses the modern freedom – the freedom that the car bestowed. And still bestows: in the words of Professor Melvin Webber, a distinguished planning theorist at the University of California at Berkeley:

[The car] is obviously an instrument of personal freedom . . . all kinds of opportunities are open to those who have discretionary use of cars to go where they want to go. It's meant the possibility of living out in a decent place in the suburbs with a lot of space around your house and a garden, and lots of people, I guess most people, are choosing that kind of suburban living arrangement and they have a choice . . . People still choose to drive when they have a choice not to drive.[111]

We must conclude that they also choose to cover the entire world with suburban development. Or perhaps – since choice assumes alternatives – this is no longer a choice. It has become an inevitability.

Chapter Five

Berlin:
The Small Car
and Fascism

In our family, no one drove German cars. If my mother caught sight of a Mercedes or a Volkswagen she would shudder and say, 'Horrible thing!' I hated the savagery in her voice, the vindictive unforgivingness. And most of all my own inability – dimmed now, but still in some degree active – to detach myself from these feelings, the chastening realization that other people's wickedness drags you down with it, persisting by proxy years after the actual event. In his novel *Ravelstein*, published in the first year of the new century, Saul Bellow, pondering his friend's acquisition of a BMW, remarks 'I wonder, did they use slave labor during the war?' My mother's reaction exactly. And now mine.

My father drove a succession of severely patriotic vehicles: a Standard 9, followed, as business improved, by a pair of stately Triumph Renowns, one black, one silver – huge square things with a boot that hinged downwards, strong enough to provide, on our annual excursion to Towcester Races, an excellent grandstand for two. Renowns were not your run-of-the-mill car – so out of the way, indeed, that I have never seen them either mentioned or pictured: were it not for a few old family photographs I might doubt their very existence. But they were

British to the core. As was the last car of my childhood, an elegant dark grey MG Magnette with walnut dashboard and spiffing acceleration, its engine continuing flawless even as its body, after two hundred thousand miles, disintegrated, finally dying an honourable death in a stock car race. Much later, when my father was safely dead, a series of sales and amalgamations saw MG, together with such ur-British symbols as the Mini and the Land-Rover, fall into the (as he would have viewed it) clutches of BMW. He had been driving a German car all the time, simply *avant la lettre*.

With such a history I felt nervous about visiting Berlin, even though more than half a century has passed since the war ended, and those now in power were children at the time. What did I expect, vampires, goose-stepping SS men, *Triumph of the Will*? Naturally not. But I am Jewish, they are German; knowing and feeling are two different things. Conditioning is not so easily shaken off.

As it happens, when the Berlin Wall finally came down in the avid presence of the world's television cameras, many of the most striking images featured cars. A crush of mingled Mercedes and Trabants caught all the years of separation, the sleek West and the drab East, in a single image. The tinny, noisy, polluting, ugly little Trabbi, surely the worst car ever designed, spoke only of the complete absence of alternatives. Comparable vehicles – early Minis, Fiat 500s, VW Beetles – remain ubiquitous even where production is long ended. They are motorized pets, coddled and primped. But the Trabant, it seems, is beyond even irony. I had expected to see some in action, but the only one I noticed was parked by a kerb in Senefelderplatz, near the arty clubland of Prenzlauerberg with its spacious streets of run-down once-bourgeois apartment houses. That's where cars mostly are in East Berlin – parked: just one of the ways in which, years after unification, it still remains separate from the West. Here, in the centre of a modern capital city

(Prenzlauerberg is ten minutes' walk from Unter den Linden), you can cross the road almost without looking, other than for trams or bikes. In the old Western sector, meanwhile, and especially at the airport, the traffic is solid all the way into the city. But no Trabants were visible there either. Universal the Trabbi may have been; people's car (except by default) it was not.

The real people's car was another matter. In engineering, pedigree, culture and popularity it was, and remains, the business. The VW Beetle ceased production in Germany in 1979, but continued elsewhere: by 1990 almost 20 million Beetles had been sold. This was the baby-boomers' car, the hipmobile of the great anti-Vietnam Nixon-baiting days, of peace, love and the counterculture. Stewart Brand's seminal *Whole Earth Catalog* featured an entire page of right-on, anthropomorphic manuals aimed at this flower-power market: *How to Keep Your Volkswagen Alive, How to Buy a Used Volkswagen in Europe, Keep It Alive and Bring It Home*, and the *Baja Bug Kit*, with a *Catalog* mention of the Volkswagen Official Service Manual 'because you can't just walk up to a 74 Super Beetle and diddle the carb screws and have it run right. No way.'[1] To own a Bug was as much a political statement as long hair, eliciting clenched-fist salutes from fellow subversives as you drove; so iconic did it become, so symbolic of its era, that the 'Volkswagens in Film and Video' website lists 512 films featuring a Beetle, including four in which it stars – the four Disney 'Love Bug' films whose central character is the eponymous lovable Beetle.

The list of Beetle-starring documentaries, however, is more ambiguous. There are five altogether, four of them dating from the hippy era: *Celebration at Big Sur, The Endless Summer, Tie-Died: Rock 'n' Roll's Most Deadicated [sic] Fans, Woodstock*, and alongside these the fifth, altogether more sinister: *Triumph des Willens*, Leni Riefenstahl's notorious celebration of Hitler's Nuremberg Rally. For by a supreme irony this emblem of peace and love started life as National Socialism's car, issued originally in a uniform field-grey. (In a neat conflation of these contrasting faces, the cover of *Autobahn*, a 1970s album by the German group Kraftwerk featured an early 1960s white Beetle with a sunroof travelling along one of the early *Autobahnen* constructed for the Third Reich by the aptly named Dr Todt – the two faces of the VW Beetle thus neatly conflated.)

» » »

What more ideologically suitable emblem for a fascist state than an automobile? In the famous words of Filippo Tommaso Marinetti, Futurist leader and ardent supporter of Benito Mussolini, 'A roaring motor car . . . is more beautiful than the *Victory of Samothrace.*' Under Mussolini Italy would blast its way into a shiny metal future free from pasta-fed decadence and stultifying Catholic tradition, machines and the death-defying romance of speed an integral part of the nascent fascist vision.

Hitler, though he too loved fast cars, did not drive. However, thanks to the friendship of a Mercedes car salesman, Jakob Werlin, whom he met in the early 1920s, he was able to travel Germany and preach the Nazi word in the splendour of a chauffeur-driven 770K supercharged eight-cylinder open-topped Mercedes, bought out of party funds. (Ironically, the marque took its name from the daughter of a Jew, Mercedes Jelinek, whose father Emil had been Daimler-Benz's first representative in Paris.) From then on Werlin became Hitler's adviser on all automotive matters, one of the very few intimates allowed unrestricted access to his presence after Hitler seized power.[2] Another was Ferdinand Porsche, designer of the Volkswagen as well as the racing cars that bore his name, and in the words of his son 'one of the half-dozen men in all Germany who dared speak his mind before Hitler' (who was

34. Kraftwerk's *Autobahn*.

'simpatico if you knew him personally'.) Cars were evidently the key to the Führer's heart.

Despite their adulation of the machine, however, the fascist (or proto-fascist) powers were comparatively unmechanized. In 1925, a year in which America produced 4,266,000 cars, Italy and Germany produced only forty thousand and fifty-six thousand respectively – fewer than Canada, Britain or France.[3] Germans preferred to buy American cars, on the whole cheaper and more reliable than the home-made product.

Hitler determined that one of his first acts after acceding to power would be to turn this situation around. There were ideological reasons for this, but also compelling economic ones. As the American experience had shown, the car industry was an incomparable industrial pump primer, creating demand not only for components and raw materials such as steel, glass and rubber but also for infrastructure, which meant great public works such as road-building. The American slump of the 1930s was due in no small part to the saturation of the first-time buyers' market that had made Henry Ford's fortune, the resulting slow-down draining impetus from the great engine that for the past twenty years had driven business expansion. But when Hitler took office in 1933 Germany had hardly embarked upon this cycle. *Motorisierung*, along with rearmament, would be the chief economic foundation of the Third Reich.[4]

In fact Germany was recovering from the Depression well before Hitler took power. By the early 1930s, ceilings on dividends were diverting profits into research and investment, prices were falling and trade booming. The transport gap at railheads had become grossly apparent, and Hitler eagerly seized this opportunity to match need with deed. Between 1933 and 1935 transportation, which mainly meant roads, consumed 60 per cent of all public investment in work projects; between 1932 and 1934, cement output doubled. In 1933 these schemes employed 727,500 men directly on the sites; a year later this had risen to 992,500. By 1938 a total of 1,150,000 men were estimated to be employed in jobs created by roads and cars.[5]

A particular feature of this frenzy of construction was the network of new high-speed *Autobahnen*. As early as 1924 a private firm had produced plans for nearly fifteen thousand miles of motorways in Germany, but by the time Hitler seized power only two stretches had been built: the AVUS (*Automobil-Verkehrs und Übungstrasse*), a combined raceway and commuter road in Berlin's Grunewald, and a short link between Cologne and Bonn. Using the existing plans and a special subsidiary of the German State Railways, a network of limited-access motorways was at once begun under the direction of the brilliant construction engineer Dr Fritz Todt, who was given the title of Inspector-General, *Reichsautobahnen Gesellschaft*, and a 250,000-strong workforce. By 1936 Todt had completed six hundred miles, by 1938, 1,900 miles; by the time World War II broke out in September 1939, 2,400 miles of motorway had been finished.[6] Todt would go on to become Minister for Armaments, in which capacity he built Hitler's submarine pens; he eventually took charge of all road construction in occupied Europe. He died in 1942, in a mysterious plane crash, after repeatedly begging Hitler to stop a war he considered unwinnable.

Many of these hastily built *Autobahnen*, especially in the east, remain unaltered – in Peter Hall's words, 'Strikingly primitive, they run like a roller-coaster over every undulation in the landscape, almost devoid of cut-and-fill techniques.'[7] They lack acceleration and deceleration lanes – unknown innovations at the time they were built – and, as with other early motorways (for instance the Arroyo Seco Parkway in Los Angeles), their access ramps are too tightly engineered for today's speeds and traffic densities. Nevertheless they created a new highway landscape that would be imitated throughout the world.

The *Autobahnen* were of course partly military in purpose. But this was by no means the only use Hitler had in mind for them. He aimed to extend car ownership to all Germans, announcing in January 1934 at the Berlin Motor Show that the Nazis would

> crank up the economy through the furthering of the motor-car sector, giving bread and work to thousands of men, but also offering ever greater masses of our people the opportunity to acquire this most modern means of transport . . . While the car is a vehicle for the rich, I bitterly resent the fact that millions of good, hard-working and industrious people are excluded from the use of a motor vehicle, which would be particularly beneficial to the less well-off, and which would not only prove useful to their way of life, but would also enhance their Sundays and holidays, giving them a great deal of future happiness.[5]

Of course mass car ownership would benefit Hitler as well as his subjects. What object could be more calculated to obscure dictatorship's rawer edges than that instrument of individual fulfilment and personal freedom, a car? Tax breaks for motorists were introduced, enrolment in the National Socialist Car Corps encouraged, and the road classification and administration system reorganized. But none of this was in itself enough to achieve Hitler's goal. What was needed was the right sort of car – German, that went without saying, small and simple – and it simply did not exist.

It was at this juncture that Dr Ferdinand Porsche entered the picture. Hitler and Porsche had met in 1924, when Porsche was working as Daimler's technical director in Stuttgart; but Porsche, more interested in his racing cars than a then obscure provincial politician, had no memory of the occasion. When in May 1933 a member of the Auto-Union board invited him to a meeting with the new Chancellor, it was Hitler, not Porsche, who recalled the occasion.

At that first meeting Porsche talked about a rear-engined racing car he was designing for Auto-Union.[9] When, some time later, Jakob Werlin visited Porsche's headquarters, Porsche thought Werlin wanted to pump him for details of this racing car. As a diversion he talked instead about another project, for a small, light car, that he had been nursing for some time. Porsche had put this project up to Daimler in 1929, but the Daimler board was not interested and refused to authorize it; upon which Porsche lost his temper, walked out and launched his own consulting firm. Between contracts he began to design his small car, using his garage as a workshop and financing the project with a loan on his life insurance.

The new car was not (as was then usual) a scaled-down large model, but was designed to be small from its inception. It would be light in weight, robust and easy to service, with four seats and a top speed of a hundred kph. Technically, it would be highly innovatory: streamlined (as were all the innovatory car designs of the period) and air-cooled, with the engine at the back, eliminating the need for a drive-shaft, independent suspension of all four wheels, and a simplified and reduced number of stamped-metal parts.

Werlin realized that Porsche's car was precisely what Hitler was looking for; and by the time Hitler addressed the 1934 motor show it is clear he knew about it. Later he and Porsche had detailed discussions regarding the specification. Hitler insisted that the new car must use no more than seven litres of fuel per hundred kilometres (one litre less than Porsche proposed, approximately forty miles per gallon). It must maintain, not just reach, a hundred kph. And it must cost less than a thousand Reichsmarks – a figure finally shaved to RM900. This was good politics – in 1934, the average German's savings were less than RM1,000 – but was far less than the 1,550 marks which on Porsche's calculations were needed to cover the car's costs.

At first Porsche was horrified. However, in the words of his son Ferry, he 'let himself be convinced' by Hitler; he thought 'it might be possible'. In June 1934 a contract was signed for the production of a prototype. There was only one problem: Porsche was a Czech citizen, born in Bohemia – and it was unthinkable that the designer of Hitler's new project not be a German national. In December 1934 Porsche was therefore instructed to apply for German citizenship – which, at the age of fifty-nine, he duly did.

The car would be called the Volkswagen or 'people's car'; it was also, at the insistence of party apparatchiks (and to the horror of marketing men) known as the KdFWagen (*Kraft durch Freude*: Strength through joy) after the recreation arm of the Nazi workers' Labour Front. By the winter of 1936 three prototypes had been built; in early 1937 it was recommended that the project be developed further, and that thirty additional prototypes be built by Daimler-Benz, with a view to mass production if they succeeded.

The new car was originally intended to be assembled from parts made in existing auto factories. But such was the success of the *Motorisierung* project that spare capacity was soon in short supply. Between 1933 and 1938 the production of private cars in Germany increased by 40 per cent per year.[10] In 1928 40 per cent of cars sold on the German market were foreign; by 1934 that figure had been reduced to 9 per cent, and Germany had overtaken France in automobile production, making 186,000 vehicles to France's 181,000. By the end of 1935 the motor industry was working at 93 per cent capacity. By 1936 Germany had become the world's third largest exporter of vehicles.[11]

In this hectic industrial climate, it was clear to Porsche that his new car would need a factory of its own. However, Germany

35. Nazi party poster extols the wonders of *Motorisierung*, 1935.

had at that time no experience of industrial mass production. So he visited the Ford factory in Detroit and other assembly-line plants before working out plans for his own plant, which would be an exemplary model of National Socialist organization. In 1937 a site was selected in a hitherto barely industrialized area on the Mittelland Kanal near the castle of Wolfsburg, just east of Hanover. The estate's owner, Count Schulenburg, furiously resisted expropriation, citing insect infestation, overload of existing railway facilities, ancient oaks and lack of camouflage: all to no avail. On 26 May 1938, a month before the invasion of Austria, a crowd seventy thousand strong watched Hitler lay the cornerstone of the new auto-town, to be called Fallersleben, in a ceremony involving trumpet fanfares, six hundred guests of honour, sixty-foot-high swastika banners and three hundred standards of the local SA, Hitler Youth, National Socialist Motorists' Corps and Labour Front. Production in the mile-long factory was slated to begin in 1939; a hundred thousand cars were to be produced in 1940, two hundred thousand in 1941, and up to 750,000 a year after that. The final goal was eight hundred thousand to a million cars a year, more than half for export, to earn currency for the new Germany. For tools, machinery, materials, supplies and personnel the new auto project took priority even over rearmament. It began with a workforce of 17,500, rising as production increased to 30,000; much of it, as in so many of Hitler's vital industrial projects, slave labour.

In January 1939, the *Manchester Guardian* ran a piece on the Volkswagen project, so grandiose and, economically speaking, so puzzling.

Considering that real wages are still low in Germany, a scheme for furnishing all members of the Labour Front with private motor-cars is definitely audacious, but if German press reports are trustworthy the plan is at least

36. Dr Porsche with his Strength-through-Joy car, 1939.

feasible, for it is stated that upwards of 200,000 cars have already been ordered. The finances of the totalitarian states continue to perplex economists, and no British authority has succeeded in solving the £.s.d. of this ambitious enterprise. It is, of course, obvious that if a dictator who periodically or continuously demands great sacrifices from his subjects desires to keep them contented he could hit on no more promising palliative than to provide a motor car for every family . . . The cars are to be purchased by their owners and payments are to be spread over four years, if desired. It is to be presumed that such payments will be made compulsory by the State and deducted from wages . . .

The price of the car has been kept down to about £80 by two expedients . . . The first is design, coupled, of course, with gigantic production. The second is the elimination of certain costs which are inevitable under the pure capitalist system . . . Expert opinion in this country will watch this experiment with intense interest . . . Since it hardly seems possible for such a car to be bought, housed and run for much less than a pound a week, it may create a new social stratum in Germany.[12]

In fact the Volkswagen project was largely financed by the public. Those who hoped eventually to own one of the cars paid in advance, purchasing weekly stamps: '5 *Mark die Woche musst Du sparen, willst Du in eigner Auto fahren*' ran the jingle ('You must save five marks a week if you want to ride in your own car'). There were eventually 336,668 subscribers, who put up RM280 million. But the contracts they took out were weighted almost exclusively in favour of the state.[13] Unlike hire-purchase contracts, in which the buyer takes delivery and pays while she uses, Volkswagen subscribers paid in first and received (they hoped) later. Purchase of a savings book was declared 'equivalent to placement of an order for delivery of a Volks-wagen'. But there was no obligation on the state to deliver a car once the last stamp had been bought and pasted in. At that point the final savings book was exchanged, not for a car, but for a certificate of ownership at the Strength-through-Joy office. Lost or misplaced savings books could not be replaced. The contract was not transferable and could not be cancelled other than in exceptional cases, when a fee amounting to 20 per cent of the payments was retained. 'For reasons of technical experiments and the consequent low price of the Volkswagen,' there was no interest on the savings.

The projected price was indeed low: a basic car would cost RM990 ($396, or £85); sixty marks more would buy a 'cabrio-Limousine' with a roll-back canvas roof, or a soft-top cabriolet. All cars, 'until further notice', would be produced in 'a deep blue-grey finish'.[14] Unfortunately, however, things did not work out according to plan. Although refinements to the car were undertaken and production begun, as World War II escalated civilian cars were abandoned in favour of the amphibious Schwimmwagen and jeep-like Kubelwagen (bucket car) (much prized by Rommel, who relied heavily on it during the desert war: where a camel could go, he declared, so too could his Kubelwagen). And far from the intended sale price of RM990, the few (210) hand-tooled Volkswagens completed before war broke out changed hands for almost ten times this, while the 630 civilian vehicles made before production halted in 1944 cost RM3,000.[15] Parts were sourced throughout Greater Germany – which at that time included much of France: the Peugeot plant at Sochaux, which became a subsidiary of the VW works in 1943, supplied twenty thousand connecting rods, three thousand flywheels and five thousand raw forgings for crankshafts.[16]

When the war ended, Porsche's plant, renamed Wolfsburg in an attempt to shed Fallersleben's unpleasant association with forced labour, was offered to anyone who cared to take it on. But although the factory was still operational, and despite its modern design and lavish equipment, it seemed nobody wanted it.

The VW had, throughout the war, been an object of intense curiosity to British intelligence, who eagerly took apart and analysed any examples that fell into their hands. An engineering team from Humber, reporting on the design and performance of a Type II saloon they had acquired, considered that 'from the Body Engineering point of view the design of this vehicle is exceptionally good, and shows a great advance on previous constructional methods'. It was much lighter than its nearest British counterpart, with 'much better fuel consumption, shifted easily, handled well and gave a good ride'. Nevertheless, the Humber team declined to credit the enemy with having produced a desirable product. 'Looking at the general picture we do not consider that the design represents any special brilliance, apart from certain of the details.' They did not recommend it as a design to be copied by British industry.[17] A senior engineer at Vauxhall confirmed these findings. He thought the VW 'noisy, uncomfortable and tricky to handle . . . Of all the pre-war cars available for resurrection, this seemed to be one of the least promising.'[18] Accordingly, when the British firm of Rootes Motors was offered the VW plant to run, either *in situ* or in the UK, Billy Rootes declined the offer, and ridiculed the product.

In November 1945 the option passed to the French. The equipment would be claimed as war reparations and moved from Wolfsburg to France, and Porsche would be offered the chance to redesign his car in a 'more French' style. But Jean-Pierre Peugeot, whose plant VW had commandeered during the war years, would have nothing to do with a French Volkswagen, and the plan fell through.

The Australians assessed it, but concluded that it would be

commercially too risky to produce the car in the high volumes its tooling justified and demanded. Would the Americans take it on? With their very different motoring tradition, they were quicker to see the VW's virtues. 'Perhaps the critics of the vehicle forget that large areas of the world are still looking for cheap transportation, and that the Model T Ford, which started world motorization, also had technical faults,' observed one GM engineer; while a team from Ford concluded that 'Compared with other automobile factories in Germany, and visualizing the original intended factory layout, the Volkswagen effort is out-standing and is the nearest approach to production as we know it.' But Sir Patrick Hennessy, head of Ford's European opera-tion, opposed the acquisition, afraid that it would make the Ford German subsidiaries too strong relative to Ford England. And when Henry Ford II asked the advice of the company president Ernest R. Breech, Breech said, 'Mr Ford, I don't think what we are being offered here is worth a damn.'

What can explain such perversity? An unwillingness to con-cede German excellence? Perhaps there was some such inad-missible bias. The old British distrust of cheap, volume products was probably also to blame, the persistence of the pre-Ford view that the best motor was a craft object, ideally a Rolls-Royce. In some circles, this ambivalence still persists. A millennium poll conducted by Lord Montagu of Beaulieu's National Motor Museum found the 1953 Volkswagen Beetle both Best Car and Worst Car of the twentieth century. 'I suppose once you become used to its rather obvious charms, you realize it really hasn't got very much else going for it,' mused the museum's film and video archivist.[19] If that was your view, 'the rough and raucous wartime Volkswagens must' (as VW's historian Karl Ludvigsen observes) 'have come as a shock'.

Fortunately for the Volkswagen, British forces personnel stationed in Wolfsburg were seduced by the Beetle's charms, and insisted it must be saved. If nobody else would have it, why not hand it back to the Germans? In September 1949, therefore, the British military authorities signed over control of the plant and its products to the Federal German government and the state of Lower Saxony. Chancellor Adenauer decreed only that the contract should not fall to Porsche, who, along with his son-in-law Anton Piech, had been accused of war crimes by the French (they were released seventeen months later on payment of FF1 million to French officials). This, however, proved an easily superable obstacle. Porsche, by then seventy-five, was indeed excluded: it was Piech who became the Volkswagen company's first chairman.

The rest is history: as everyone knows, Volkswagen became, and remains, one of the most successful auto manufacturers in the world.

» » »

The Volkswagen's strategy of low pricing based on volume production of a single model in a single colour was of course not new. This had been Henry Ford's strategy for the Model T thirty years before. And this similarity was no coincidence. While in prison in 1924 following the failed Munich *putsch*, Hitler wrote one book – *Mein Kampf* – and read another: Ford's bestselling autobiography *My Life and Work*. Ford immediately became one of his heroes. Dietrich Eckart, to whom *Mein Kampf* is dedicated, tells in his memoirs that Hitler had Ford and his philosophy much in mind as he wrote.

It is easy to see why Hitler might admire Ford in general terms. Both were romantic populists, with extravagant social schemas fuelled by improbable personal success – though when Hitler read Ford's book, his own glory days were yet to come. Indeed, Ford's first principle, 'an absence of fear of the future and of veneration for the past',[20] encapsulated much of what both Hitler and Mussolini set out to achieve.

But Hitler was drawn to Ford by more than a common world-view. They also shared a deeply held prejudice: anti-semitism, pushed to the verge of madness and beyond.

In Hitler's case this was not particularly surprising. German Jewry had been a scapegoat in bad times ever since the Crusades; in the status-ridden, deeply Catholic Austria of Hitler's adolescence Jews were both culturally dominant and socially equivocal – a natural focus for resentment. But they could hardly have figured very largely in the life of Henry Ford. In 1863, when he was born, there were less than a quarter of a million Jews in America; only four hundred out of fifty-three thousand Detroiters. Indeed, it is a testimony to the abstract purity of Ford's prejudice – its lack of connection with any actual person or experience – that he was surprised when, after his anti-semitic newspaper campaign began, Rabbi Leo Franklin, the leader of the Detroit Jewish community, a one-time neighbour and an old friend, returned Ford's gift of a new Model T. Ford felt that 'good' Jews should rejoice in his exposure of their less admirable co-religionists, though his secretary Liebold acknowledged that 'it is possible that all Jews may temporarily feel the sting' of the campaign.[21]

Of course, the fact that Ford had encountered few actual Jews did not diminish the likelihood of prejudice (and, following the assassination of Tsar Alexander II of Russia in 1881 and the ensuing pogroms, more than 2 million Jews arrived in America – so many that one professor predicted that in a hundred years America would be populated primarily by Slavs, Negroes and Jews).[22] In the Populist movement that swept the Midwest between 1870 and 1896, feeding on the fears and frustrations of farmers like Ford's father, the Jew as distant financial parasite had long been a hate figure. For the Populists, the gold standard was the root of all evil, and the Jews – 'the Rothschilds across the water,' to quote the Central Greenback Club of Detroit – were at the bottom of it. Like Ford, the Populists distrusted city slickers and thought the true American was one who worked with his hands. As Ford put it, 'The foundations of society are the men and means to *grow* things, to *make* things, and to *carry* things.'[23] Everything else was suspect, especially financiers and intellectuals. And historically few Jews grew or made things, while many were financiers and intellectuals.

Ford's campaign was begun as a circulation booster for his newspaper, the *Dearborn Independent*. This had been acquired in 1919, as a vehicle to promote his philosophy of life. But since he had nothing in particular to say, and that strictly uplifting, the paper was deathly dull. Not surprisingly, therefore, nobody bought it. So a journalist named Joseph J. O'Neill suggested a crusade. The *Independent* took no advertising because it had Ford's guaranteed backing; it was therefore uniquely placed to conduct fearless campaigns. It should 'find an evil to attack, go after it and stay after it . . . name names and tell actual facts . . . If we get and print the right stuff, ONE SINGLE SERIES may make us known to millions. A succession of FEARLESS, TRUTHFUL, INTERESTING, PLAIN-SPOKEN articles, if properly handled . . . will make a lasting reputation . . . LET'S HAVE SOME SENSATIONALISM.'[24] Any target would have done, but Ford, possibly egged on by his pan-Germanist secretary Ernest Liebold, picked the Jews. 'International financiers are behind all war,' he declared. 'They are what is called the international Jew: German Jews, French Jews, English Jews, American Jews. I believe that in all those countries except our own the Jewish financier is supreme . . . here the Jew is a threat.'[25]

From May 1920, for ninety-one weeks, the *Independent* chronicled the Jewish menace – the worldwide conspiracy of Jewish super-capitalists, the 'gentile boobs' they subjugated, their control of the press, this 'Asiatic' people's monopoly of the movies 'reeking of filth . . . slimy with sex plays', their infiltration of organized crime; above all, their stubborn clannishness and refusal to become complete Americans. Articles included 'The Jewish Associates of Benedict Arnold', 'The Gentle Art of Changing Jewish Names', 'What Jews Attempted When They Had Power', 'The All-Jewish Mark On Red Russia', 'Taft Once Tried to Resist the Jews – and Failed'. Bernard Baruch was called 'the pro-consul of Judah in America', 'A Jew of Super-Power' and 'the most powerful man' of World War I. Asked by news reporters to comment on these charges, Baruch quipped, 'Now, boys, you wouldn't expect me to deny them, would you?'[26] But few of his co-religionists were able to dismiss them so lightly. There were riots in Pittsburgh, and Toledo, Ohio; in Cincinnati, Jewish citizens persuaded the city council to ban street sales of the *Independent*, reducing them so much that Ford had to obtain an injunction. The newspaper's sales-men were threatened and assaulted; the theatrical producer Morris Gest filed a $5 million libel suit against Ford.

This campaign ended abruptly in January 1922. But the poison continued to spread. The most aggressive of the articles were reprinted in a volume entitled *The International Jew*. An estimated 10 million copies of this publication were sold in America; it was translated into sixteen languages, including Arabic. *The International Jew* sold for 25¢, the *Independent* for 5¢ a copy – heavily subsidized prices that cost Ford $4,795,000 over eight years: his donation to world anti-semitism.[27] 'You have no idea what a great influence this book had on the thinking of German youth,' said Baldur von Schirach, testifying at the Nuremberg war crimes trials after World War II. 'The younger generation looked with envy to the symbols of success and prosperity like Henry Ford, and if he said the Jews were to blame, why, naturally we believed him.'

Ford, however, supplied Hitler with more than mere ideas. 'That Henry Ford, the famous automobile manufacturer, gave money to the National Socialists directly or indirectly has never been disputed,' wrote Konrad Heiden, one of Hitler's first biographers.[28] When the American Ambassador to Germany, William E. Dodd, referred in an interview to 'certain American industrialists [who] had a great deal to do with bringing fascist regimes into being in both Germany and Italy',[29] everyone knew that this was a coded reference to Ford. On the occasion of Ford's seventy-fifth birthday in 1938, Hitler thanked him with the Grand Cross of the German Eagle, the highest decoration Germany could bestow on a foreigner.[30]

Did these political enthusiasms affect day-to-day life at Dearborn? By the end of the 20s, this had become a matter of public concern and discussion. In an article entitled 'The Mussolini of Highland Park', which appeared in the *New York Times* on 8 January 1928 to mark the 15 millionth Model T and the end of its long reign, Waldemar Kaempffert wrote:

Probably Henry Ford would resent being called a despot – even a beneficial despot. For all that he is an industrial Fascist . . . No man in contemporary industry wields such dictatorial power . . . Ford is not only Chairman of the Board: he is the board itself . . . the Ford Organization is unique in that it is one man's realization of what an enterprise should be.[31]

Such concentration of power in any one man's hands, the article implied, had to be dangerous.

Aldous Huxley's novel *Brave New World,* published four years later, carried Kaempffert's reservations to an extreme conclusion. Huxley's book is a meditation on the new industrial methods and their consequences. In his tightly controlled, conveyor-belt dystopia whose inhabitants worship Our Ford at the sign of the T, mass production has been extended to humans, this being the only way of ensuring that society's dirty work gets done. 'An Alpha-decanted, Alpha-conditioned man would go mad if he had to do Epsilon semi-moron work – go mad, or

37. Henry Ford receives Hitler's medal.

start smashing things up.' Such a world has of course required a shift in human values – first instigated by 'Our Ford' himself – 'from truth and beauty to comfort and happiness. Mass production demanded the shift. Universal happiness keeps the wheels steadily turning; truth and beauty can't.'[32] Consequently all independent thought must be stifled – for independent thought may rock the boat, the one eventuality that must never be permitted. Seen through Huxley's eyes, Ford, in his control of both production and society, was as much a totalitarian dictator as Hitler, Mussolini or Stalin. What was Dearborn but the prototype of the fascist or National Socialist state?

In fact, when it had started out, a more apposite comparison might have been with a welfare state. But by the time Huxley wrote his book Ford's empire had taken a more sinister turn. Although opinion polls throughout the 20s and 30s continued to credit him with the best and most enlightened labour relations in America, Dearborn had become a dark place.

This was largely due to the activities of the company's 'Service Department' and its chief, Harry Bennett. Service Department sounds relatively benign – not unlike the Sociological Department that had once looked after the workers' interests. But nothing could have been more different. Bennett was a vicious man well known for his connections with gangsters and racketeers, and the Service Department, set up to co-ordinate the protection of the plant, became as time went on a private police force, the corrupt underside of that quasi-fascist state sensed by Huxley and Kaempffert. 'Detroit is a city of hate and fear,' wrote Jonathan Leonard in *The Tragedy of Henry Ford*, published in 1932 (the same year as *Brave New World*). 'And the major focus of that hatred and fear is the astonishing plant on the River Rouge . . . Over the Ford plant hangs the menace of the "Service Department", the spies and stool pigeons who report every action, every remark, every expression.' The Rouge, once a benign dictatorship, had transmuted into a place of totalitarian terror: the parallel with Nazi Germany was drawn by many of those who worked there. And, in the words of one ex-member, the Service Department was 'Our Gestapo'. It

> covered Dearborn with a thick web of corruption, intimidation, and intrigue. The spy net was all-embracing. My own agents reported back to me conversations in grocery stores, meat markets, and restaurants, gambling joints, beer gardens, social groups, boys' clubs, and even churches. Women waiting in markets buying something might discuss their husbands' jobs and activities; if they did, I soon heard what they said. To those who have never lived under dictatorship, it is difficult to convey the sense of fear which is part of the Ford system.[33]

The most notorious example of Bennett's brutality is the infamous 'Battle of the Overpass'. The automobile industry had long resisted unionization, but as the Depression deepened so, too, did labour unrest. During 1932 and 1933 there were sporadic strikes and marches, and at the end of 1936 the United Automobile Workers of America (UAW) brought most of General Motors to a standstill with a sit-down strike in which workers occupied the plants so that strike breakers could not be brought in. Governor Frank Murphy refused to call out the National Guard to evict the strikers, and Frances Perkins, Roosevelt's Secretary of Labor, supported him. On 11 February 1937 GM capitulated to the UAW, and so, two months later, did Chrysler. On 1 April Alfred Sloan, GM's president, furiously informed stockholders that the strike had not been 'actuated by any fundamental causes that affected, in an important degree, the welfare of the workers' and expressed his opinion that the unionization of GM 'means the economic and political slavery of the worker, and an important step toward an economic and political dictatorship'.[34]

38. Harry Bennett.

Now only Ford held out against the unions, in violation of the National Labor Relations Act, which established workers' rights to collective bargaining. The UAW felt it had a sufficient base for membership at the Rouge, and in May 1937 union organizers obtained a permit to distribute handbills at the gates of the plant. Over fifty union representatives arrived with circulars citing the NLRA and urging workers to join the UAW. They were led by Walter Reuther and Richard Frankensteen, and arrived at the main entrance to the Rouge an hour before the change of shifts. The entrance gate was at the end of an overpass built so that shift-changing would not interfere with traffic running along the road beneath.

Frankensteen, Reuther and their friends talked with reporters and posed for photographs. Then they were approached by a group of Service Department employees and set upon without warning. Frankensteen's coat was pulled over his arms, and he was kicked in the head, kidneys and groin. Reuther was repeatedly picked up and thrown down, and kicked in the face and body. Their colleague Richard Merriweather had his back broken, and others were severely injured.

The 'Battle of the Overpass', pictured in magazines and newspapers up and down the country, was as brutal an example of industrial fascism as could well be imagined. But in the public mind, Ford retained his place as the most benevolent of dictators: that same year, an opinion poll conducted by the Curtis Publishing Company found that 59.1 per cent of Americans still believed that the Ford company treated its labour better than any other firm.

» » »

Henry Ford's anti-semitism and support for Hitler are a matter of record, as are the brutalities of his henchmen at the Rouge. The name of William Morris, Lord Nuffield, creator of the

39. 'The Battle of the Overpass'. Reuther and Frankensteen approach Bennett's goons; they are attacked without warning. Later, a dazed Reuther and Frankensteen show their bruises.

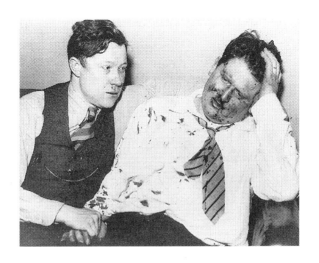

Morris Oxford and Morris Minor, and Ford's nearest European equivalent, has more benign associations. Nuffield College, Oxford, was endowed by him; the Nuffield Foundation is one of the largest medical charities in Britain. Childless, he gave away most of the millions he made out of Morris Motors, and in return received the public acclaim and recognition he craved. But Morris, too, was tempted by fascism.

Like Ford, William Morris was a country boy, attracted to machines. He grew up in the Oxfordshire countryside, and began by building and repairing bicycles, later opening a shop in Oxford itself. Moving, like so many cyclists, into the new and expanding world of cars, in 1913 he produced the four-cylinder, 8.5-horsepower Morris Oxford, the first European car to compete directly with the Model T. Success seemed assured; but then came war. Morris, deeply patriotic, gave his factory over to the war effort. And after the war had ended, it was clear that his customer base had evaporated. The Morris works, now back in civilian production, was crammed with unsold cars. 'I therefore sent for my manager,' Morris recalled,

> and suggested to him that the price should be dropped by a hundred pounds per model, and he said, 'How can you do that with the profit you're making today?' And I said, 'Well, *you* are making no profit at all because you're selling no cars. I therefore give you instructions to go and do exactly what I've suggested, and also to double up the supplies.' He then went to the door, and stood in the door and looked at me as much as to say, he's gone at last! With that he slammed the door and went out.[35]

In three weeks not a car was left in the place.

Superficially, the histories of Morris and Ford have much in common: country boy makes good in the motor trade, sees the future in large numbers and small margins, becomes national

40. William Morris.

figure. But no two men could have been more different. Ford's deep romantic conviction that he alone could set the world to rights – perhaps most apparent in his impulsive excursions into pacifism, social welfare and soybeans – is visible in every line of his oddly delicate face as, elegantly soy-suited, he lifts the sledgehammer that will, to his chagrin, crack his supposedly unbreakable soy-built car. Morris, on the other hand, square-jawed, hair slicked back, is firmly down to earth. Who would dare propose soybean suits and weed sandwiches to this no-nonsense figure?

Morris's approach to manufacturing was as diametrically different from Ford's as his appearance. Ford demanded total control, producing all he needed within his own empire: cars entered the Rouge as ore, sand, wood and rubber (grown on his own plantations) and left it running on four wheels. Morris, however, felt that 'there is no point in producing any article yourself which you can buy from a concern specializing in that work. I only buy a concern when they tell me they cannot produce enough of the article in question for our programme.'[36] And the product that emerged also differed from Ford's, in both its design and its appeal: a divergence in style that to this day separates European and American cars. The Model T was robust, powerful and durable, suitable for America's tough roads and long distances. But European roads, winding and congested, demanded manoeuvrable, light cars that would run in high gear at low speeds, with quick acceleration when the opportunity offered. And where in wide-open America gasoline was expendable and large engines an asset, non-oil-producing Europe preferred small engines and good fuel economy. In Britain petrol was heavily taxed, and France, Germany and Italy soon followed the British lead. When the Morris Minor appeared in 1929, advertisements coupled its top speed of a hundred mph with its hundred-mpg fuel consumption and £100 price.

41. Ford attacks the soy bean car.

If the cars differed, so too did the public at which they were aimed. The Model T offered itself to improvement and adaptation: owners' ingenuities, from mattress supports to heaters, were celebrated in the company magazine, *Ford News*. Devotees of the Sears catalogue and unfazed by technicalities, its owners often lived far from a garage and enjoyed tinkering and experimenting. Morris, however, aimed his cars at the generally unmechanical suburban middle classes, who had no wish to spend their weekends in oily overalls wrestling with gaskets; a pitch epitomized in his insistence that on the 1914 London-to-Edinburgh run, his entrants wear straw hats and ordinary suits, not the special motoring gear associated with running repairs.

> If one bought a car [wrote S. F. Edge, one of the great early motoring pioneers], it was always delivered minus lamps, horn, windscreen, hood, spare wheel, luggage grid and all the 1001 refinements which are found on even the cheapest car today. The purchaser discovered that even after he had put his cheque down for his car, he was very far from being out of the wood; he required all these accessories and they usually involved a further expenditure of the best part of £100. [Morris] was one of the first to appreciate the great drawback of this system. Shortly after the termination of the war he began to equip his cars with all the necessary fitments; first one accessory and then another was included without additional cost; and to these he gradually added certain refinements which were not essential, but useful and much appreciated by every car owner.[37]

The policy paid off handsomely: Morris was soon a rich man. And he needed no prompting when it came to taking up the public position indicated by this newfound wealth and power.

Only ill-health prevented him standing as Conservative candidate for Oxford in 1924.

But even though he did not become a Member of Parliament, politics continued to preoccupy him.

I find it hard to avoid politics [he wrote three years later]. Politics are bound up so intimately in the lives of all of us. I look upon life essentially as a practical man. Frankly I have not much use for philosophies. Theories of any sort leave me cold . . . Life is a practical job. Thinking about it may help some people but the longer I live the more certain I become that a man can only find himself in the work to be done.

Needless to say, I am an individualist.[35]

The election of a Labour government in 1929 signalled, in his view, a sinister lurch towards socialism and trade union domination. As the Depression deepened, he began to take steps, in association with other industrialists including Alfred Mond of ICI, towards the establishment of a National Council of Industry and Commerce which would take over economic and industrial policy and set it upon the right (in every sense) road.

In 1930 Oswald Mosley, one of Labour's brightest sparks, resigned over the government's non-acceptance of his proposals to deal with the rapidly worsening situation. Mosley mooted, among other things, a five-man Cabinet ruling by order with only a veto from the House of Commons. For Morris the authoritarian this was 'a ray of hope'. He considered Mosley 'a courageous young man'; while he himself was 'harassed day and night by the plight into which this England of ours is rapidly falling', the 'one bright spot [was] this forceful gesture of a young and virile section of the Labour Party, providing concrete evidence of the possibility of the formation of the foundation

of a vigorous Industrial Party'. Parliament, he thought, had out-
lived its time. 'Show me a successful business anywhere in the
world that is operating on the principles utilized a century ago.
You cannot. Then what hope is there of a Parliamentary system
which has remained unchanged for so long?'[39] The next step
was obvious. Mosley needed money to set up his new party and
(hopefully) impose his authority; Morris would provide it.

Mosley was at this point considered one of the most brilliant of the younger British politicians. His friends included
radicals from both sides of the House – Conservatives such as
Harold Macmillan and Robert Boothby and Labourites such
as Aneurin Bevan. His concept of a New Party attracted many
who would later regret the move. Morris, however, was not one
of these. He and Mosley met several times to discuss the project; but no cheques were forthcoming, and Mosley had more
or less given up hope when a telegram suddenly arrived inviting
him to lunch at Morris's golf club.

> We lunched alone and as usual the conversation roamed
> widely over general political questions. Like Lord Rother-
> mere he was a genuine and ardent patriot, but he was even
> less well versed in the technique of politics, a business
> genius who seemed rather lost outside his own sphere.
> His success rested on an extraordinary and inventive flair
> for mechanical processes . . . and a remarkable capacity for
> picking men, particularly business executives. Political con-
> versation tended consequently to be tedious, as the only
> real contribution he could make was through the power
> of his money, and that point seemed never likely to be
> reached.
>
> However ennui flew out of the window when at the
> end of lunch he pulled a cheque from his pocket and
> handed it to me across the table. It was for £50,000. He
> said he had been studying me for a long time – the object

of the seemingly pointless conversations was now clear – had developed full confidence in me and had decided to back me. Then came one of those white-light observations which reveal a whole career, in this case the long and dusty road from the little bicycle shop to the motor empire. 'Don't think my boy that money like this grows on gooseberry bushes. The first ten thousand took me a lot of getting.' I bet it did, I thought, and was deeply touched. He was a good and honest man, as well as a business genius; a combination which can occur.[40]

Mosley describes Morris as 'our chief backer' at the start of his party, and Morris never disputed this. But by the end of 1931 the New Party was finished. A National Government came to power that August, and in the October general election Mosley and his supporters did not win a single seat. Mosley's career now took an extreme direction, and many of his earlier supporters no longer wished their names to be associated with his cause. Morris withdrew his support. That, he always averred, was the end of his involvement with Mosley.

Mosley was secretive about his benefactors, and in the case of Morris claimed that the total extent of his support had been a substantial sum to the boys' clubs Mosley planned as part of his New Party youth movement. But Morris's biographer Martin Adeney, citing some mysterious entries in Morris's private cash books, thinks Morris gave Mosley a great deal more money than was ever admitted.

In the middle of 1931, Morris agreed to back the weekly newspaper *Action* which the party was starting to try to get round what it saw as a press boycott and the refusal of the BBC to give the party airtime.

He provided £5000 for launch costs and guaranteed £15,000 a year for two years.

He had also guaranteed several years' salary for one of
Mosley's working class Labour MP supporters, W.J. Brown,
the MP for Wolverhampton West . . . In the event Morris's
pledge was not redeemed. Although Brown resigned he
decided at the last moment not to join the New Party.

Morris also provided money to support the controversial youth clubs . . . the mix of political and physical
training they were to provide seemed to some early supporters such as John Strachey to be a potentially explosive
combination with fascist overtones . . .'[41]

In July 1934 Morris wrote to the *Jewish Chronicle* denying
'rumours to the effect that I have given financial support to the
Fascist movement in this country and that my tendencies are
therefore anti-Jewish . . . There is not an item of truth in these
allegations. I never subscribed to the Fascist movement nor
supported it in any way neither do I have the least antipathy to
the Jewish race. It occurs to me that the best way of evidencing
the foregoing statements may be for me to make a subscription
to a Jewish charity.'[42] He enclosed a cheque for £250 – for him,
a derisory amount: consider, for example, an announcement
two years later to the effect that 'The congregation at Oxford
was taken by surprise this afternoon when Lord Nuffield, chairman of Morris Motors Ltd., announced he would add £750,000
to his recent gift to the university, making the total of his gift
£2,000,000.'[43] Later there were contributions to other Jewish
causes – small amounts in 1938 to a Jewish art exhibition and
the London Jewish Hospital, and £5000 to the Jewish Refugee
Fund at the end of 1939.

These were real enough, but that they were for public
consumption can hardly be doubted. Morris's genuine feelings
were expressed more privately – for instance, in annotations
to his copies of *The Patriot*, a sheet published by the Duke of
Northumberland to promote the views of the so-called 'Die-

hard Conservatives' – anti-socialist, pro-empire, anti-semitic. An item in the August 1937 issue recording Harold Laski's address to the Durham Miner's Gala is marked: *Jew*. In the margin of an article on Bolshevism: 'It is a well-known <u>fact</u> that <u>every</u> govt of my England is Jew-controlled regardless of the Party in power.'[44]

» » »

Henry Ford's arbitrary lurch into anti-semitism was the apolitical impulse of an impressionable man drawn to extreme positions. The story of Morris's dalliance with Mosley tells another tale – of the slippery slope, the blurred frontier between legitimate authority and dictatorship. Democracy was not his style in business and he did not see it as an efficient road to the right politics: he told Miles Thomas, an employee who later went on to become chairman of BOAC, that he believed in 'benevolent dictatorship'.[45] This, of course, might describe any dictatorship – from the standpoint of the dictator. And the identity of the dictator Morris had in mind was not far to seek.

The association of the small-car project with such extreme views and brutality is disturbing. The Model T and Morris Minor are innocent, benign, universal – toys provided for our pleasure by some jolly uncle. Benevolent Uncle Morris and romantic Uncle Ford are part of the family. You don't look for skeletons in *those* cupboards. Yet, for that very reason, these unexpected and disreputable histories throw an instructive light on their time. They express the defining tragedy of the 1920s and 30s: the ease with which idealism becomes corrupted by power without anyone realizing what is taking place under their noses (see, for instance, the extraordinary persistence of Ford's reputation as a benevolent employer). For that both Ford and Nuffield were in their different ways idealists no one could deny; and the same was true of the dictators of those terrifying decades – Lenin, Stalin, Mussolini, even Hitler. The difference, of course, was that Ford and Nuffield were not politicians (though both made abortive forays into politics: Ford stood twice as a senator, though without campaigning and always at others' urging, and there was even, briefly, talk of Ford for President). But, even though not in office, they enjoyed the public power wealth confers. And as Lord Acton put it,[46] 'Great men are almost always bad men, even when they exercise influence and not authority.'

For that 'even' one might substitute 'especially'. All of us have whims and prejudices; very rich men – like politicians, unlike the rest of us – are in a position to indulge those whims at a national, perhaps even an international level. But unlike politicians (although like dictators) they cannot be deposed at the ballot box. Indeed, entrepreneurs have much in common with dictators, scorning what they see as mediocrity's rules, impatient with democracy's delays, preferring to trust instinct, *diktat*, bluff and occasional intimidation. Think (to name but three) of Ross Perot, Jimmy Goldsmith, Silvio Berlusconi. Beneath those perfectly cut suits, dark agendas lurk.

Of course not all politically inclined plutocrats wield their wealth in the same way. Some use it to cushion a new career in conventional politics. Some buy titles, either directly or (like Nuffield through his medical and educational largesses) indirectly. But Ford and Nuffield were a very particular type of businessman. Not only had they climbed a ladder of their own making from utter obscurity to unimaginable wealth, they had set in motion cataclysmic and universally welcomed social change – an experience given to few (Bill Gates comes to mind, although, unlike Ford or Morris, he made his fortune on the back of other people's ideas). Like the dictators they admired, they were little men propelled to a pre-eminent position by daring combined with faultless reading of the popular mind; they inhabited the popular imagination more fully, more adventurously than their contemporaries. And the popular mind can be a grim place. The Model T and the Morris Minor were populism made flesh – but so, in their disgusting way, were the concentration camps.

Naturally this does not mean that Ford and Morris would have endorsed the camps. To rant in private, or even in public, is one thing; to carry the fantasy to its bitter conclusion is altogether another. Even the deposed Kaiser, whose obsessive views on Jews much resembled Hitler's, was appalled when he heard the news of *Kristallnacht*, declaring it made him feel 'ashamed to be a German'.[47] To act in this way required a psychotic political determination possessed, fortunately, by few. Certainly not Morris: as Mosley observed, he had no political vision at all, viewing government's chief task as the enabling of business. And Ford was little different. 'The slogan of "less government in business and more business in government" is a very good one,' he wrote. 'We may help the Government; the Government cannot help us.'[48] When it seemed possible he might become President he gave no thought whatever to political programmes, but imagined he would govern the country as he governed his factories, by moving his proxies into office and sitting back while they dealt with contingencies. In his view, professional politicians were parasites in the same way as speculators and intellectuals. If he supported Hitler, who was undeniably a politician, it was not for political reasons but on the emotional ground of a shared prejudice. Indeed, Hitler's policies (other than anti-semitism) were ones that, nearer to home, Ford viewed with horror. Roosevelt's New Deal, with its job-creating public works, its support of trade unions, its non-profit ethos, was anathema to him. And the Volkswagen operation – indeed, the whole *Motorisierung* programme, from the *Autobahnen* up – was the New Deal in spades. The VW, as the *Manchester Guardian* recognized, was not a matter of profit and loss. It was a political tool, a stepping-stone to non-commercial ends – in this case, Hitler's establishment as dictator of the Thousand Year Reich. The Romans offered bread and circuses, Hitler proposed motoring for all (along with a generous helping of your subhuman neighbour's property).

Given that Ford and Morris disliked the Jews because they were shadowy financiers, watching in the wings while others took the real risks, their own fates can be seen as richly ironic when compared with what happened to those who actually took the risk of basing policy upon such views. Ford's mansion and his personal historical monument at Greenfield Village are visited each year by wondering millions; Morris is remembered for his Oxford college and his medical endowments. But Hitler and Mosley, whom they supported, who embodied their prejudices and misjudgements and acted them out to the nth degree, have been less successful with posterity. Mosley died in ignominious exile. In the great construction site that is post-communist Berlin, the bunker, now grassed over, where Hitler put a bullet through his temple while his staff played dance tunes on the gramophone constitutes a stage on the Third Reich tourist circuit between Gestapo Headquarters and Göring's grandiose Air Ministry. And the most extraordinary new building in this city of virtuoso architecture is Daniel Libeskind's strange and poetic Jewish Museum, overrun by visitors before any exhibits are even installed.

Chapter Six

Harley Earl vs Norman Bel Geddes: The Future is Streamlined

Nothing is harder to predict than the future; yet on correct prediction business success depends. In 1908, it had enabled Henry Ford to create a mass market in automobiles. But the future soon becomes the past. By the mid-20s, 1908's future was history. In 1926, with 16.8 million cars in operation on American roads,[1] Ford was still selling twice as many as his nearest rival, Chevrolet. But two years earlier the proportion had been six to one. The Model T's day was done.

Some of the reasons were technical. For example, the T was essentially an open-car design, although an awkward closed body was grafted on to it in 1925. As late as 1919 this was no disadvantage: 87 per cent of new cars were still open, closed models costing from $500 to $1,500 more than the touring model of the same make.[2] But by 1931, 92 per cent were closed.[3] Manufacturers had been forced to look for real improvements if they were to keep on selling new cars during the Depression, and the closed roof was one of the most important, made possible by new steel-manufacturing techniques developed during the 1920s. The open car, uncomfortable in all but the kindest weather, and especially in the freezing American winter, died the death as the price differential narrowed. As with the self-starter, this improvement was at first presented as a slightly shameful concession to feminine demands. Thus a Colorado man, admitting that his next car would be a closed model, gave the reason for this preference as 'my wife. I personally prefer an open model, as I drive a lot in the mountains.'⁴ But, again as with the self-starter, feminine weakness swiftly prevailed over macho discomfort.

Ford's vision was overtaken by other innovations. Model Ts had been black because only black enamel dried fast enough for the Ford production schedule. But in 1924 du Pont introduced its quick-drying Duco polychrome synthetic lacquers, so that colour was no longer constrained by speed. And although the T's low price had given it an essential edge in a society that assumed cars would be bought cash-down, such a principle was not inevitable – as had been evident since 1856, the year Edward Clark invented hire-purchase in order to sell another expensive domestic item, the Singer sewing machine: a device that trebled sales within a year. Now Alfred P. Sloan, president of General Motors, rediscovered this strategy: by 1925, around 65 per cent of new cars were being sold on the instalment plan. So buyers were no longer constrained to buy the cheapest possible car.

Commercially, however, the most important change was the establishment of the used-car trade-in. In 1927, for the first time, more than half the new cars bought in America were replacements for old ones. And this had revolutionary implications for the first-time buyer market at which the Model T had been aimed. The T was still the cheapest new car around. But now even less money would buy, as Charles Sorensen recalled, 'a not-too-elderly Buick [with] such conveniences as a self-starter, demountable rims, and a smoother ride on the road'.⁵ And this, Sloan recognized, 'had revolutionary significance'. The first-time buyer had usually been looking for basic transportation. But now this constituency was more likely to turn to the used-car market. The buyer who traded in his still-serviceable car for something new was looking for something better – 'for comfort, convenience, power and style. This was the actual trend of American life, and those who adapted to it, prospered.'[6]

On 26 May 1927, after producing more than 15 million Tin Lizzies, the Model T assembly lines finally shut down to retool for a new model. The Model A would incorporate every possible significant improvement: self-starter, stick-shift gears, hydraulic shock absorbers, rubber insulated cushioning, balloon tyres. It had excellent acceleration, swiftly reaching and maintaining fifty-five mph. It had a safety-glass windscreen, then a notable innovation. And it was cheap: at $495, $100 cheaper than the equivalent Chevrolet and less expensive, weight for weight, than the T. But though new, the Model A was still a variant of Ford's original vision, in which utility and cheapness compensated for lack of choice. This was the policy that had made him the richest man in America, and he was not about to abandon it.

His competitors, however, were less constrained. 'We had no stake in the old ways of the automobile business,' wrote Alfred Sloan. 'For us change meant opportunity . . . As fine a little car as [the Model A] was in its time, it . . . was another expression of [Ford's] concept of a static model utility car.'[7] And, despite the ballyhoo that greeted the Model A's appearance, Sloan knew this was a concept whose time had passed.

Sloan's great *aperçu* – as fundamental as Ford's twenty years earlier – was that the car had become a fashion item. The nature of the market was transformed; it must be wooed in entirely new ways. Last year's dress is rarely worn out, but it still won't do. It has a knee-length skirt and this year everything's halfway up the thighs; it's green, and this year's colour is grey. From now on General Motors, like any other fashion business, would introduce new models every year.

They would not, however, be new in the way the Model A was new – a total rethink requiring top-to-bottom retooling. No one could afford that sort of investment, nor was there any need for it. 'Only occasionally in any one year do we introduce changes in all the chassis units – the frame, engine, transmission, front and rear suspensions,' Sloan observed.[8] GM's new models, introduced annually, would ideally change just enough to make last year's model unsatisfactory.

What this meant was that the emphasis would inevitably be on appearance. Sloan – small, dark-suited, as stiff as his literary style – was an unlikely advocate for frills. But frills were the future now. Ford's approach to motoring had been, like Ford himself, ascetic: the minimum working wheels. But ascetics are not consumers, and in Sloan's view future profits lay in the cultivation of consumerism. Far from seeking cheapness, he proposed that GM should, as a matter of principle, position its cars at the top end of the price range. And, that being so, the customer would require more than an efficient tin box. 'For the first Cadillac car that I ever had . . . I purchased small wire wheels in order to get the car down nearer the ground and I never could see why, as motor car people, we have apparently been so loath to do a thing which contributed probably more to the appearance of the car from the attractive standpoint than any other single thing,' Sloan complained to Buick's general manager in July 1926. '. . . The question arises – Are we as advanced from the standpoint of beauty of design, harmony of lines, attractiveness of color schemes and general contour of the whole piece of apparatus as we are in the soundness of workmanship and the other elements of a more mechanical nature?'[9]

They were not; but thanks to that other great American business, the movie industry, they very soon would be.

» » »

The brilliant light and constant sunshine that made driving in California such a pleasure also attracted the budding movie industry. In 1911, the Horsley brothers rented an abandoned tavern on the corner of Sunset and Gower in a real-estate tract called Hollywoodland to shoot stories on film using Edison's new moving-picture camera. And that same year the combination of automotive fun and the movies' particular combination of easy money and creative self-advertisement saw the start of what would become a Los Angeles cultural tradition – the customization of automobile accessories. Cinema stars were the new gods, the world's royalty; and kings and gods don't just buy their chariots off the shelf. In the customized automobile, at the same time public and personal, the movie industry could express its newfound wealth and status with all the visible extravagance money could buy. By the time Tom Wolfe published *The Kandy-Kolored Tangerine-Flake Streamline Baby* in 1965, Californians had been customizing their cars for over fifty years.

One of the first firms to cater to this specifically Hollywood need was the Earl Automobile Works. This had started out in the 1880s as a coach-building operation. But as early as 1911 it was offering bespoke bodies for cars and trucks. At first these were just modified standard models, but customers soon arrived who both demanded and could pay for something out of the ordinary. When Harley Earl, then aged twenty-five, joined his father's business in 1918, he specialized in extravagant cars for the stars. For cowboy star Tom Mix he fastened a real leather saddle to the roof; for Fatty Arbuckle he made 'the most streamlined vehicle anywhere', long, low and softly moulded ('*and* it cost him $28,000');[10] another client selected the colour of his car by pouring cream into his coffee until just the right shade of brown was achieved.

In 1919 the Earl Automobile Works was bought by Don Lee, a local Cadillac dealer. Seven years later Lawrence P. Fisher, general manager of Cadillac, paid Lee a visit. And as soon as the flamboyant Fisher saw Harley Earl's creations he knew that this was the man General Motors needed. Earl was at once invited to Detroit to design for General Motors 'a production automobile that was as beautiful as the custom cars of the period'.[11]

Before Harley Earl's arrival, design as a specific discipline had not been part of the Detroit equation. What was required was that a car went, and kept on going. Advertising stressed reliability and technical innovation: the notion of *style* simply did not arise. As a GM executive put it, 'Engineering was the all-absorbing activity and the engineer was usually the dominant personality, often to the point of unreasonable insistence on having his ideas . . . followed to the letter regardless of manufacturing feasibility or ease of maintenance.'[12]

Earl's first car for General Motors, the La Salle, was destined to fill the gap between the most expensive Buick, the $1,295 Buick 6, and the $2,985 Cadillac. He modelled his design upon the super-aristocratic Hispano Suiza, which he referred to as the 'Hisso'. Now anyone with a little money would be able to buy Hisso styling in the shape of Earl's La Salle. It appeared in March 1927, and caused a sensation. Nothing like it had been seen before. Corners had been abolished in favour of curves; a patched-together conglomeration of engineering necessities had given way to an artistically satisfying whole. Harley Earl's entire career in auto design would be devoted to lowering and lengthening the silhouette to give an impression of speed, and the La Salle began this process. Later, Earl would dismiss it as 'slab sided, top-heavy and stiff-shouldered'.[13] But at the time it was the last word in elegance.

Tremendously pleased with what he had done (he said he 'felt like a quarter-back who had just thrown a pass for a touchdown')[14] Earl returned to California. But Alfred Sloan at once called him back. On the strength of the La Salle, he had, in Sloan-speak, decided 'to obtain the advantages of [Earl's] talent

42. Harley Earl (seated) and Larry Fisher with the 1927 La Salle.

43. The pregnant Buick.

for other General Motors divisions'.[15] A special new department would be set up, officially named the 'Art and Color Section', unofficially known as the Beauty Parlor. It began with fifty people, ten of whom were designers. Later it would grow to fourteen hundred. Here Earl held court, in Sloan's words, 'selling progress'. 'We were all window-shoppers in the Art and Color "sales" rooms,' said Sloan.[16]

The Art and Color Section did not achieve instant success. Its first effort, the 1929 Buick, was, as Sloan put it, 'a tremendous flop from the public standpoint'. Introduced in July 1928, it was soon dubbed 'the pregnant Buick' and quickly withdrawn from production. The problem, said Sloan, 'was a slight bulge or roll just below the belt line, which started at the hood and continued around the entire car. By actual measurement, this curvature extended one and a quarter inches from the side of the belt line . . . In modern cars we tolerate a bulge of three to five and a half inches. The "pregnant Buick" . . . is a classic example of how the public generally prefers gradual rather than drastic changes of design.'[17]

'Mr Earl' (as he was invariably known) placed responsibility for this flop squarely upon the unfortunate engineers.

I designed the 1929 Buick with a slight roundness both ways from the beltline highlight, and it went into production. Unfortunately the factory, for operational reasons, pulled the side panels in at the bottom more than the design called for. In addition, five inches were added in vertical height, with the result that the arc I had plotted was pulled out of shape in two directions, the highlight line was unpleasantly located, and the effect was bulgy. The Styling Section then had not been as well integrated into other company operations as it is now, and I was unaware of what had happened until I later saw the completed cars. Of course I roared like a Ventura sea lion, but it was too late to keep car buyers from having a lot of fun naming the poor *enceinte* Buick.[18]

As Earl's chronicler Stephen Bayley remarks, 'It said something for the degree to which Art and Color had been resisted by other divisions in the corporation that the car could go from concept to production without Earl being aware of the changes made to his design.'[19]

It would never happen again. From now on Art and Color would become increasingly integrated into the company's mainstream, and Harley Earl would wield more influence than any mere engineer. Style rather than substance would be the dictator. Most notorious would be Earl's demand for a curved, wraparound windshield – a technical impossibility, as the despairing engineers insisted, and, even when achieved, distorting. But achieved it was, distortions and all, to become a status symbol for a generation, 'illustrat[ing] the extent to which a public experienced in the business of consumption could apply subtle degrees of social evaluation to degrees of curvature in glass'.[20] As a paper delivered to the Society of Automotive Engineers in 1962 put it,

> Previously, functional improvement or cost reduction was a good reason for component redesign, but [in the 30s] the engineer had to learn to appreciate new reasons for redesigns . . . The designer [is] the architect of the car, the coordinator of all the elements that make up the complete car, and the artist who gives it form. He stands at the beginning, his approach to and responsibility for the design of the vehicle is parallel to that of an architect for a building.[21]

The analogy, however, is misleading. The architect of a building must consider its functioning as well as its appearance. The automobile designer, by contrast, was (at least in Earl's day) concerned exclusively with appearance: it was up to other people to make his concept work.

Earl himself ranked among the most baroque of his creations. He was a very large, tall man, always dressed to kill, the impression of superhumanity sustained by a duplicate wardrobe kept in his office closet so that at the end of the longest, hottest day he would miraculously shed all trace of creasing and perspiration, without apparently changing his clothes. He kept himself portentously separate from his subordinates, rarely smiling, never visibly raising a pencil, pointing out design details with a languid, perfectly shod toe, ruling by intimidation. In the words of a colleague, 'He looked like he could kill you, a near miss might have done.'[22] In the technological universe that had, until his arrival, been General Motors, he was a living statement of intent, a theatrical novelty, his Hollywood ideas unsullied by engineering compromise or the European good taste of those he dismissed as 'design eunuchs'.[23] His fantasies were fleshed out in full-scale models prepared with clay on a wooden armature, then japanned and sprayed lightly with Duco for a glassy finish. 'The trouble with small models,' he told the *Detroit Free Press*, referring ostensibly to the prototypes but surely also to himself, 'is that your eyes don't shrink with the model.'[24] As for his cars, they bore the same relation to production models as his persona to the average Joe. Harley Earl drove cars no public would ever buy, most famously the 1937 Y Job, a two-passenger sports convertible based on a standard Buick chassis, just under twenty feet long. The Y Job took to its furthest extreme Earl's mission to lengthen and lower the American automobile. 'If 1937 trends were extrapolated,' observes Stephen Bayley, 'the 1965 Buick would be about the size and height of a tennis court.'[25] This did not happen – quite. But Earl's advent meant that anyone with

44. The Y Job.

enough money for a car could buy a piece of the Hollywood dream.

» » »

In 1929, three years after Harley Earl's arrival in Detroit, the stock market crashed and the world's economies screamed to a halt.

Ironically, the Depression, at least in America, was due in large part to that agent of freedom and business expansion, the internal combustion engine: in particular, its effect on agriculture. The automobile, and later the truck, had enlarged the farmer's potential market and improved his quality of life. ('It's the fun of the thing that appeals to him,' said a Studebaker agent. 'He's tickled to death with the sport.')[26] But though cars rapidly became indispensable, both for economic reasons and because the newly hard-surfaced roads made the use of horses and wagons expensive and dangerous, whether they increased the farmer's profits was doubtful. They saved time, so that more hours could be devoted to work and output increased; but, reflected an analyst in 1928, since the farmers were already producing all that could be sold at an advantage, this meant lower prices for agricultural commodities.[27]

Cars and trucks increased farm output indirectly, as well. Before 1920 most of a farmer's time and acreage had been used to produce feed for workhorses. But now the workhorse was superseded just as the carriage horse had been. In 1919 there were 147,600 tractors in use, in 1929, 825,900.[28] Land once devoted to grazing and hay could thus be used for marketable crops: the result was the first American farm surplus.

Henry Ford's vision of a soybean universe was one response to this. But it would take more than soybeans to restore the family farm to its pre-tractor level of prosperity. Tractors were expensive to run, not only because of the initial outlay (often obtained by mortgaging the farm) but because they required pricy accessories and artificial fertilizers to replace what horses had produced for free. Anything dispensable had to be dispensed with; and this meant labour. A farm had once guaranteed employment for all the family and more, but now that a larger acreage could be managed with far fewer hands, the traditional small family farm was becoming obsolete. And the stock-market crash finished the job. In 1929 farm income was $13 billion; by 1932 it had dropped to $5.5 billion, 'the lowest ebb since the days of George Washington, while wheat touched the lowest level since the days of William Shakespeare'.[29] Small-town bankers, wiped out in the crash, took the farmers' savings down with them. Banks, loan agencies and insurance companies, facing a liquidity crisis, refused to let farmers renew promissory notes by paying interest, as they had done before, but foreclosed on mortgages and sold the farmer's property for what it would bring. An Iowa lawyer writing in 1931, at the end of two years which had seen 25 per cent of the mortgaged farm real estate in Iowa go under the hammer, described how farmers were required to pay their debts with oats selling at 10¢ a bushel, corn 12¢ a bushel and hogs at 2¢ a pound. 'In the fall of 1932,' writes Reynold Wik, the product of a South Dakota family farm, 'it took a wagon load of oats to buy a pair of shoes, and a truck load of hogs would not bring enough money to pay the interest on a $1,000 note.'[30] He describes the consequences:

> A family at Norbeck, South Dakota, had lived on their farm for half a century. Their parents had homesteaded, built large farm buildings, planted trees, broken 600 acres of prairie sod, and paid their taxes. When the crash came, loans were secured to buy seed, feed, and fuel for the tractors. One day the agent for the land bank drove into the yard, presented a court order demanding full payment or evacuation of the home within twenty-four hours . . .

Conditions seemed to get worse. In Washington, forest fires raged because unemployed lumber jacks and farmers had set them in order to get jobs as firefighters. In Oregon, thousands of bushels of apples rotted because they were not worth picking, while women in Seattle searched garbage cans for food. In Southern states, cotton went unpicked because workers could make only 70 cents a day, not enough to keep them in pork and beans. Seventy per cent of the farmers in Oklahoma were unable to pay interest in the mortgages. Roads in the West and Southwest teemed with hungry hitchhikers, while camp fires of the homeless could be seen along every railroad track. Most of them were tenant farmers who had lost everything. As if to add realism to Dante's *Inferno*, even nature turned against the midwest farmers. In a region requiring 30 inches of rainfall annually to raise grain crops, only 10 inches fell in 1931, creating a drought which dried up water holes and ruined gardens, crops, and hay land. A shortage of pasture necessitated selling livestock or trucking in straw from as far as 200 miles away. Some cut green thistles for hay. Groves of trees died. Grasshoppers thrived on the heat and drouth, stripping corn fields and alfalfa, and in gale winds they rattled against the sidings of farmhouses like hail. In 1933 soil began blowing into the air, eventually causing 50 million acres to be blighted by dust storms which reached from Canada to Mexico . . .[31]

Naturally this misery had its effect on business, including automobiles. Between 1929 and 1930 Ford's profits dropped from $1,145 million to $874 million; by 1931 the plant was operating at one-third capacity and the balance had dropped into the red.[32] 4,587,400 new cars were made in 1929, fewer than 2 million in 1931. 1930 saw the first-ever decline in registrations.[33] And the custom- and luxury-car market virtually disappeared. Luxury car sales peaked at about 150,000 (about 5 per cent of American demand) in 1928 and 1929, but declined to 30,000 in 1933; in 1937, when the rest of the automobile industry had begun to recover, they dropped still further, to 10,000.[34] This was partly because Duco lacquer and the all-steel body meant that ordinary cars had become better-looking and more comfortable, but partly too for social reasons. During the 1920s enormous popular prestige had attached to the ownership of a custom-built car; now owners of such vehicles were stoned if they dared drive past breadlines. Meanwhile Harley Earl surged on undaunted, purveying ever more extravagant fantasies.

In a sense this might be seen as surprising: GM fiddling while the Midwest burned. On the other hand, in hard times people look for escape. The Lynds, revisiting Middletown (Muncie, Indiana) in 1935, found that although purchases of new cars were down (from 2,401 in 1929 to 1,162 in 1930 and 556 in 1932) there was only a 4 per cent drop in the dollar value of gasoline sales between 1929 and 1933: 'People manifestly continued to ride.' Car ownership was, they observed, 'one of the most depression-proof elements in the city's life in the years following 1929 – far less vulnerable, apparently, than marriages, divorces, new babies, clothing, jewelry, and most other measurable things'. Many businessmen thought it scandalous that some people on relief still managed to run their cars, and that no formal effort had been made by the relief authorities to discourage this. 'The depression hasn't changed materially the value Middletown people set on home ownership, but *that's* not their primary desire, as the automobile always comes first,' commented a local banker acidly. But the relief authorities took a different view, encouraging car ownership so that people might get to work if they could find it; if that meant the car was also available for recreation, so be it. A local paper estimated that '10,000 persons leave Middletown for other towns and resorts every fine Sunday.' And as soon as they could, people began to buy cars once more. In 1935 General Motors, already the largest local employer, 'passed an all-time employment peak' and, that November, broke ground for a plant enlargement.[35]

But where cars had once sold themselves, now customers had to be tempted by every means possible. 'As an incentive to buying, automobile manufacturers in their models for 1932 are offering attractive new features, beautiful cars and exceptional value,' concluded a report on the passenger car industry published that year.[36] The 1932 Plymouth introduced hydraulic brakes, and was much lower-slung. In 1934 independent front suspension was introduced by GM and Chrysler; in 1935 GM, desperate to stay ahead of the competition, introduced the solid steel roof, made with the body in a single pressing – something nobody had tried before. Only something exceptional would persuade customers to part with their money.

Design was a vital part of this inducement package. In 1925 America had officially declined an invitation to exhibit at the Paris exposition on the grounds that American craftsmen and manufacturers produced only 'reproductions, imitations and counterfeits of ancient styles'.[37] But in 1933 an executive whose profits doubled after Joseph Sinel restyled a hearing-aid declared that a 'redesign movement' would solve the nation's economic problems.[38] A whole new discipline – Industrial Design – was in the process of defining itself. The Art and Color Section at GM was only one of the famous design studios set up at this time; others bore the names of Raymond Loewy, Walter Dorwin Teague and Norman Bel Geddes. These freelance industrial designers were an altogether new species: between them, they would influence the look of a generation.

Their approach, however, was for the most part very different from Harley Earl's – a difference perhaps most clearly seen in the influence of the aeroplane, one of the most powerful shapers of 1930s visual thinking. Lindbergh's epic trans-Atlantic crossing in 1927 symbolized all that was daring, thrilling and new, bringing aviation into the forefront of public consciousness. Now man had entered territory hitherto wholly metaphorical: 'free as air, free as a bird' had become actual, possible states. When Middletown's inhabitants drove out of town on those pleasant Sunday excursions the local airport was an overwhelmingly popular destination, for psychological as well as touristic reasons. People's present circumstances might be dire, but the aeroplane represented escape into a new future full of undreamed-of possibilities. 'With each new thrilling invention of this sort, the imperatives in the psychological standard of living of a portion of the population increase.'[39]

The combination of speed, freedom and modern design represented by the plane gave rise to that hallmark 1930s style known as 'streamlining'. Everything that could be streamlined was, from armchairs to pencil sharpeners. But how deep did the streamlining go? Was it just another mode, or was it something more?

For Harley Earl streamlining was strictly a visual matter. True child of Hollywood, of back-lot sets and plasterboard fronts, he saw design as part of the entertainment business, a question of externals, of beauty, novelty and 'a visible receipt for the customer's dollars'.[40] And the planes he saw ready for flight on airfields across the States were above all a source of visual ideas with which to achieve the impression of speed he was constantly trying for. The idea of the wraparound panoramic windshield came from the bubble canopy of the Lockheed P38.[41] And the fin, that archetypal badge of the 1950s glamour car, resulted from a wartime glimpse of the then brand-new and top-secret Lockheed Interceptor pursuit plane.

They got to see it because the General's [GM's] Allison division made the engines. It was under security when they saw it and no-one, not even Earl, was allowed to go nearer than thirty feet. This prevented them taking in all the radical details which the plane sported: its projectile-shaped nose, its cockpit greenhouse, its beautifully contoured stream-lining and its twin tail booms. Not all of them, however. The admiring party led by Earl stood afar, and what they took in was the *twin tail booms.* At thirty feet only the big details are noticeable, and it was the tail booms that got through the broad gauze that was Earl's filter on the world of experience.

At the end of hostilities . . . the first fresh design which Earl pulled out of the plan chest was as radical in its way as Kelly Johnson's pursuit plane. Earl even called it the 'Interceptor'. He was never one to deny the source of a good idea. From thirty feet he had soaked up the lines of the Lockheed plane and found the source of the style for the next decade. Those twin booms were to become the celebrated and then infamous fishtail fenders, or tail fins.[42]

For designers such as Norman Bel Geddes, however, streamlining meant far more than low lines or fins. For him the notion that a piece of engineering such as a car should be designed from the outside in, dressed up in some preti-fying disguise, however streamlined, was anathema. Instead of enhancing merely the *perception* of speed, streamlining should enhance speed itself; instead of fighting against the specification, it should be part of it, design and engineering one inseparable whole. Geddes was (as we shall see) no more an engineer by training than Earl – if anything less so. But for him, as for many other designers at this time, engineering products were desirable in themselves, *because* they were functional. The better a thing worked, the more beautiful it became. Engineering technique held the same glamour for Geddes as Hollywood did for Earl; his admiration for the

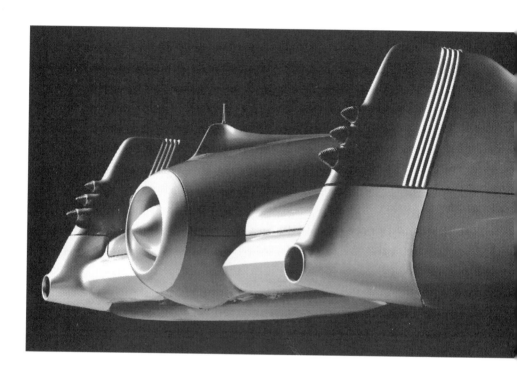

45. Fins! 1951 Buick LeSabre.

plane's shape was dictated not by aesthetics (although it was beautiful) but because, in the words of the design cliché, form followed function. When Geddes applied elements of aero-nautic design to other forms of transport such as cars, trains and ships, it was in the form of aerodynamic principles to improve performance, not fins and wraparounds. 'The executive may think that by minor changes here and there, after the manner of fashion designers with women's clothes, by changing the shape of moldings or of hardware, and by adding new gadgets, he is improving the design of the car,' wrote Geddes in 1934, perhaps with Harley Earl in mind. 'When visual design gives major emphasis to details, the result can only be mediocre.'[43]

Geddes' view of what design ought to be doing was at that very moment being demonstrated by some wind-tunnel experiments conducted on automobiles by the aviation designer Glenn Curtiss.

[Curtiss] took a stock coupe, which as delivered from the factory ran at a maximum speed of seventy-four miles per hour, and removed the body superstructure. He replaced it on the body backwards and driving it with the same motor, he was able to increase the speed of the car to over eighty-seven miles an hour. He then built a trailer which weighed fifteen hundred pounds and fastened it to the rear of the car. The trailer was built in a streamline form to eliminate the vacuum at the rear of the coupe. Despite doubling the weight that the engine had to pull, the streamlining increased the speed of the car eleven per cent. Further tests by Curtiss proved that the speed of the average automobile could be increased twenty per cent when going only twenty-five miles an hour merely by streamlining. This ratio increases considerably as the speed increases.[44]

In fact Curtiss's conclusions about the relation of shape to speed were not new, though they had never been so spectacularly demonstrated. The problem of drag had concerned racing car designers ever since Camille Jenatzy's *Jamais Contente* had topped a hundred kph in 1899, the first automobile to do so. That had been torpedo-shaped, the model that intuitively represented speed. But as early as 1911 the optimum shape was recognized as being counter-intuitive, with the point at the back rather than the front. Geddes' innovation was to apply these principles to a normal passenger car – his Car No. 1, designed in 1929 for the Graham-Paige company, whose president, Ray Graham, had been instrumental in attracting him to the industrial design field. Geddes began with Car No. 5, i.e. a car of five years from then; and working back in four stages each representing a 20 per cent change, he arrived at Car No. 1, 'an automobile which, except for its extreme simplicity, would resemble present-day cars'.[45]

Car No. 1 was never built, owing 'to psychological factors in the human make-up that have to do with timidity'.[46] Another and perhaps more potent factor was the 1929 crash, which swallowed the Graham-Paige company – though had the crash happened a week later a first test body of Car No. 1 would have been built and road-tested – or so Geddes liked to think. Meantime he kept his office busy designing the futuristic Car No. 8, its design based upon the falling drop of water – the illustration used by the architect Le Corbusier in *Towards a New Architecture* to exemplify the principle of streamlining in its ultimate natural form.

Inevitably, others were working along similar lines. The first actually to produce a finished low-drag vehicle was A. E. Palmer in 1930, whose design, resembling an extremely elongated VW Beetle, was built in Britain for Sir Dennistoun Burney. It was a bizarre-looking thing, but undoubtedly advanced, and a focus of tremendous excitement at the January

46. Not what you'd expect. Glen Curtiss's experiment in streamlining.

47. *Jamais Contente.*

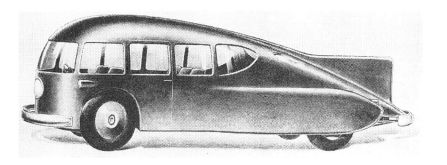

48. Car No. 8.

1931 meeting of the Society of Automotive Engineers in Detroit, where 'an abundance of pungent engineering ideas dart[ed] about the sessions with something like the speed and power of electrons being ejected from a radio-active substance' – the tremendous modernity of those sessions evident from the metaphor. By the time the meeting ended, the teardrop form had been unanimously accepted as the 'final evolution' of the automobile body.[47]

» » »

All these different groups converged upon Chicago for the 1933 Century of Progress Fair, held to mark the hundredth anniversary of Chicago's incorporation as a village. Far from having nothing to contribute, as in 1925, now America's designers had a plethora of exciting new ideas to show.

The planning of the Chicago fair had inevitably been affected by the crash, but its promoters evoked the spirit of the great fire which had destroyed their city in 1870, only for it to rise from the ashes stronger and more vigorous than ever. 'The forces of progress sweep on,' they declared. 'They are the forces of science, linked with the forces of industry.' And those forces, in 1933, were streamlined. Streamlining was the fair's defining style; the irresistible, onrushing force of modernity would whoosh America out of depression. 38.6 million people visited the fairgrounds to absorb this uplifting message before the gates finally closed in October 1934, the fair's popularity having extended it into a second season.

The Earl camp's bow to streamlining was represented in Chicago by Cadillac's 1933 V-16 Fastback Coupé, fresh from the Art and Color Section. This had an all-steel roof that flowed into the tail, teardrop fenders, an integrated rear luggage compartment and concealed spare wheel. But it was still, underneath the new visual language, a direct descendant of the horseless

49. Sir Dennistoun Burney's streamlined car.

carriage, its lines bearing little more relation to its functioning than the exterior of the new Super-Six Coldspot Refrigerator designed by Raymond Loewy ('. . . new in design – modern – streamlined – arrestingly beautiful') bore to the chilling of food. As Alfred Sloan put it in a letter to GM stockholders in 1935, 'The contribution of streamlining is definitely limited to the question of styling.' Belief that streamlining would reduce operating costs or increase efficiency reflected 'popular misunderstanding'.[48]

Other models, however, hinted at less cosmetic possibilities. 'Pierce-Arrow gives you in 1933 the car of 1940!' crowed the publicity for the 1933 Silver Arrow, emphasizing the role of wind-tunnel experiments in its 'scientifically accurate streamlining'. And in 1934, the fair's second year, Chrysler introduced its revolutionary Airflow, displayed next to the new Union Pacific M-10,000 Streamliner to emphasize the similarity in their design concepts. The Airflow was 'a modern aero-dynamic car', its welded unitary body designed by the chief engineer at the Guggenheim Foundation for Aeronautics. For the first time the body and chassis frame were made as a single integral whole, rather than the body being a separate structure bolted on to the chassis frame: the concept of streamlining was built into the very structure of the car. Carl Breer, Chrysler's chief engineer, described it as 'a totally engineered car designed from the inside out'.[49] Powered by a 4.4 litre engine and selling at a moderate $1,345, the Airflow, with its deco grille, flush headlights, split slanted windscreen, integral trunk and seating entirely within the wheelbase, developed 40 per cent less drag than existing models. Norman Bel Geddes, who was involved in its design, thought its 'basic body design . . . the best compromise between the present 1933 type body and the completely streamlined car of ultimate use'. It was both beautiful and efficient, riding 'more smooth on a rough dirt road than a Packard car does on a smooth concrete road. Another feature of the car

50. The Silver Arrow.

51. The Airflow and the Steamliner.

. . . was the fact that, after driving for many miles over this extremely rough road, the rear of the Packard car was entirely caked with mud, while the [Airflow] . . . did not suffer any splashes of mud at all.'[50]

Ten years later, such features of both the Airflow and the Silver Arrow as the all-steel frame and body, the forward relocation of engine and passengers, the lowering of the body in relation to the frame and the unified outer shell had become standard elements in most production cars. But at the time they were revolutionary – in Walter Chrysler's view, too revolutionary. Despite having initiated the Airflow project, when push came to shove he favoured something less extreme – for instance a La Salle-like torpedo front to make the car appear less unfamiliar: an initiative firmly squashed by Breer and Geddes in favour of a fully streamlined bonnet.[51] But the defensive marketing of both the Airflow and the Silver Arrow reflected managerial nervousness, with diagrams comparing the wind resistance of a conventional automobile to that of a streamlined profile in an effort to convince the public that the Silver Arrow's unusual appearance was 'a concrete vision of the automobile of the future' rather than a foolish aberration.

As Chrysler had feared, the public remained unconvinced: as with the pregnant Buick in 1928, it resisted sudden change. These might be tomorrow's cars, but when it came to parting with their money people preferred today's. Fewer than eleven thousand Airflows were sold before the model was withdrawn from the market in 1937. And the fabulous Silver Arrow never took off, partly due to financial troubles at its parent company Studebaker, and also because it was a luxury car selling for $10,000 at a time when all luxury cars were failing.

However, both the Airflow and the Silver Arrow paled by comparison with Buckminster Fuller's Dymaxion Car, first demonstrated to the public on 12 July 1933 and by some way the most spectacular exhibit at the Chicago fair.

The Dymaxion Car carried streamlining as far as it was possible to imagine. Where Harley Earl saw auto design as a branch of art, for Buckminster Fuller it was an aspect of philosophy. The form of an object followed not only from engineering imperatives, but from its place in a whole world-view. Through correct design, the world might be transformed.

> He envisaged the contemporary living pattern as local spherical control systems, everywhere surrounded by an air ocean . . . If shelter was to be given the economic advantages which derived from mass production, entire houses and apartment houses must be constructed in factories and delivered as totally assembled products, like automobiles . . .[52]

During the 1960s, Fuller would become world-famous for his geodesic dome, a framework of hexagons and pentagons that could be (and was) used to construct everything from a hippy camp to airport radomes. But until this belated recognition his life had been spent, in every sense, on the edge.

Born in 1895 to an old Nonconformist New England family, Buckminster Fuller made two brief attempts at a Harvard engineering degree. But he could never fit in with other people's structures, intellectual or material. After a spell meat-lugging for Armour's, in 1917 he joined the Navy, where he made vital improvements to seaplane rescue tackle and was seconded for a while to the US Naval Academy at Annapolis – the only formal engineering training he ever received. When the war ended he worked briefly in industry, then founded, in Chicago and in partnership with his architect father-in-law James Monroe Hewlett, the Stockade Building System, a new flat-packed fibrous acoustical building block. Five years later, however, Hewlett, the company's majority shareholder, found it necessary to sell his stock, and Fuller was sacked by the new management.

He and his wife had already lost a daughter. Now they moved with their new baby to a cheap tenement on Chicago's Northwest Side, where their next door neighbour was an Al Capone trigger man. In despair, Fuller toyed with the idea of sending his family to New York and quietly doing away with himself. There seemed to be only one argument against this. 'Bucky,' he said to himself,

> 'you've had many more industrial, scientific and social experiences than most of your steadier contemporaries. And if these experiences are put in order, they might be of use to others. Through them you might be able to discern and design environment controlling mechanics and structures that would provide spontaneously travelled bridges for mankind, which completely span the canyons of pain into which you have gropingly fallen. Whether you care to be or not, you are the custodian of a vital resource.'

From now on he would dedicate himself to a 'persistent search for the all-over social design factors'.[53]

Fuller gave his ideas the name 4D, for fourth dimension. At the time this was a buzz-word, like 'atomic' in the 50s or 'cyber' today, indicating intense modernity. It permeated the thought of such diverse sages as Einstein and Ouspensky – though meaning different things to each of them: for Einstein it was time, for the Theosophists some vague, pastel environment peopled by indistinct souls and angels. For Marshall Field's marketing department, however, 4D smacked of grade school; so, when they decided to use Fuller's 4D house to promote their first stock of 'modern' furniture purchased in Europe following the 1926 Paris Exposition, they called it 'Dymaxion', an equally forward-looking fusion of syllables derived from 'dynamic', 'maximum' and 'ions'. And despite its basely commercial origins, the name stuck. As well as a Dymaxion House – light, prefabricated, roomy and comfortable – there would be a Dymaxion Car, a Dymaxion Bathroom, a Dymaxion Deployment Unit – basic dwelling-units portable by helicopter – a rowing-boat, a new geometry, a new structural principle called 'tensegrity' . . . But the world – or at any rate its commercial elements – remained obstinately blind to what Fuller had to offer.

This was partly because of bad luck. But it was also a result of the grandiose and revolutionary nature of Bucky's ideas, and his uncompromising nature. When a backer of the Chicago fair asked how much it would cost to produce a Dymaxion House that was more than window-dressing, Bucky told him $100 million at which the backer, who had been thinking of a prototype rather than a production line, hurriedly withdrew.

In January 1933, however, a friend offered to put up some money to test out some of the Dymaxion ideas. It was not enough to finance the house as Bucky envisaged it. However, he was also interested in an aeroplane based upon the aeronautics of the duck – in his words, a '4D twin, angularly-orientable, individually throttleable, jet-stilt, controlled-plummeting transport'.[54] This would ideally burn liquid oxygen. Unfortunately, no alloys were yet available that would withstand the extreme combustion temperatures liquid oxygen generated. Nevertheless Bucky decided to conduct some preliminary investigation into the ground taxiing capabilities of this unprecedented vehicle. He rented the Dynamometer Building belonging to the recently defunct Locomobile Company in Bridgeport, Connecticut, a city where many skilled mechanics and engineers had been left idle by the Depression, and engaged a crew of twenty-seven to work under the direction of Starling Burgess, a renowned naval architect and aeronautical engineer. A thousand men applied for the jobs: those chosen included Polish sheet-metal experts, Italian machine-tool men, Scandinavian carpenters and former Rolls-Royce coach builders. The Dymaxion Car was under way.

Bucky's car was and remains an engineering phenomenon. It had a fully streamlined aluminium body and a chrome-molybdenum aircraft-steel chassis, with all the running gear except the lower half of the three wheels and the air-scoop enclosed within the belly. The engine was at the rear; the two front wheels were the car's tractors, the steerable rear wheel its rudder. It carried ten passengers in addition to the driver, and featured air nostrils, air-conditioning and rear-view periscopes for both front and back seats. Its ninety-horsepower Ford V8 engine gave a top speed of 120 mph – a performance which, in an ordinary 1933 sedan, would have required a three-hundred-horsepower engine. And although at nineteen and a half feet it was four feet longer than such a sedan, its steerable back wheel made it stunningly manoeuvrable: to park, you just headed directly into the kerb then tailed in sideways.

> One day [recounts Robert Marks] when he had the car filled with *New Yorker* and *Fortune* editors . . . Fuller made a sharp turn from 57th Street into Fifth Avenue. A traffic officer signalled for him to stop. 'What the hell is this?' the cop asked.
>
> Fuller opened the window. Then, while patiently explaining to the cop what the Dymaxion was about, he slowly rotated the car in a complete circle around him. The astonished officer demanded a repeat performance. This was noontime in New York in the era before stop-lights; a policeman was on duty at each intersection. The cop at 56th Street witnessed the performance at 57th and demanded a demonstration for his own pleasure. The 55th Street cop was not to be undone by his colleague a block above. Fuller was called on to perform by every cop on duty, from 57th Street to Washington Square.[55]

52. Buckminster Fuller with his Dymaxion Car.

Many aspects of the Dymaxion Car were eccentric and over-complex. For instance, there were several separate frames. Paradoxically, this was in order to reduce weight while giving a comfortable ride. Hitherto, railroad and automobile designers had improved riding quality by adding weight to the sprung part of the vehicle so that it should not bounce around too much. Bucky characteristically approached the problem as a plane builder, aiming for as light a vehicle as possible; and he saw that comfort could be increased while decreasing the total sprung weight, if the *un*sprung proportion of the vehicle was reduced to zero. The resulting multi-hinged, multi-spring arrangement 'could zoom across open fields with the agility of a light plane, yet provide a ride as smooth as any cruise on a highway'.[56]

Despite its complicated design, the car attracted various potential investors, including some who proposed selling a Dymaxion car with a Curtis-Wright aircraft engine as the top-line Studebaker. But it died a tragic death almost as soon as it appeared. The first car made its sensation, but was rather unstable; a second, improved car was ordered by a group of English automobile enthusiasts who commissioned Col. William Francis Forbes-Sempill of the RAF to visit America and test Dymaxion No. 1. This had been bought by Captain Alford Williams, then holder of the world's speed record for seaplanes and manager of the Aviation Fuel Department of the Gulf Refining Company, who called it 'aviation's greatest contribution to the auto industry' and drove it across the country in a nationwide campaign to promote the sale of aircraft fuel.

Forbes-Sempill crossed the Atlantic in the *Graf Zeppelin*, and was met at Chicago Airport by No. 1, sent over for the purpose by Williams. It was placed at his disposal; when he was ready to leave, arrangements were made to have him driven in it to the airport. On the way there, it was rammed by another car. Both cars overturned, but the Dymaxion's driver was killed and Forbes-Sempill severely injured – virtually at the entrance to the World's Fair. Reporters arrived; but by then the other car, which belonged to a Chicago South Park commissioner, had been removed. The headlines at once condemned the Dymaxion. TWO ZEP RIDERS KILLED AS FREAK CAR CRASHES read one; THREE-WHEELED CAR KILLS DRIVER, another. No mention was made of the other car. At the coroner's inquest, which was postponed on account of Forbes-Sempill's injuries, it was established that the accident was the result of a collision of two cars racing each other and weaving through traffic at seventy mph. But in the public mind the Dymaxion had become established as a dangerous freak. Nobody wanted it any more. Bucky's luck had struck again.

Car No. 1 was repaired and subsequently sold to the director of the Automotive Division of the US Bureau of Standards; it burned ten years later in a garage fire. No. 2 was no longer wanted by the English group; to pay his debts, Bucky gave it to the men who had made it, sold his tools and laid off his team. No. 3, already produced, was bought by the conductor Leopold Stokowski and his wife Evangeline Johnson, painted emerald green, and placed on exhibition in Chicago during the second year of the World's Fair, where it aroused tremendous interest and enthusiasm. Later it disappeared from sight, surfacing in 1946 in Wichita, Kansas, where it was used, among other things, as a henhouse. Aviatrix Amelia Earhart had ordered one, and the Russian Embassy wanted three, but the money had run out and they could not be built.

In 1943 Bucky redesigned the Dymaxion Car for industrialist Henry Kaiser, who thought the end of World War II would be a good time to challenge Detroit's stagnated dominance. This was a much smaller design, with a tiny engine at each wheel, in which four or five passengers sat abreast in the single front seat. Stability was increased by mounting the tail-wheel on an extensible boom, which stretched out to give the car a larger wheelbase at high speed and retracted automatically when it decelerated. Unfortunately the proposed car was so advanced that an affordable, road-testable prototype could not be constructed from existing mechanical parts, as Bucky had promised; like the other Dymaxion cars it came to nothing.

» » »

During the prosperous 20s, figures such as Buckminster Fuller were in a sense sidelined by plenty. Why redesign society when it was doing so well already? But after 1929 the mood of the times – embodied in the Century of Progress, and even more in the decade's second great fair, the New York World's Fair of 1939 – was very different. Previous fairs (such as the 1926 Paris Exposition) had been shop windows for the latest developments. But Chicago in 1933 and, in particular, New York in 1939, were about changing the world, or visualizing how the world might change. Times might be bad, but they need not stay bad. Developments in science and technology had brought within reach a material utopia that had hitherto seemed an unattainable dream.

How, though, could this dream best be realized? Not, as the Depression proved, through laissez-faire capitalism. In the words of M. King Hubbert, later to become the world's most respected oil industry theorist, then a young geophysicist working at Columbia University, 'I had a box seat at the Depression . . . We shut the country down because of monetary reasons. We had manpower and abundant raw materials. Yet we shut the country down.'[57] Yet any other solution implied a level of social prescription unacceptable to independent Americans and those Europeans still free from totalitarianism. What was needed was some middle way. This of course was exactly what Roosevelt's

New Deal tried to deliver. But it was a delicate path to tread. The organizers of the 1939 New York World's Fair, calling for a 'consumer's fair', stated, 'We must demonstrate an American Way of Living.' The *Official Guide Book* openly claimed that 'the fair exalts and glorifies democracy as a way of government and a way of life'.[58]

Streamlining was an integral part of this vision. The long, low lines of the buildings at both fairs, with their bright colours and rounded corners, spoke of technical precision and efficiency, optimistically projecting a unified, smoothly functioning future. This was the look of tomorrow's technological wonderland. But it also echoed ideas familiar from the literary utopias that had illuminated people's imagination since the beginning of the century: Edward Bellamy's *Looking Backwards*, with its hopeful urban vision, written 'in the belief that the Golden Age lies before us and not behind us, and is not far away'; H. G. Wells's *Modern Utopia*, with its 'dynamic technological society of joy and endless movement', and his *When the Sleeper Wakes*, whose hero, entranced in 1897, wakes two hundred years later in a high-tech city possessing such details as electrically lit, windowless, air-conditioned houses: exactly the buildings visible throughout the fairgrounds.

Between the Century of Progress Exhibition in 1933 and the New York 'World of Tomorrow' fair in 1939, this ideal future drew nearer at speed. The Chicago planners posited it for 'a generation that has not yet been born'. But, for the planners of the New York fair, 'The tools for building the world of tomorrow are already in our hands.'[59] Nevertheless, this was still the future, it had not yet happened. And an exhibition consists, *ipso facto*, of *stuff*: solid artefacts in a visible setting. Hitherto stands had presented the latest offerings, and this had been enough to make people marvel. Now their minds had to be directed through what was currently available in the spectacularly unmarvellous present, towards possibilities as yet unrealized. And this required new skills of presentation and imaginative extrapolation – just the skills, in fact, offered by those Wellses and Bellamys of their day, the industrial designers. Could they steer a middle course between the alluring superficiality of Harley Earl's automobile fantasies and the apparent lunacy of Buckminster Fuller's 'spherical control systems'?

Norman Bel Geddes, the designer most in view at both the Century of Progress (where he acted as a consultant to the Architectural Commission) and New York's World of Tomorrow, typified both the attributes and the deficiencies of this new breed. He designed cars, aeroplanes, ships and buildings, but (like most of his compeers) was neither an engineer nor an architect – a fact that architects, envious of his success in (as they saw it) taking bread from their mouths, were not slow to point out, refusing his application to register as an architect in 1931 on the grounds that, artistic though he might be, 'no one could be registered in this state as an architect who couldn't comply with the requirements of the law, and I complied with none of them'.[60]

He certainly did not. Geddes was a one-off, a phenomenon of continuous reinvention, no sooner established in one field than eager to try something new, bigger and more exciting. Adventuring through eighteenth-century Europe, Casanova, an impoverished ex-seminarian, discovered that you can be anything you wish: founder of the French state lottery, general of an army, Dutch banker, favourite of the German Court, Voltairean wit, multiple lover. All you need is charm, conviction and ability: above all the ability, *in extremis*, not to panic. Twentieth-century America was a very different place but, as Norman Bel Geddes found, human nature had not changed.

Born in 1883, Geddes' first job, after a spell at the Chicago Art Institute, had been with a poster-design firm in Detroit.

After a few weeks this came to an end. But a competition had been announced, to design covers for theatre programmes, and Geddes persuaded his employers to let him stay in the building and prepare some entries. His covers won. 'Dear Mother,' he wrote, 'I won four contests and I think I will get my job back with a salary.'[61] Within six months he had doubled his salary at the poster firm by working out his value to the company and threatening to go into competition, freelance. 'But you're not a salesman!' exclaimed his boss. 'No, and I wasn't a poster-designer six months ago,' Geddes unarguably retorted.[62]

Poster design soon palled. He became a stage designer, spent some time in Los Angeles working in both theatre and film (for Carl Laemmle, then just starting out at Universal), and by the mid-20s had arrived in New York, where he designed Max Reinhardt's sensational stage production of *The Miracle*. Soon he was established as a man about town, known by everyone, seen everywhere. But, restless as ever, he once again felt the need to expand his professional horizons. 'Until recently,' he wrote, 'artists have been disposed to isolate themselves upon the side of life, apart from business . . . I was drawn to industry by the great opportunities it offered *creatively* . . . In 1927 I decided I would no longer devote myself exclusively to theater, but would experiment in designing motor cars, ships, factories, railways . . .'[63] Once again he was reborn – this time as an industrial designer.

Geddes saw design as central to every aspect of the new era: 'in social structure, to insure the organisation of people, work, wealth, leisure . . . In machines that shall improve working conditions by eliminating drudgery . . . In all objects of daily use that shall make them economic, durable, convenient, congenial to every one . . . In the arts, painting, sculpture, music, literature and architecture.'[64] His projects became ever larger: an enormous airliner, a four-thousand-seat theatre with room onstage for five thousand artistes, a single skyscraper that would contain all a town's shops, a one-block skyscraper city . . .

When design reaches this kind of scale it becomes a form of social engineering, and the implications may be alarming. Such constructions formed the setting for many early twentieth-century dystopias – Fritz Lang's *Metropolis*, Wells's *Time Machine*, E. M. Forster's *The Machine Stops*; in real life one has only to think of Speer's Hitlerian grandiosities and Stalin's palaces of culture. It is not surprising, therefore, that democracies tend to view grand designs with suspicion. As Geddes observed, 'The basic idea which differentiates the way the Russian Government undertakes to organize and operate its affairs from the way other governments try to run theirs is that they have a definite plan.'[65] Americans, to his regret, did not have such a plan: indeed, they rejected any such notion.

That, however, was before the crash. Between 1929 and 1932 net income from manufacturing in the United States fell by more than two-thirds. And with stockbrokers jumping from high windows and farmers wandering the roads homeless, a planned economy capable of commissioning four-thousand-seat theatres (Geddes' had been designed for the Ukrainian State Theatre in Kharkov) seemed suddenly more attractive. Or so the American public evidently thought: for in 1932 Franklin D. Roosevelt was elected President. America had embarked for Utopia, and Norman Bel Geddes was going to design it.

» » »

In his book *Magic Motorways* Geddes speaks of 'highway progress – highways to new horizons of a country's welfare and happiness'. No vision could more absolutely have encapsulated his view of the world and design's role within it. And in 1936 he was asked to give that vision concrete form. That year, Shell Oil commissioned a new advertising campaign from J. Walter

Thompson, who decided to make their concept 'Traffic Conditions of the Future'. Geddes was to design an interstate highway system and an entire metropolis, with a view to building a scale model from which photographs could be taken for the advertisements. He set his staff to collect statistics on population trends and automobile registrations, photos of highways and cities, books and articles on city planning. 'Speed is the cry of our era, and greater speed one of the goals of to-morrow,' he declared.[66] But speed, although theoretically attainable, was rarely achieved on the American highways of the 1930s. Cities were choked by cars; even rural roads were becoming clogged. And to Geddes (as to Dr Todt, who began constructing his *Autobahn* network this same year) the solution was clear: a system of limited-access motorways with no bordering shops or houses. The old main transport network – the railways – no longer answered twentieth-century needs or priorities. If the car's increasing importance was to be used to greatest effect, a new network was needed – of roads.

Several such motorways had already been built. The first, the Bronx River Parkway, was conceived in 1906, though not completed until 1923. Three other New York parkways followed in swift succession – the Hutchinson River in 1928, the Saw Mill River in 1929 and the Cross Country in 1931. In Los Angeles the Arroyo Seco Parkway, fifteen years in the building and finally opened in 1940, was under construction. And across the Atlantic, as well as the Berlin AVUS built in 1921, Hilaire Belloc had in 1924 prefigured today's M1:

A man living at Windsor and desiring to reach Coventry, and using the new method of fast travel, would seek this main road at its nearest point and leave it again at the nearest point to his terminus. It would be a less picturesque, but a much safer and quicker way of doing his business. It would add a dozen miles to his total trajectory, but it would save a much more than corresponding amount of strain and expense of energy in following the series of narrow and winding roads most nearly connecting the two points . . . The final effect would be the relief of congestion upon the typically narrow, winding roads which cover the surface of England.[67]

Geddes' scheme, however, was bigger and grander than anything yet conceived. The ads were to depict the world as it would be twenty years on: 1957. And for that date he envisioned a continent-wide network of limited-access roads – what he would later term 'Magic Motorways' – with three lanes in each direction, the outer lane for speeds up to a hundred mph ('In 1960, 100 mph will seem no faster than the motor speeds we now take for granted'),[68] with service stations and rest areas spaced along the route. Technicians in elevated bridges would monitor the traffic and provide lane-changing directions to motorists by radio; at night, photo-electrically sensor-triggered lighting systems in the road itself would light up when a car passed. 'It took years to get the automobile out of the horseless carriage stage. The incredible conclusion is that highways will have to go through the same upheaval – sooner or later. And it can be done more safely if it is done soon.'[69]

This part of the vision, though grandiose, was comparatively straightforward. The space and expertise to build such roads were amply available: as Dr Todt's experience in Germany so impressively showed, with money and political will they could be put in place at once. The metropolis, however, was more problematic. For cities already exist. Was Geddes' city to be an adaptation of some city already built? Or was it to be entirely new, some city of the mind presaging future trends? Above all, how to create an acceptable symbiosis between cities and cars? This had been the unresolved question since automobiles were invented, as it still is. Within existing cities cars created unacceptable congestion and danger: in New York City, 65 per cent of traffic fatalities involved pedestrians.[70] Something clearly had to give – but what? The pedestrian, the car, the city itself? A series of conferences now took place at Geddes' offices to discuss the latest thinking on these issues.

Some of the ideas put forward were already venerable: for example, wings. 'In 1960 . . . the average person will be flying about in a small mosquito plane, the roadster of the air,' Geddes declared.[71] The notion that private aircraft would increasingly replace cars, thus relieving congestion on the ground, was first put forward in 1901, and ever since has hovered tantalizingly just over the horizon. This dream featured in Le Corbusier's *City of Tomorrow*, translated into English in 1929 and immediately bought by Geddes, whose well-thumbed copy now resides in the University of Texas, and in Frank Lloyd Wright's 'Broadacre City' of the early 1930s. In 1943, *Scientific American* predicted that after the war there would be 'an airplane in every garage'. In 1999 the Moller Skycar briefly hit the headlines, offering 'no traffic, no red lights, no speeding tickets . . .';[72] another Californian company hopes soon to offer the SoloTrek, a strap-on helicopter designed to fly at speeds up to 120 kph.[73] A poll conducted in Britain at the end of 2000 found a sense of 'let-down' among people aged over thirty when they were asked to compare the reality of the new century with the science fiction dream; 17 per cent had believed that they would by now own flying cars. Why traffic jams in the sky, mid-air collisions and constant noise above our heads should be intrinsically more desirable or less dangerous than the same things at ground level are questions significantly unaddressed.

Other still-familiar scenarios were discussed. William Day of J. Walter Thompson suggested that 'the simplest method of eliminating cars in New York City or elsewhere would be to pass a law prohibiting private ownership'. Everyone agreed (as they still do) that this might work practically if it could be politically enforced. But the different interests at work in any city make this a big 'if', as the meeting went on to demonstrate. It was agreed that this suggestion 'tend[ed] too much towards the socialistic' to make a good ad.[74] And in any case, the Shell campaign's whole intention was to sell cars, or at any rate fuel. What worried the auto interests was not congestion, but the low take-up of cars in inner-city areas. Dr Miller McClintock, whose Harvard traffic-study unit was funded by auto manufacturers, described his patrons' concern at the 'submerged market' of traffic-jammed New York City. The average overall speed of travel on Manhattan's north–south avenues was eleven mph, and on the east–west streets between five and six mph – just about the same as in the days of horse-drawn vehicles. As a result many people who could afford to own cars declined to do so. Car ownership on Park Avenue was, McClintock reported, very low, 'and this condition, from the point of view of the automobile manufacturers, is so important that they give Harvard $100,000 a year just to study the congestion problem.' There would also, he remarked, be more cars bought for young people if parents were not so afraid and so aware of the danger of accidents.[75]

So controlling the people was not an option. And in that case only one possibility remained: to control the environment. If cars could not be eliminated from cities, cities would have to be redesigned around cars.

Fantastic dreams of future cities had permeated the imagination of both filmmakers and architects during the century's first three decades. The catacombs of Fritz Lang's expressionist Metropolis underpin a city of bridges and swooping 'mosquito-planes'; the multi-levelled visions of *Scientific American*'s 1908 New York envisage trains on five levels, three below ground, two above, with a pedestrian bridge atop the lot; the same magazine's 1913 version, by Harvey Wiley Corbett, is another spectacular multi-storey fantasy, its ground level devoted to cars and buses, with two subterranean levels for trains, pedestrian walkways on the second and third storeys, and three levels of pedestrian bridges. There were also monumental futurist projections by Antonio Sant'Elia, Umberto Boccioni and their friends.

Today we are beginning to have around us an architectural environment that develops in all directions [wrote Boccioni in 1914]: from the well-lighted basement floors of the big department stores, from the various levels of tunnels in the city subway systems, to the gigantic leap upward of the American skyscrapers. The future will bring constant and ever-increasing progress to architectural possibilities, both in height and depth. Life itself will shape the age-old horizontal line of the earth's surface, with the infinite perpendicular in height and depth of the elevator, and with the spirals of the airplane and dirigible. The future is preparing for us a sky invaded by architectonic scaffoldings.[76]

Most of these 'vertical city' visions were based explicitly upon New York. But some rejected Manhattan's Art Deco assortment for an altogether new beginning: chief among them Le Corbusier, for whom New York's chaos discredited the whole pristine notion of the skyscraper:

In New York 20,000 people invade a narrow street at practically one moment, and the result is complete chaos; all fast traffic is paralyzed and the idea for which the sky-scraper stands is robbed of all significance. Created for the purpose of de-congestion, actually it slows up all traffic and is, in fact, a powerful factor for congestion. The result is that people cry out against the sky-scraper and the vertically-built city; and because of the need to get about

53. Harvey Wiley Corbett's City of the Future.

quickly, against the type of city which is spread out over a large area. So we have a new paradox. Since New York (Manhattan) is to some extent an absurdity, the whole idea is vehemently attacked . . .[77]

Faced, in the 1920s, with the problem of adapting the old city to the all-conquering automobile, Le Corbusier had offered radical solutions. In his plan for Paris, the Marais, the Archives, the Temple, are all torn down, and only the ancient churches preserved, 'surrounded by verdure; what could be more charming!', with wide car-friendly boulevards and acres of green grass in which 'one might find . . . an exciting and delightful relic [such] as, say, some fine Renaissance house, now to be used as library, lecture hall or what not'.[78]

It was to Le Corbusier that Geddes turned for his chief inspiration when it came to building his model. His vision of evenly spaced skyscrapers, administrative, commercial and cultural, recalls Le Corbusier's 'Panorama of the "Voisin" scheme for Paris', pictured in his *City of Tomorrow*. People would park on the outskirts and would enter the buildings by moving sidewalks, subways and pneumatic tube trains. Sidewalks would be elevated above street level, with streets bridged four ways at each intersection and commercial entrances and display windows moved to second-storey level. All streets would be one-way only, with only right turns permitted (America, then as now, driving on the right). Every tenth street would be an elevated limited-access artery.[79] And zoning would be total. 'The city is used only as a place to work. No homes are within its limits, no owner-driven automobiles are permitted within its boundary.'[80]

Le Corbusier had seen big business as the financial power behind his proposed politico-aesthetic urban salvation: it alone possessed the necessary resources and, once it had 'modified its customs' to become 'a healthy and moral organism', would be

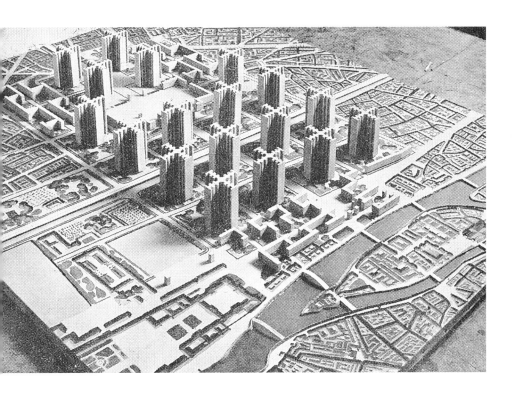

54. Le Corbusier's view of the Voisin plan for Paris.

happy to use them in this way.[81] Geddes, on the other hand, showed a New Deal faith in government. 'In the future,' he declared, 'a city will be composed of sections laid out from the sociological point of view . . . The use each block is put to (and it is probable that each block will be a single building) will be thoroughly worked out and organized, and it will operate as a unit. In cities where this ideal situation exists . . . people will arrive at the desired zone . . . in buses, taxi-buses or de luxe subways.'[82]

Geddes' monumental blocks and wide green spaces clearly echoed Le Corbusier's 'contemporary city'. But they also reflected his own preoccupations. The sweeping expressways recalled his previous career as an expressionist stage designer. And where Le Corbusier had demanded, 'Physic or surgery?', extolling Voisin's 'frontal attack' on the centre of Paris in his *City of Tomorrow* (and clearly coming down on the side of surgery), Geddes was less brutal, recognizing that everything could not be achieved at once. 'The [new] city makes no claim to being ideal. It [would] not [be] financially possible to rebuild the city completely, swapping its original layout. In the densest central portion, where development and values were at their highest, there [would have] to be many compromises.' But in general, this was the way forward. 'It is apparent that the city has not been redesigned for any one set of interests – either commercial or realty – or for the interests of certain individuals. It has been designed for communal use and . . . the automobile.'[83] Zoning already separated industry, commerce and recreation from living space. Now it would be extended one step further, separating people from wheels.

Geddes' model contained four existing buildings to give a sense of scale – the Woolworth Building, Trinity Church, the National Archives and Notre Dame Cathedral (with a parking garage beneath). Its highest building measured 1,500 scale feet – 250 feet higher than the Empire State Building. Ninety thousand pedestrians were represented on it, each one requiring four operations to put in place: a hole drilled into the brass sidewalk with a dentist's drill, a pin inserted and soldered, the solder polished off, and the pin clipped to the height of a person. There were eleven thousand vehicles of five different sizes: private cars, taxis, trucks, city buses and rural buses, all of the most modern teardrop design, each cemented to the sheets before the sidewalks and buildings were assembled . . .

The Shell Oil campaign ran through 1937 as a series of apparent articles.

TOMORROW'S CHILDREN WON'T PLAY IN THE STREETS
SAYS NORMAN BEL GEDDES

[ran the ad's headline, above a picture of the model].

'One half the space of the city of 1960 will be used for parks and playgrounds,' predicts Norman Bel Geddes, authority on future trends.

'Pedestrians will move quickly and safely on elevated sidewalks above the traffic level.

Streets will be made much wider by eliminating present-day sidewalks . . . Parking, loading and unloading will be done in side buildings. Traffic going 10 blocks or more will use high-speed Express Streets. No stop lights . . . no intersections . . . no stop and go!'

But no advertising campaign continues indefinitely. And then what? Was all this effort and expertise to be dissipated?

Geddes was determined it should not. After it had been photographed and filmed, his model was first of all installed at J. Walter Thompson's headquarters, then toured around the country as an educational exhibit, with filmed presentations for the use of smaller communities. Its genesis as an advertising tool fell into the background, so that it now appeared wholly visionary. And its creator, too, was transmuted. He was no longer a mere designer; he had become a sage.

It was in this purified form that, early in 1938, Norman Bel Geddes' model city came to the attention of General Motors' William Knudsen. General Motors was at this time preparing its pavilion for the 1939 New York World's Fair, whose theme was 'The World of Tomorrow'. Albert Kahn, the veteran architect who had designed Ford's Highland Park factory, had been commissioned to design it, and was preparing to install a model assembly line. But when Knudsen saw Geddes' model, a far more arresting possibility began to take shape in his mind. Would Geddes be able to construct a City of the Future for General Motors? On 28 January, Geddes circulated an excited memo to his staff.

> There are only two important obstacles: one is that we must use the material in such a way that it will in no way recall the Shell Advertising campaign; the other is that we must find out what Teague is doing for Ford, because if it in any way conflicts, General Motors will not be interested.[84]

It was of course inevitable, given the fair's theme, that Geddes' would not be the only 'ideal city' exhibit. Walter Dorwin Teague was indeed designing one, though for US Steel, not Ford. And the fair's central building housed yet another, 'Democracity', by designer Henry Dreyfuss, representing a city of 2039. This drew upon different utopian concepts, from the French revolutionary architect Ledoux to Ebenezer Howard. Viewed from peripheral balconies, it reproduced a twenty-four-hour day in five and a half minutes, ending with a heavenly chorus in which marchers, appearing from equidistant points in the heavens, converged upon the centre singing the fair's theme song. But neither of these rivalled Geddes' scheme for grandeur of conception and thoroughness of research.

Geddes prepared a twenty-two-page script for his presentation to Knudsen. It reflected his theatrical background, with
precisely indicated pauses and emphases, and firmly linked his
project in with government – dissociating it, by omission, from
the nasty commercialities of advertising: a year later he would
tell the *New York Herald Tribune* that the project had originated at a time when he had no work for his staff, and instead
of sacking them he had set a series of traffic problems and told
them to find answers, spending $100,000 of his own money in
the process.[85] The script quoted recent front-page newspaper
headlines:

$8,000,000,000 HIGHWAY PROJECT WINS
ROOSEVELT ENCOURAGEMENT

BUCKLEY SHAPES BILL FOR EAST–WEST AND
NORTH–SOUTH TRANSCONTINENTAL TOLL SPANS

ROOSEVELT FAVORS SELF-PAYING ROADS
SUPER HIGHWAY BILLS IN CONGRESS GAIN SUPPORT

It also underlined its begetter's showbusiness credentials:

A method of presentation has been devised
which will provide the spectator with
constant thrills and entertainment
IN RESTFUL COMFORT

This was no exaggeration. Geddes had devised a sort of
armchair-train in which viewers would ride into and around the
diorama, now enormously increased in size. As they rode, a
commentary would explain what they were seeing: first a huge
relief map, then momentary darkness, then 'a beautiful realistic
landscape – an animated scale model . . . seen in terms of 1960'.

The one-way traffic system would be described, then the spectator's chair would climb a hill and a small white farmhouse would appear. The viewer would whizz past it along the super-highway with its disciplined lanes and traffic towers, then night would fall, and 'the road itself seems to glow . . . He hears the rush of the car's slipstream. He has a sense of smooth running power, high speed.' Then he would climb from an apparent vantage-point of five hundred feet into mountainous country, finally arriving at an apparent twenty thousand feet elevation. 'The visitor looks toward a far horizon. In the distance, beyond the lower hills and plains, are the tall buildings of a vast city.'

> A super-highway runs past the city in a great by-pass, fed from mid-town and suburban feeder roads. The city has a great area of open parks. The towers of several great suspension bridges can be seen, spanning a river that runs along the city's edge. Around the outskirts are large spaces given to automobile parking, garages and comfortable depots . . . Down over the foothills the landscape is a patchwork of farms. Inns, resort hotels, golf courses and lakes are seen . . . The city river front, its docks, and shipping, and housing developments come clearly into view . . . Slowly the visitor circles down toward the street level. He sees an elevated grid of express boulevards, running through the several hundred blocks of low buildings. There are vast park areas which throw into prominence the new building forms . . .[86]

The presentation worked: the commission was landed. Now Geddes had just twenty-eight days to complete the design job, including not only the general plan of the diorama, but the building that was to house it. 'I had thirty draughtsmen on my staff – damned good men,' he told the *New York Herald Tribune*.

55. Geddes shows Knudsen (centre) the Futurama model.

56. Spectators on the Futurama ride.

I called each one of them in and told them to get two more draughtsmen . . . so in a couple of days each of those thirty had two assistants, then I told them all to go out and get two more. When they did start, the drawings came in so fast it would have been impossible for me to go over each detail and check them all. So we started a model, about nine foot square. At 6.00 every night all the day's drawings went to the model makers, and they built it up to scale, working all night. Then, the next morning at ten o'clock, I could see the work in solid, three-dimensional form.[57]

Time was too short to create an imaginary landscape, so it was drawn variously from life. The first scene, a long valley with gently rolling hills, represented land recently covered by the Ashokan Reservoir in the Catskills; the cities and towns were taken from St Louis, Missouri, Council Bluffs, Iowa, New Bedford, Connecticut, Concord, New Hampshire, Rutland, Vermont, Oneida, New York, Colorado Springs (the model for the area of lakes and ski-slopes Geddes christened Vacationland) and Omaha, Nebraska. The mountains were taken from the Yellowstone range, and the big lake from Yosemite. The diorama itself was built at the old Cosmopolitan Motion Picture Studio on more than four hundred twenty-by-five-foot work-tables, with four feet of working space between them. The display was then mounted on legs of iron pipe, threaded together so that the top surface could be inclined or levelled to hairline accuracy by a turn of the threaded joint. Twenty-seven thousand people a day could ride its conveyor belts of easy chairs into the future; as many as fifteen thousand might be waiting in line at any one time to make the fifteen-minute journey, progressing along streamlined ramps across the white façade from which a locomotive dramatically jutted (enclosing the generator from which the building drew its power). Knudsen had been against the ramps, but Geddes insisted the showmanship was

57. Part of the Futurama model.

worth the expense. And on opening day, Knudsen acknowledged he had been wrong: 'I've been watching them for over an hour, Norman, and the crowds are swarming in!'[88]

One critic compared Futurama's 'strange power' to 'some vast carburetor, sucking in the crowd by fascination into its feeding tubes, carrying the people through the prescribed route, and finally whirling them out' – 'a striking image', comments Robert Hughes, 'of subjugation to the Machine'.[89] But the crowd experienced something altogether more inspiring: a sense of new possibilities, of a new life almost within their grasp, of streamlined certainties and grand designs surrounding them like an invigorating bath. In Futurama the present is a mess to be cleared up, the sharp-edged, speedy world of 1960 a comprehensive vision to which all may aspire. 'Come,' invites the clipped, optimistic, unmistakably inter-war voice as we mount the armchairs.

> Let's travel into the future. What will we see in the wonder world of 1960? This world of tomorrow is a world of beauty – hills and valleys, flowers and flowing streams . . . Over space, man has begun to win victory – Space for all! . . . The farmer of 1960 works in greater security! Science and research control the risks of agriculture! Orchards are protected against insects, pollination is controlled – Physics and chemistry have joined hands with the farmer in help and friendship! . . . Strange? Fantastic? Unbelievable? Remember, this is the world of 1960!

The city fully participates in this relentlessly upbeat vision.

> Twenty years ago, the population of this city was approximately one million persons. Now it is much larger. Residential, commercial and industrial uses are separated for

greater efficiency and convenience . . . Parks are united to form green strips around each community. Along the banks of the river, landscaped parks replace outworn neighborhoods of an earlier day. Outmoded business sections and slum areas have been replaced where possible. Man always strives to replace the old with the new!

But even as Futurama's eager viewers queued on the ramps, war was engulfing Europe – and reinvigorating the American economy. All at once the Depression was over. And the future? Its shape was anybody's guess.

» » »

Harley Earl and Norman Bel Geddes represent not only two extremes of design philosophy, but two opposing world-views. Earl was preoccupied with detail and the indulgence of individual preference, Geddes swept away by planning on the grand scale; Earl confined himself to surfaces, Geddes struggled with fundamentals. They were opposite in appearance – Earl tall, suave, blond and dandified, Geddes small, dark, round and rumpled – and temperament: Earl blasé and cynical, Geddes enthusiastic and romantic (on marrying his adolescent sweetheart Bel Schneider, he insisted on changing his name from Geddes to Bel Geddes, to show the world that they two were now one; retaining the 'Bel' even after they divorced). Their approach to the automobile naturally reflected this baggage. For Earl cars were a commercial proposition, a means of pleasure and self-expression, to be dressed up, used, and discarded when the new model came along. For Geddes, the automobile was the scientifically perfect embodiment of design principles, a pod in which to race, under controlled conditions, towards the perfect future that hovered so tantalizingly just over the horizon.

Geddes was through-and-through a man of the New Deal, trying to steer a mid-way between capitalist freedom and the state-led mitigation of its more brutal consequences. But America's embrace of welfarism was never whole-hearted. Roosevelt was beloved by many, but almost as many more regarded him and all his quasi-socialist works with deep suspicion – a desperate remedy to be discarded as soon as times got better. And by the time the war ended, they had got better. People were prosperous again. They had had enough of being ordered about, of frugality and making do; capitalism could let rip once more. The New Look, with its nipped-in waists and yards of swirling skirts, spoke of a new light-heartedness, a pleasure in attainable excess. And the tailfins which were Harley Earl's every year more exaggerated tribute to aeronautics did the same. They were symbols of the good life explicitly associated, in ad after ad, film after film, with sex and pleasure; they symbolized, perhaps more than any other single image, the joyous extravagance of post-war America.

But although it might seem that the Earl view of life had won out over that proposed by Geddes, the facts, as always, were less simple. For the stunning paradox of the McCarthy period and the Cold War years that followed it is that this era of flaming anti-collectivist rhetoric saw the greatest public investment, in both housing and transport, that America had ever known. Even as the black lists were drawn up and the witch hunt intensified, Futurama was materializing in the shape of the interstate highway system, built almost exactly as and when Geddes had predicted twenty years earlier: in the words of planner Peter Calthorpe, 'the largest public works system in the history of mankind'.[90] It was acceptable because (like the *Autobahnen*) it was a defence priority, the decision to build highways rather than rail lines taken for military reasons, in order to spread possible bomb targets more widely. Civilian use was incidental – though, again as

58. Let the good times roll: Harley Earl and friends
with the Buick LeSabre.

59. You can do anything in your Buick.

with the *Autobahnen*, civilians would form the overwhelming majority of the system's users.

What happened next, of course, did not accord with Geddes' neat vision. In Calthorpe's words, 'Without that armature of freeways none of the suburban sprawl would have happened.'[91] And the question of how to reconcile the car with the older cities built before its advent remained – and remains – unsolved. In 1944, the Executive Office of the President wrote Geddes a letter about planning possibilities. 'I have been terribly interested for some time in trying to get that imagination of yours working on city planning,' it begins, outlining intentions 'to get a law passed whereby the Federal Government will furnish money for [city] plans . . .'[92] But whether Geddes' solutions would have been any more successful than the other doomed attempts to bring order to this chaos remains unknown. FDR died, the war ended – and Norman Bel Geddes' name was no longer one to conjure with.

The *Saturday Review of Literature*'s critic put the position starkly in a review of Geddes' book *Magic Motorways*, published in 1940. The book was

styled out of concepts in which most of vocable America does not believe. If we are to renew our embrace of *laissez faire*, of individualism, of competition, rejecting collectivism, planning, overhead direction, we are not entitled to the beauty which the Futurama had or that which 'Magic Motorways' forecasts. It has no relation with that aspiration . . . A nation fitted out with Norman Bel Geddes's Magic Motorways could not tolerate the slums of Brooklyn or of the Mississippi Delta, the miseries of California ditchbanks, or of Pennsylvania coal-towns. Nor, Mr Geddes and Mr Sloan, the particular profession of General Motors. Either this book is nonsense, or most of solemn industrial America is; how shall we choose?[93]

In the end, of course, the choice proved not to exist. The motorways remain, the poverty continues unabated. Laissez-faire gathered Futurama into its bosom: the result was the usual unsatisfactory compromise.

As the twentieth century drew to a close, however, it turned out that in car design, as in so much else, Geddes – and Buckminster Fuller – had been more prescient than anyone supposed. Sixty years after the Dymaxion Car and Geddes' teardrop designs, vehicles began to appear which might have rolled directly off the streamliners' drawing-boards. After seventy years, Car No. 8 is enjoying its day in the sun.

Chapter Seven

Detroit to Dunmurry: John DeLorean - A Study in Fantasy

Get your kicks on Route 66, sang Chuck Berry; but for those who restrict their on-road activities to simply driving, one of that route's more interesting features, certainly its only intentional artwork, is the Ant Farm's *Cadillac Ranch*: ten Caddies headed west and buried hood-down in a row, a decade's models in chronological order, their tail-fins silhouetted against the endless sky of the Texas Panhandle. Cadillac Ranch is sited eight miles west of Amarillo, a town otherwise notable only for its helium storage facility and the Pantex nuclear weapons factory. It was made in 1974 for oil magnate Stanley Marsh III, aficionado of giant artworks and Amarillo's solitary liberal: he once memorably remarked of Pantex that it was 'like living down the road from Auschwitz'. But if Pantex represents the dark side of the American dream, cars fuel its fondest fantasies. 'What makes America the best country in the world is the car,' Marsh says. 'In Germany, Africa, China or Russia kids grow up thinking they'll have a house someday. But American kids dream that they'll have a car.'[1]

And in the 50s and 60s, that car would have been a Caddie. Cadillacs, in particular Cadillac Eldorados, took glamour to its ultimate limits. They had white-wall tyres and bench seats for

60. An Ant Farmer at the *Cadillac Ranch*.

heavy petting, not to speak of 'power train, outriggers, pillarless styling, gull-wing bumpers, outboard exhaust parts, four metal magnetized fold-finished drinking cups, a perfume bottle, an antenna which automatically rises to urban height, ventipanes, and a sound wave opening for the horn.'[2] They were more than eighteen feet long and six and a half feet wide. They also cost $13,000, had less than five and a half inches road clearance, a three-foot seat ceiling, and not quite forty-four inches for your legs: 'a thing built for very rich, very short people who have no parking problems'.[3]

'The real reason Detroit builds dreamboats,' thought John Keats, whose view of the Eldorado this was, '[is] so that it can sell six million $2500 cars on the installment plan, and thus make *five billion more dollars* than if it sold twenty million $500 cars.' But although that was undoubtedly true, it was not by any means the whole truth. These were the days when Detroit's product not only chimed with the moment, it *was* the moment, post-war America as the promised land, a Big Rock Candy Mountain of extravagant delights and inexhaustible possibilities. 'Today the American road has no end,' said a 1951 Ford advertisement. 'The road that went nowhere now goes everywhere . . . The wheels move endlessly, always moving, always forward – and always lengthening the American Road. On that road the nation is steadily traveling beyond the troubles of this century, constantly heading towards finer tomorrows. The American Road is paved with hope.'

Cars are one of the two great symbols of the post-war United States – the other, of course, being rock 'n' roll. Wind down the windows, set a tape in the deck and, wherever your corporeal actuality, your soul is instantly Stateside. For post-war America, and for all those non-American millions whose imaginations Hollywood formed, the car was desire on wheels. 'I can remember standing on Miller Road while new Dodges and Plymouths were driven to the convoy lot,' recalls Robert

Szudarek, a Detroiter. 'I was awestruck every year, thinking there would never be a car again that would be better than what I was seeing. The magnificent chrome trim, spinner, hubcaps, two-tone paint, even three-tone paint. Then I would see the next year's offering and start all over again thinking this would be the ultimate. You know, I am still wondering when the ultimate car will be formulated.'[4] The answer, inevitably, was never: in real life your car, like every car, was inexorably surpassable. But that didn't matter; once you were in it life became a dream – even if you were just a little old lady from Pasadena (*Go granny, go granny, go granny go*).

The Beach Boys celebrated fun and status, Chuck Berry hymned dubious sex (*Can you imagine the way I felt / I couldn't unfasten her safety belt . . .*). But more seductive even than sex or status was freedom, the all-American possibility of moving on. The western frontier was officially declared no longer to exist in 1890. Here, though, was a frontier on wheels, the ever-present escape hatch so poignantly celebrated by Jack Kerouac:

> Do you know there's a road that goes down Mexico and all the way to Panama? – and maybe all the way to the bottom of South America where the Indians are seven feet tall and eat cocaine on the mountainside? Yes! You and I, Sal, we'd dig the whole world with a car like this because, man, the road must eventually lead to the whole world. Ain't nowhere else it can go – right?[5]

This remained true even if (like most people) you didn't have a Cadillac Eldorado – even if, like the Okies twenty years earlier, all you had was a fourth-hand Model T with a rickety home-built superstructure. That was still something – more than something. When *The Grapes of Wrath* was made into a film, its audience outside America did *not* see Steinbeck's 'thousands of dilapidated automobiles' as poverty incarnate, the detritus of a sick society. Rather, they saw a society where even the poorest farmer owned a car.

And if all else failed there was danger – the greatest and possibly the last thrill of all: the twentieth-century version of Russian roulette. Kerouac took you along for the existential ride:

> There was absolutely no room on the bridge for the truck and any cars going the other direction. Behind the truck cars pulled out and peeked for a chance to get by it. In front of the slow cars other slow cars were pushing along. The road was crowded and everyone exploding to pass. Dean came down on all this at 110 miles an hour and never hesitated. He passed the slow cars, swerved, and almost hit the left rail of the bridge, went head-on into the shadow of the unslowing truck, cut right sharply, just missed the truck's left front wheel, almost hit the first slow car, pulled out to pass, and then had to cut back in line when another car came out from behind the truck to look, all in a matter of two seconds, flashing by and leaving nothing more than a cloud of dust instead of a horrible five-way crash with cars lurching in every direction and the great truck humping its back in the fatal red afternoon of Illinois with its dreaming fields . . .[6]

Death on wheels became the stuff of legend – James Dean's final, fatal sulk in his beloved Porsche Spyder *Little Bastard*; Albert Camus's classy exit in his publisher's Facel Vega; Jackson Pollock drunkenly obliterating himself in his Ford aged forty-four ('A romantic way to die,' said his lover Ruth Kligman); Princess Grace of Monaco, *née* Kelly, opting out in style on the Grand Corniche. And the culmination of all these, crash to end all crashes, apotheosis of auto death, Princess Di obliterated in the tunnel beside the Seine, her questionable lover beside her, their driver allegedly high on drink and drugs, gory reality buried in a blur of deliciously unanswerable questions. Was it a deliberate murder cooked up by MI5 to save the future king from the shame of his mother's morganatic association with a disreputable Egyptian? What of the mysterious white Fiat seen by some speeding away from the scene? The flash of blinding light registered by a pursuing paparazzo? It was a paradigm of thanatic romance, a life petrified at its fragile peak of glamour and mystery, factitious, irresistible: as that connoisseur of crashes J. G. Ballard observed, 'an accelerated death in both senses of the word'.[7]

But legend is, precisely, not reality. On the contrary, it is there to obscure and override all that tiresome, downbeat detail. Pounding along in the automobile with Chuck Berry, what does it matter that the baby beside him at the wheel was probably aged no more than thirteen? *I'll go you one better if you've got the nerve / Let's race all the way / To Dead Man's Curve*, sang Jan and Dean – but who knew, or cared, that Jan was brain-damaged in an auto accident soon after 'Dead Man's Curve' hit the charts? Jayne Mansfield, though also killed in her prime while driving an automobile, never made the legendary-death charts because hers was simply too gruesome – her head torn off as she leaned out of the window and met an oncoming vehicle. There's no making a myth out of that. It brings the horrific actuality too brutally home.

And in 1965 Detroit's legend foundered as unromantic reality hit the headlines. For this was the year Ralph Nader published his shattering indictment of the American automobile, *Unsafe at Any Speed* – a study, amongst other things, of fantasy's deadly effects when given pride of place in a life-or-death business like the motor industry. Danger, it seemed, was built into the very details with which dreamboats were most joyfully identified – the fins, the chrome, Harley Earl's high

61. 1959 Cadillac tail light.

style. When Ford's vice-president in charge of styling referred to the 'leading edges of the blade-like front fenders' on the Lincoln Continental,[8] this was no mere hyperbole: it was the exact truth. A textbook on preventive medicine observed that 'If one were to attempt to produce a pedestrian-injuring mechanism, one of the most theoretically efficient designs which might be developed would closely approach that of the front end of some present-day automobiles.'[9]

Nader provided numerous examples of such injuries. A motorcyclist, boxed in on a freeway merger lane, hit the rear bumper of a Cadillac and was 'hurled into the tail fin, which pierced his body below the heart and cut him all the way down to the thigh bone in a large circular gash'. A nine-year-old girl cyclist bumped into a parked car, a 1962 Cadillac, whose tailfin 'ripped into her body below the throat' and killed her. An old woman in New York City was hit by a Cadillac rolling slowly backwards after its power brakes failed: the blow of the tailfin killed her. A thirteen-year-old Chicago boy, running to catch a ball, ran into a 1961 Cadillac fin, which pierced his heart . . .'[10]

The industry, it emerged, was well aware of these dangers. Early in 1962 an independent automotive engineer called Henry Wakeland had sent by registered mail a formal advisory note to General Motors and its chief safety engineer, Howard Gandelot: 'This letter is to insure that you as an engineer and the General Motors Corporation are advised of the hazard to pedestrians which exists in the sharp-pointed tail fins of recent production 1962 Cadillac automobiles and other recent models of Cadillacs. The ability of the sharp and pointed tail fins to cause injury when they contact a pedestrian is visually apparent.' Wakeland had studied accident and autopsy reports of about 230 consecutive pedestrian fatalities occurring in Manhattan during 1958 and early 1959, and case after case showed the victim's body penetrated by ornaments, sharp bumper and fender edges, headlight hoods, medallions and fins. In response

Gandelot vouchsafed the 'confidential information' that 'The fins [of the 1963 Cadillac] were lowered to bring them closer to the bumper and positioned a little farther forward so that the bumper face now affords more protection.'[11] The killer fins were eventually removed, but only to conform to a new styling fad, the 'clean look'. Harley Earl's battle had been so unconditionally won that, even in the face of evidence like this, engineers could do nothing until the stylists approved.

Perhaps the most extreme example of this hegemony was the phenomenally successful Ford Mustang. The Mustang was a triumph of design detail. Appearance, not performance, was its selling point. Ford's Product Planning Committee, working closely with the stylists, chose the prototype and approved the basic sheet metal and two body styles *before* informing the development engineers. And it worked.

> Even before the press coverage and massive advertising campaigns were under way, Ford began receiving thousands of letters from people who had never even seen the Mustang. On the day the car was introduced, almost four million people went to Ford dealers to look at it . . . One woman wrote to the company to confide that the 'Mustang is as exciting as sex.' A woman from St. Louis maintained, 'Yes it is true that blondes have more fun in a new Mustang.' A massive 'after-market' sprang up quickly, anxious to be part of the Mustang boom.[12]

Given all that, what could the engineers say? The motoring magazines said it for them. The independent automotive evaluation magazine *Road Test* described the car as 'A hoked-up Falcon with inadequate brakes, poor handling, and marvelous promotion . . . Like most American cars the Mustang abounds with new and startling engineering features carried over from 1910.' It cited the 'very bad' glare from windshield-wiper arms

62. The Ford Mustang.

and blades, found its shock control dangerous on railroad crossings, and described its 'rear-axle hop and instability'. Another
report called it 'the quintessence of what's generally wrong with
American cars. It's a heavy-nosed blunderbuss with a teen-age
rear suspension.'[13]

None of this was news to Ford's engineers. In January 1963,
one of them delivered a technical paper to the Society of Automotive Engineers on the subject of an experimental model of
the Mustang then on display in various parts of the country. The
paper included references to a number of safety features incor-
porated in the operational model (and now, largely thanks to
Nader, standard in all cars): a 'fail-safe' dual braking system,
integrated headrests to prevent or minimize neck and spinal
injuries, a roll-bar to strengthen the roof structure in the event
of rollovers, a steering column preventing rearward displace-
ment into the driver during a front-end collision, a collapsible
steering-shaft, shoulder harness and lap belts, strongly anchored
seats, and bucket seats with internal holding power. 'In the
production-model Mustang . . . introduced in April, 1964 (and
of which nearly half a million were sold in twelve months) *every
one of these features had been eliminated.*'[15]

Nader's most devastating criticisms, however, were reserved
for the Chevrolet Corvair. In order to be killed by a tailfin you
had actually to impale yourself upon it; the Mustang might
be less safe in a crash than you would hope and expect, but the
Corvair was actively dangerous all on its own. It had a terrifying
tendency to flip over without warning, and could kill you for
no apparent reason at all. Nader described it as 'the "one-car"
accident'. General Motors' response was to have Nader tailed,
in the (unfulfilled) hope of turning up some scandal that would
destroy his public image and discredit his findings – a tactic that
backfired spectacularly, affording Nader unlimited publicity
and throwing GM even further into disrepute.

The Corvair was a rear-engined car with a swing-axle suspension; a combination well-known to have several unnerving habits. In the words of a GM senior manager, 'In turns at high speed they tend to become directionally unstable and, therefore, difficult to control. The rear of the car lifts or "jacks" and the rear wheels tend to tuck under the car, which encourages the car to flip over. In the high-performance Corvair, the car conveyed a false sense of control to the driver, when in fact he may have been very close to losing control of the vehicle.'

This same manager went on to reveal that all this was known at GM well before the Corvair was launched. But the then general manager of Chevrolet, Ed Cole, who went on to become president of General Motors, was 'enthralled with the idea of building the first modern, rear-engine American car', and refused to alter the suspension because it would increase costs. That was scandalous, of course; but, amazingly, this prior knowledge of the Corvair's potential dangers had not deterred GM's own managerial staff from driving the car. The problem, it seemed, was less cynicism than psychological blindness: they all believed their own propaganda. As a result a number had lost children or, in some cases, their own lives in Corvairs. The son of Cal Werner, general manager of the Cadillac Division, was killed in a Corvair; the son of Cy Osborne, an executive vice-president of GM, was critically injured in a Corvair and suffered irreparable brain damage; the niece of 'Bunkie' Knudsen, son of a one-time GM president and himself a lifelong GM man, was 'brutally injured' in a Corvair.[15] Such was the fantasy's power that it seduced even those who should have known better – who surely *did*, in some part of themselves, know better.

The narrator of these misadventures took a highly moral, indeed self-righteous, view of these goings-on – from which, naturally, he dissociated himself. He reflected on the schizophrenic nature of the American way of business, with its huge impersonal corporations and relentless reliance on stock

dividends as the sole measure of success. This, as GM's experience showed, could lead to highly dubious practices 'even
though the personal morality of the people running the businesses is often above reproach'.[16] He himself was on the side
of the dealers and engineers, honest and competent fellows
unable to do their job as they would wish because of the unreasonable demands and impositions of top management. He
was in a position to know: before his departure from General
Motors, he had been in line for the chief executive's chair. His
name was John DeLorean.

» » »

Speed and risk (as *Ben Hur* recognized) were addictive long
before the motor car. Rome's Circus Maximus accommodated
more spectators than Wembley Stadium and the Houston
Astrodome combined.[17] Dr Johnson's alarm – 'Fie, sir – twenty
miles in one hour upon a coach? No man could rush as fast
through the air and continue to draw breath!' – only goes to
show the relative nature of perception. But the internal combustion engine introduced a new dimension of thrill. Richard
Noble, holder as I write of the world land speed record,
remembers his first view, aged six, of John Cobb's *Crusader*,
then about to try for the water speed record. 'Suddenly I felt
myself gripped with this tremendous excitement. The whole
thing was just so fabulous. It wasn't the boat itself that was to
prove my inspiration, though *Crusader* was a sleek beauty . . .
It was the enormous power that was so appealing.'[18] Cobb was
killed a few days later, when *Crusader* broke up travelling
at more than two hundred mph – the first time anyone had
achieved such a speed on water. But in the face of such god-like
possibilities, death, as is its wont, lost all substance. Young
Richard was hooked by the idea of speed – addicted, like the

charioteers, to the rush that comes at the ultimate limits of acceleration and control.

Nothing is harder to analyse than the essence of an entirely unmediated thrill, and few speedsters are deep thinkers. An exception was T. E. Lawrence, romantic, writer and motor-bike enthusiast, who described a race he once had – and won – with a Bristol fighter-plane: 'A skittish motor-bike with a touch of blood in it is better than all the riding animals on earth, because of its logical extension of our faculties, and the hint, the provocation to excess conferred by its honeyed untiring smoothness . . .'[19] Anyone who rides in an open-top car will recognize this sensation. The rush of air past your ears, the sound of the wind, feel exactly as Lawrence describes. And although for Lawrence risk was an essential part of pleasure, I can testify that the sensations he evokes may be experienced in perfect safety. For those unequipped with goggles and helmets, anything much over forty mph becomes distinctly uncomfortable once the hood is down. And who wants goggles and helmets? Nothing could be less necessary: driving is headier with the top down at thirty than at a hundred in a standard saloon, a machine so insulated from the road beneath and the air above that velocity barely impinges.

John DeLorean's stern demolition of the Corvair and the business ethic that gave rise to it might lead one to assume that prudence and safety were his chief concerns. His success at General Motors, however, had little to do with either. On the contrary, it was unashamedly founded upon the macho addiction to power, and also to risk.

Born in 1925, DeLorean was a true son of Detroit. His mother assembled tools for General Electric and his father, an immigrant from Alsace, was sporadically employed as a millwright at Ford's during the dark days of Harry Bennett's Service Department.

I was probably six or seven and was awakened in the early morning by loud banging on the front door. My dad answered the door and was pushed aside by a couple of the legendary Harry Bennett's goons who proceeded to ransack the home in search of tools or auto parts they thought were stolen from the Ford foundry. My dad never took as much as a wrench from the plant, but this didn't preclude him from a random search. I can remember peering down the hallway and seeing these big men in dark clothing throwing things around our house. My mother rushed all of us into a bedroom and shut the door. We sat there in silence listening to the crashing of furniture and banging of doors as they went through the house. Later we were too afraid to ask any questions. I guess we just accepted it as part of my father's working life.[20]

Eventually the parents split up, and the children left for California with their mother. Returning to Detroit after a year, John found he had fallen behind in his schoolwork, but was accepted on probation at Cass Tech, the city's most competitive high school. There he worked hard, caught up, and won an engineering scholarship to Lawrence Institute of Technology. After a number of unsatisfactory jobs (time and motion studies, selling insurance) he realized that his real interest was automotive engineering, and was accepted at the Chrysler Institute, graduating with a master's degree in 1952 at the age of twenty-seven. A short time later he took a job as assistant to Forest McFarland, the head of research and development at Packard.

Packard was a small company, and this meant that the job still remained satisfyingly complete. 'An engineer had to . . . design a part, work with the machinist as he built the first part (I even machined a few myself), help put the part together with the car and then test it. If everything worked out, then I'd go to the guys in production and work with them to make sure the part was built and assembled properly.'[22] It was exciting work, and he threw himself into it. When McFarland moved four years later, DeLorean was named to succeed him. Later he moved to Pontiac as head of advanced engineering, and by 1961, aged thirty-six, had become Pontiac's chief engineer.

It was a classic American story, and a picture taken at this time shows a face to fit it, a serious-looking young man staring squarely at the camera. Honest, talented and hard-working, he has seized his opportunities and is poised to reap his just rewards. And there the key to DeLorean's story lies, in the ambivalent nature of those rewards as he envisioned them – and as Detroit tried to embody them.

In a revealing passage describing his impoverished early life, DeLorean says: 'I thought we had a pretty happy childhood. Part of the reason is that while we had the humble surroundings that come with lower middle-class existence, we didn't know we were being deprived of some of the great fruits of American life because we didn't have the means of instant communication then as we do today. So while we didn't have a lot, we also weren't aware of what other people had.'[22] But it was of course impossible to be wholly unaware of life's possibilities in a country where Hollywood daily dangled its version of paradise before the world. And nowhere was this celluloid vision more inescapable, more relevant to everyday life, than in Harley Earl's Detroit.

John DeLorean's life, as he went on to fashion it, is a kind of paean to the pervasiveness of the Hollywood fantasy. And appropriately, his first great automotive success was a bow towards that fantasy – though, since he was an engineer, it was not an anti-mechanical ribbons-and-bows film-star creation *à la* Earl. Under Earl's direction Detroit produced sheep in wolve's clothing, sedate sedans with speedy accessories. DeLorean would do just the reverse: his great winner, the foundation of his future career, was a racing car in dowdy sedan disguise.

The Pontiac Division, when he arrived there, was known for its staid solidity. DeLorean and his friend Bunkie Knudsen, then general manager, decided to revitalize it by aiming at the youth market, then acquiring both purchasing and trend-setting power as the baby-boom generation grew up. And DeLorean hit upon the idea of 'muscle cars' – standard production cars fitted with outsize engines.

The idea came to him as he watched boys illegally drag-racing along Woodward Avenue, Detroit's main street, in souped-up production models. Why should not Pontiac soup up its own uninspired saloons for this enthusiasts' market? He tried out his idea on a Pontiac Tempest, a car described by *Road Test* magazine as 'the worst all-around handling car available to the American public'.[23] And it worked. 'We put a 326 cubic-inch V-8 engine in this lightweight Tempest, tested it, and discovered that the car was surprisingly quick and exciting to drive. When we put a big 400 cubic-inch V-8 into the car, it was even more exciting. It was an electrifying car. It gave you the feeling and performance of an expensive foreign sports car. But it was basically a low-cost car to build.'[24]

They took the Tempest with the two big optional engines, stripped it down to essentials, added heavy-duty brakes and suspension and three two-barrel carburettors: and, presto! the new car was ready for production. DeLorean suggested they call it the GTO after a Ferrari then being raced in Europe, the Gran Turismo Omologate, and introduced it as a 1964 model without waiting for corporate approval. Management 'was mad', and Pontiac's head of sales refused to schedule more than five thousand for production. But it was too late to stop the line – and the car was an instant success. It sold thirty-one thousand the first year, sixty thousand the second year and eighty-four thousand the third. It was copied throughout the industry: it became iconic. Just as the Cadillac purveyed instant glamour, transforming any suburban housewife as if by magic

63. Honest John: DeLorean aged 36.

into Marilyn Monroe, so the GTO shouted streetwise tough. You opened your garage door an accountant and rolled out ready to cut the meanest deal in town. Starsky and Hutch's 1971 Ford Torino was a GTO copy; so was the Dukes of Hazzard's 1969 Dodge Charger Daytona. Shops were flooded with GTO shirts, shoes and emblems; there was even a hit record, 'Little GTO' by Ronnie and the Daytonas.

DeLorean's reputation was made. Knudsen moved to Chevrolet and then to a group vice-presidency; and in 1965 DeLorean, still not quite forty, took the general manager's job at Pontiac. The great fruits of American life were his to enjoy at last.

Enjoyment, though, hardly begins to describe DeLorean's reaction to this transmogrification. He was intoxicated, bewitched, entranced, overwhelmed. 'The trouble with being a manager of a major automobile division is the sudden celebrity that goes with the job,' Bunkie Knudsen observed. Cars mean big bucks advertising – and that means showbiz power. For example, Chevrolet sponsored *The Dinah Shore Show*, with its 'See the U.S.A. in your Chevrolet' song; and on the first day Knudsen took over Chevrolet he got a call from Dinah Shore, asking him to Hollywood for a party at which she would introduce him to Gregory Peck and various other stars.[25]

Knudsen, son of a GM chief executive and familiar with this ballyhoo since childhood, was not dazzled. He declined Ms Shore's invitation, observing that it might one day be in Chevrolet's best interests to fire her, and he wouldn't want a social friendship to cloud his judgement. But DeLorean, receiving similar approaches, was bowled over. His feet left the ground, never to return. He knew what the real world was: he had grown up in it. But now he had been admitted into the paradise that was Hollywood and need never enter reality again. In Knudsen's words, 'He got in with that crowd and went through all sorts of changes.'[26]

64. Starsky and Hutch's Gran Torino.

It is possible to mark this moment photographically. The earnest engineer was not a bad-looking fellow. True, he had a somewhat weak jawline; but engineers' jawlines are less important than their mechanical training – not, that is to say, matters of life and death. In Hollywood, however, bodily perfection is the first requirement. And all of a sudden DeLorean acquired extra jaw in the shape of a chin implant. The result, perfection in, say, *High Noon*, as Gary Cooper in the empty square braces himself for the bad guy's gunshot, was oddly worrying in an automotive context. You couldn't put your finger on it, but the niggle was there – as when you suddenly realize that the taut, wrinkle-free cheeks of the woman opposite don't go with her sixty-year-old hands. Down-to-earth solidity is what you want in an auto man; and something about DeLorean didn't look real. As of course it wasn't. The secret of those unreal manly looks lay in their genuine unreality. He had been restyled.

DeLorean's new look, however, differed from a Harley Earl job in that the transmutation was not merely external: it was a true mirror of the upheaval within. Where until now his concerns had been strictly precise and mechanical, now the emphasis was all the other way. In the words of David E. Davis, the man who ran his advertising campaigns, he 'bought the entire California package of the youth culture – being intuitive, letting your feelings hang out, that sort of thing'. He directed a promotional film 'and it was what everyone was supposed to look at to learn "where John was coming from" so it would guide us in dealing with him. It was a nicely photographed job showing beautiful cars smoking down the road with gorgeous young people at the wheel. The background music was the theme . . . from the French film *A Man and a Woman* . . . John had seen *A Man and a Woman* and went nuts over the picture.'[27] Filmgoers will remember the music in question, unsurpassably swoony as the couple leap towards each other in slow motion and soft focus along the beach.

65. A restyled DeLorean, jaw newly squared,
shares a ball with O. J. Simpson.

It was an extreme reaction. But in many ways DeLorean's new responsibilities demanded this divorce from reality. As divisional chief executive he was responsible for every aspect of his cars, image as well as performance. And in post-Nader General Motors, this was an extremely complex assignment. The company, smarting from the terrible publicity, was doing everything possible to emphasize its commitment to safety. In late 1965 it issued a booklet, 'Design for Safety', which closed with the statement: 'In all aspects of producing automobiles no consideration is more important than safety. This has been true in the past and will continue in the future.' But DeLorean had been propelled to the top job on account of the GTO – a car almost explicitly designed for street racing, its enormous power available to any would-be Schumacher able to afford $3,200. An ad put out at almost the same moment as 'Design for Safety' made this quite clear: 'There's a live one under the hood. Have you priced a tiger lately? Purrs if you're nice. Snarls when you prod it. Trophy V8 standard in Pontiac GTO. 386 cubic inches. 335 horsepower. 431 pound feet of torque. Want something wilder? Got it. 360 horsepower. Then prowl around in a wide track awhile. You'll know who is a tiger.'[28] Grrr!

It was clearly impossible for a company to be committed to both safety *and* the GTO. Executives above a certain level – the policy-making level – were therefore living a schizoid life, asserting one thing and doing quite another. And this split, whose results Nader had so mercilessly pinpointed, was reflected in DeLorean's activities as he rose up the GM hierarchy during the late 60s and early 70s. The quality that had got him where he was – his engineering talent – became devalued in his eyes, dismissed as 'Detroit talking'.[29] He found the mundane business of day-to-day management unbearably tedious. His organization, said Davis, was 'just nightmarish – John would take a dislike to a guy and cut him out of the decision-making process whether he really knew anything or not'.[30] On the public relations front, meanwhile, as mechanical practicalities receded and inchoate feelings took over, his pronouncements became almost entirely meaningless. When he talked about compact cars, Detroit's attempted answer to the flood of Japanese and European imports which had sent its profits tumbling, there was no mention of small cars' genuine advantages – reduced fuel consumption (an important issue, given increasingly stringent pollution controls, and soon to become vital when the oil price quintupled following the Yom Kippur War in 1973) and greater manoeuvrability. Instead, 'The small car concept is more than just a matter of size,' DeLorean said. '. . . What it really means is a new way of looking at transportation.' Small-car buyers 'look for a car that represents their life style – which is practical, fun-loving, simple, and outgoing'.[31] 'Automotive size, including smaller size, refers to a concept and not merely to physical facts.'[32] He even delved into sociology: 'At one time, family unity was most important in this country . . . today, family ties have loosened. There is no dramatic reason for having a large automobile.'[33]

Nevertheless Pontiac's sales continued to rise and profits burgeoned, largely on the back of the GTOs and such spin-off lines as the Bonneville, Firebird and Catalina. Chevrolet, by contrast, was in the doldrums following the Corvair fiasco that had provided Nader with so much of his material. So in 1969 DeLorean was made general manager of Chevrolet, to see if he could pull off the same trick there.

And pull it off he did. He infuriated union officials by demanding that styling and tooling changes be done at night or at weekends to cut lost production time – an order countermanded by senior management. He promised new designs that failed to materialize, and spent wildly on lavish television shows whose viewing figures did not justify the outlay; there were even rumours of kickbacks.[34] But Chevrolet – in the words of its departing general manager 'Such a big monster that you twist its tail and nothing happens at the other end for months and months . . . there isn't any way to really run it. You just try to keep track of it'[35] – did well. Profits soared. Somehow DeLorean, the modern-minded hipster at the heart of GM, the only senior manager who never wore a suit, had out-suited the suits. Management was dazzled. In the words of Arvid Jouppi, Wall Street's leading auto industry analyst:

> John DeLorean was the most exciting thing going in Detroit . . . He was the new generation of engineer-executive the industry needed. After all, he was projecting this image of being pro-civil rights, pro-consumer, pro-safety and fuel efficiency; and yet, he was making his numbers. The stuff with the clothes and the sideburns and the dyed hair didn't count against him with these people. If you want to know how John got away with it, ask the people at GM who knew better but kept promoting him.[36]

It is a measure of Detroit's uncertainty that by 1972 he was spoken of as the next president of General Motors, and promoted to the fabled fourteenth floor, home of the company's senior management.

He was where he'd always wanted to be; and he hated it. The new job was about all the things he couldn't do – committees, organization, policy-making – with none of the hands-on stuff at which he still excelled. His lifestyle spun increasingly out of control; wives and girlfriends came and went; he sank into depression. He talked of resignation: the vice-chairman dissuaded him (or so DeLorean said) with the words, 'Jeez, I don't see why you want to leave. Nine chances out of ten, when Cole leaves you'll be the next president.'[37] However, not long afterwards he did indeed resign: 'I figured I had to leave quickly, because if I stayed on the job much longer the attempts to discredit my business reputation would hurt me.'[38]

'He says he left to start his own auto company,' *Automotive News* reported. 'Insiders say he was fired.'[39]

» » »

By the time he resigned in April 1973, DeLorean had for years been living an almost entirely fantasy-based life. But his credibility within the industry still, almost unbelievably, remained intact. Indeed, 'His most important attribute is, simply, credibility,' editorialized *Automotive News* on the occasion of his resignation. 'People believe him – his co-workers, his dealers and his suppliers . . . perhaps even government and the consumer, too . . . If his style set a pattern for the future, the auto business will be better off. If he is one of a kind, the auto industry has lost more than it realizes.'[40]

However, he was not yet lost to the auto industry. His new ambition was to set up his own company and manufacture his own cars. It was a Hollywood scenario, with himself as hero: DeLorean takes on the world. He would show them – he would dazzle them all.

The starting capital for the DeLorean Motor Company was DeLorean himself – his managerial skills, automotive expertise, the 'rights' to his new sports car, and his time. A famous Italian designer was commissioned to create a body; DeLorean insisted on the soon-to-be-notorious gullwing doors, both because this would make the car stand out and because potential customers were ageing executives who needed all the help they could get if they were to climb into a low two-seater. All this, costed at GM rates, was declared to be worth $10 million. This was a purely notional sum: it wouldn't actually *buy* a single rubber band. However, on the basis of the sports car rights $3.5 million was raised from a handful of 'partners', later to become shareholders in the DeLorean Motor Company. These same rights were then sold for $18 million to a group of 134 investors assembled by Oppenheimer & Co., who would be entitled to royalties on every car sold. Stock in the company went on sale, at $5 a share in the first offering and $10 a share in the second offering, to the 360 car dealers who had indicated (on the basis of his success at Chevrolet and Pontiac) that they wanted to sell DeLorean cars: another $8.6 million. And 250,000 shares at $2 each went to Johnny Carson the talk-show host and another investor.[41] That made just over $30 million – $40 million if you counted DeLorean's wholly notional contribution.

The car, however, still did not exist except on paper; and meanwhile DeLorean, who now had no income from General Motors, was running a classy New York office and living his now habitual life of conspicuous wealth. There were two ranches in Idaho, a new wife half his age, a San Diego avocado and citrus farm, a string of twenty-five automobiles ... As to how it was all sustained, any movie-goer could write the script. Here's the stuff we've all seen a thousand times, the rumours of extortion and embezzlement, of unpleasantnesses conducted by a heavy front-man, of millions that vanish into mysterious Swiss accounts, of shell companies between which worthless cheques freely flow. All this had to be kept from the eyes not only of the law but also of the Securities and Exchange Commission, who would have to ratify an investor prospectus if DeLorean wanted to go public. Meanwhile, armed with his design and with a set of sales projections, he set about raising the real money.

And this was easier than you might think; for cars encompass every size of fantasy. If owning an automobile is every schoolboy's desire, and designing one every engineer's dream, the establishment of a successful car plant on their home patch tops the wish-list of every impoverished region. Accordingly DeLorean now began to alternate the California high life with flying visits to world centres of deprivation, places in need of jobs and prepared to offer tempting deals to secure them. 'We had people coming through the door all the time who wanted to tell us about their state or country and all their attributes,' said Bob Dewey, employed by DeLorean to work these prospects. The chief contenders were Puerto Rico and Detroit, burned out in the 1968 riots and recently assigned $300 million under the federal government's new Urban Development Action Grant Program. Texas, Pennsylvania, Kansas, Georgia, Louisiana and Maine also made approaches, as did the Irish Republic and Spain – 'always John's great fall-back', said Dewey, perhaps because its climate resembled California's.[42] In the end, however, the choice seemed to be between Detroit and Puerto Rico. But both required more money from DeLorean himself – to be precise, $25 million more – and he could see no way of raising it.

It was at this point that his project came to the attention of the Northern Ireland Development Authority.

The situation in Northern Ireland at this time was desperate in almost any terms imaginable. It was languishing amid recession, civil unrest and (in some places) 50 per cent male unemployment: a sad picture however you viewed it, and especially by contrast with the Irish Republic across the border, then as now enjoying the fastest growth rate in Western Europe. The region's traditional ship-building and textile industries were all but wiped out, each remaining shipyard job state-subsidized to the tune of £5,000 a year.[43] Its engineering firms were suffering from the decline of British car manufacturing. And there were the Troubles, a low-key civil war whose fatalities mounted daily. Fifty per cent unemployment meant an almost infinite supply of bored young men with time on their hands, ideal recruits for the IRA and its Protestant counterparts. 'Jobs, homes and hope – that's the way to beat the IRA,' said Northern Ireland Secretary Roy Mason as he readied himself to fall for the great car chimera – the perennial hope that history will repeat itself, that the great pump-primer will work its magic once again. Cars had unleashed unprecedented prosperity in

America before the Depression, in Europe during the 1950s, in Japan during the 1960s; they would do it again in south-east Asia during the 1980s. In each case, an eager market of first-time buyers yearned to be supplied. But this market, though huge, is by definition finite; after the first fine flush, everything becomes harder. Hope nevertheless persists – surely all those enormous factories with their suppliers, their dependent communities, their huge sales networks, can't *really* be finished? The delusion was paraded yet again during the 1999 Rover saga, when BMW wanted to close its Longbridge plant, whose losses were running at millions of pounds a day in a saturated market. BMW, unsurprisingly unable to find a buyer, were vilified throughout the British press; the plant was finally given away to a would-be rescuer, and, a year later, once again seeks survival in the shape of a wealthy partner. But survive it must: closure is too terrible to contemplate. When a car factory dies, so does the economy of an entire region.

Conversely, the opening of a new car plant offers hope in the midst of desolation. If once the factory can be established, the rest (it is hoped) will follow. Accordingly, in June 1978 Northern Ireland Development Authority officials visited DeLorean in his New York office. He showed them his investors' prospectus, recently passed as bona fide by the SEC; they reported to Roy Mason, who was enthusiastic. But they would have to act quickly. DeLorean had asked for 'a decision in principle' by 28 June; he had received 'other offers of assistance' from Detroit, Puerto Rico and the Irish Republic. By the end of July, minds must be made up. This was the Puerto Ricans' final signing date for their contract with DeLorean; it was also the start of the British parliamentary recess, after which nothing could be done until September. 'When it comes to dealing with industrial projects with competitors, we are both involved in a fairly massive poker game,' said Kenneth Bloomfield, the civil servant responsible.[44]

DeLorean's hand was not devoid of trumps. He could show a network of four hundred dealers and long lists of orders, each order carrying a thousand-dollar deposit. The project's many delays had merely ripened customer anticipation. One Detroit man had ordered three of the still-phantom vehicles: he declined to identify himself to the *Detroit Free Press*, citing discretion. 'What if I ordered one for my wife and one for my girlfriend?' So impatient were potential customers that a bidding war had opened. Some saw it as a speculative investment that could not fail: if the firm did not last, then any car that did exist would acquire rarity value. 'There's a lot of mystique with the DeLorean,' said a dealer. 'People have followed the man and his reputation for many years.'

A report was hastily commissioned from John Banham, then working for the management consultants McKinsey, later to become chairman of the Confederation of British Industry. It was not favourable. 'This project is very risky, and it is not difficult to see why Mr DeLorean has found it hard to raise private risk capital,' Banham wrote. DeLorean hoped to sell twenty thousand cars a year immediately, rising to thirty thousand. But Banham pointed out that the Porsche 924, which was cheaper than the DeLorean, had sold only 13,657 in 1977, the Porsche 911 only 5,709 and the Lancia Beta Scorpion only 1,375. And these all came in any colour you chose, while DeLorean was offering only one colour – stainless steel. He had made no allowance for competition, left no margin for error or a slow start-up; all the figures assumed that nothing would go wrong. There was also a section headed 'Undue Dependence on One Man' – DeLorean himself, of whom Banham was deeply suspicious.[45]

Despite this, NIDA decided to go ahead, and the west-Belfast suburb of Dunmurry was chosen as the new car plant's lucky home. Roy Mason agreed to provide £52 million of aid to help build the factory; it would employ, in the first instance,

1,300 people, but there were hopes for more if things went well. The cars it was to manufacture seemed unlikely to find a large local market in prim Northern Ireland, a region apparently marooned in the 1950s. But what do local sales matter these international days? Work on the factory began in late July 1978, immediately the contract was signed. Within eighteen months, a soggy pasture with grazing cows – 'not only no buildings and production lines, but no engines and transmissions that were now stacked floor to ceiling, no bins of the thousands of parts . . . no letterhead stationery, no paper clips, no note pads, no employees'[46] – had been transformed into a smoothly functioning plant. The dream had come true.

The first car appeared in December 1980, followed by a slow stream the following March. But these long-awaited first attempts were highly imperfect. The happy-go-lucky Irish, it appeared, had failed to take car-building entirely seriously. 'You couldn't ride in them . . . All the components were stuffed in. They weren't built in, they were stuffed in,' said C. R. Brown, head of North American operations.[47]

These doomed efforts should have been junked, written down to experience. But customers were getting impatient, and cash flow was becoming critical. Against everyone's better judgement, the cars, with all their faults, were sent to the dealers. Inevitably, problems followed: the gullwing doors leaked and wouldn't open, there were problems with the electronics, the batteries weren't powerful enough to do all that was required of them: tales multiplied of dead DeLoreans stranded by the roadside, unable to move because they didn't have the juice for the starter motor . . . And these were not just turkeys, they were very expensive turkeys indeed. Between the car's conception and its appearance the pound had risen: a vehicle once estimated to cost $13,000 was actually selling for $25,000.

By the time the faults were ironed out the damage was done. Deposits were returned and orders cancelled; cars piled up in

66. Fantasy car: the DeLorean.

the company lot. In February 1982 the British government pulled the plug. Faced with a choice between two catastrophes – to precipitate massive job losses at a delicate moment or continue subsidizing a wholly uneconomic enterprise – they had been hesitant, their indecision aggravated by DeLorean's tactic of hiring more workers and notionally raising the annual production rate every time the question arose. But finally, to a chorus of 'I told you so', the Northern Ireland Office foreclosed, citing the company's inability to pay £800,000 interest owed. A total of £80 million had been put in – and lost. Enough was finally enough.

People still talk about DeLorean at Dunmurry, almost twenty years after his plant closed for the last time. He was the most exciting thing ever to hit these parts, if you don't count the bombs and shootings. In the drab streets of west Belfast the signposts read like a litany of newscasts – Divis, Falls Road, Ormeau Road, Lisburn. In 1979, the Troubles were at their height: almost every day the news reported a policeman killed, a man shot. Now an uneasy peace reigns, though Union Jacks still flutter from the lampposts and walls urge passers-by to 'Support Drumcree' and 'Remember 1689!' – which many evidently do, as though it were yesterday. 1689! What can John DeLorean have thought, driving through these shabby streets to his promised field amid the deceptively peaceful splendour of Belfast's hills and lough? By then he was living in Malibu, a place where 1689 is quite simply a notion beyond conception. Dreams take you to bizarre places, but this, surely, was the most outlandish yet. Although he came from Detroit, a town where I was advised not to walk down the main street in the early evening, and lived in Los Angeles, also not devoid of the odd shooting, Belfast quite simply terrified him – a haunt of savages bent on assassination. He flew in and flew out again, never setting foot outside the factory compound: there was a house there, where he lived; he even built himself a private cinema.

It might as well have been Mars. But where else could he go? 'The deal was too good to pass up,' wrote Mike Knepper, who became DeLorean's director of public relations, 'a 550,000 square foot factory on 72 acres of land and $160 million in grants, equities and loans, most of which didn't have to be paid back.'[48] Or, as *Automotive News* put it, 'It is not unusual for cities, states, or countries to induce factories to locate in their environs in this age of capital scarcity. It is, however, unusual for a country to provide a company with 70 per cent of its capitalization.'[49]

So DeLorean faded from the scene, only to re-emerge six months later in even more bizarre circumstances, arrested for cocaine-dealing in a Los Angeles airport hotel. Government agents, posing as drug dealers, had arrived at the hotel room with a suitcase full of white powder. Inside, waiting for them, was DeLorean: he had arranged a £16 million deal to bail out his sinking car factory. Opening one of the suitcases, he chuckled delightedly and said, 'It's as good as gold!' Champagne corks popped, DeLorean raised his glass and offered a toast to 'a lot of success for everyone'. At that moment there was another knock on the door and a man entered with the words, 'Hi, John, I'm Jerry West with the FBI. You are under arrest for narcotics smuggling.'

A year later, when DeLorean came to trial, the world's television viewers watched this scene open-mouthed, courtesy of the well-known pornographer Larry Flynt. Flynt, publisher of *Hustler* magazine, said he had bought the tapes from a government employee. 'Everyone has his price,' he observed. They were screened on CBS just as the trial was about to begin, together with another tape, made in Washington a month before DeLorean's arrest. In it the car manufacturer explained the financing for the drug deal. The money, he said, had been provided by the IRA, who were also protecting his factory.

The script now descended into farce as Larry Flynt, ordered to pay $6,500 a day until he revealed the source of the tapes, sent in a first instalment of $10,000 in used notes, which were carried into court by a posse of scantily clad beauties. The court, outraged, ordered him to count the notes in person – a task so dull that he fell asleep before it was completed. Arraigned for defiling the American flag, which he happened to be wearing at the time, he ripped it up and threw the pieces on the floor, denouncing the federal prosecutors as 'fascist closet faggots'.[50]

DeLorean was eventually cleared of all charges.

>> >> >>

Deception is rarely a simple who/whom affair. For a truly successful con one party must wish to be deceived, while the other must, to some degree, be convinced by his own story. Even as he plundered his employees' pension funds in a last vain effort to keep afloat, in one part of himself Robert Maxwell undoubtedly believed in the reality of his business empire. And when the pretence could no longer be sustained he died – leaving his confidants protesting his probity.

In Detroit, this symbiotic acquiescence in unreality had become a tacitly accepted part of the relationship between the automobile industry and its customers. It was this habit of doublethink, as much as the shocking product, that Nader exposed. But the habit survived even Nader. And DeLorean became one of its most accomplished practitioners. His plastic surgery was worrying because it was more than just vanity: it was a metaphor. He had forgotten what reality looked like, and had no wish to be reminded of it. Who believed in his venture? He did, for a start – and still, apparently, does. Interviewed in 1995, he blithely asserted that 'if we had built [the car] in

Detroit or the States . . . it would still be going today', and grumbled that '[the British government] owned every lot, the factory, all the tools, all the equipment, all the furniture – every pencil. So we couldn't borrow money anywhere. We had to rely on their living up to their end of the contract, and of course they refused . . .'[51] In this scenario the decision to withhold further funds had nothing to do with a lack of demand for his factory's product but happened because the incoming Conservative government was determined that their defeated Labour opponents should not be allowed a retrospective success.

When he left General Motors, more than one person compared DeLorean to William C. Durant, the legendary risk taker and automotive visionary who first formed General Motors from a few small manufacturers and $10 million capitalization. As Arvid Jouppi remarked after the final calamity, 'Not since Billy Durant has anyone tried to start a major competitive large production car company in [America].'[52]

Durant, like DeLorean, had been both a brilliant engineer and a swashbuckler. But Durant dealt with actual cash and companies that made actual cars. The history of the DeLorean Motor Company, on the other hand, is a lesson in sleight of hand: now you see it, now you don't. With doubtless unintentional appositeness, DeLorean always said that the best moment of his life was the day they chose his car as the time travel machine in the Hollywood hit film *Back to the Future*. If you move fast enough, who knows where you might not end up? The DeLorean stand in the Ulster Transport Museum just outside Belfast carries a quote from a psychologist at California State University: 'He's probably one of the great entrepreneurs of our time. Anybody who can gather together nearly $200 million of other people's money – getting the confidence of the kind of people he did – is a master.'

Here, where history's superseded wheels herd together in a giant pavilion amid an aura of Jeyes' Fluid, a sleek steel

DeLorean nestles incongruously alongside assorted MGs, Rileys and Hillman Imps. In a glass display case, beside a DMC internal phone directory, the company's Articles of Association are laid out, rescued from the solicitor's office after the fall. And behind all this a film poster depicts a tanned DeLorean, a pretty girl leaning on his shoulder, advertising the film that tells it as it really was: *John DeLorean Wheels and Deals – A Story of Money! Power!! Ambition!!!*

Chapter Eight

Rolling Alone: A Cruise Around the Freeways

ONE DIRECTION! toots Walt in the car, whizzing along it . . .

ONE DIRECTION! whoops America, and sets off also in an automobile.

ALLNESS! shrieks Walt at a cross-road, going whizz over an unwary Red Indian.

ONE IDENTITY! chants democratic En Masse, pelting behind in motorcars, oblivious of the corpses under the wheels . . .[1]

It was 1923 when D. H. Lawrence famously visualized Walt Whitman as prophet of a motorized America. Now the car has the whole world enthralled. And, now as then, Los Angeles leads the pack: first metropolis of the automobile. By 1970 more than one-third of the Los Angeles region was covered by streets, parking lots and driveways – an estimated 250 tons of concrete per inhabitant. It seems only appropriate that the exhibits in the Petersen Automotive Museum on Wilshire Boulevard should be labelled 'Property of the Los Angeles

67. The Stack.

Museum of Natural History'. Coyotes, eat your hearts out! Legs are finished, gone the way of all flesh. Only wheels count now.

I'm standing high above the city on the merciless white terraces of the Getty Museum, bathed in sunlight so brutal that even if you wear a hat the reflected rays will burn your chin. Below me, nose to tail like ants in a nest, maggots on a corpse, microbes in a bloodstream, the tin boxes progress in purpose-ful alignment along their preordained courses, each individual following its own programme yet the whole clearly controlled by some communal, centrally directed brain. Los Angeles without cars, like the Sahara without sand, is quite simply unimaginable.

Pelting along, however, is another matter. On the streets it's illegal; and the freeways, where in theory you can pelt to your heart's content, are solid with vehicles. Constituting only 4 per cent of the city's total area of paved road, the freeways carry more than 40 per cent of its traffic. This is Los Angeles' transport system, and also (LA in this if in no other respect resembling Moscow) its defining urban monument. Architect Charles Moore speaks for many when he locates the centre of Southern California at the spectacular and much-photographed three-level freeway interchange near Los Angeles City Hall. For Moore spots like this are 'the monuments of the future, the places set aside for special celebration by people able to experi-ence space and light and motion and relationships to other people and things at a speed that only this century has allowed'.[2]

The first freeway of all, the eight-mile Arroyo Seco Park-way (now part of the Pasadena Freeway), was mooted as early as 1911 but not completed until thirty years later, its opening in 1940 appropriately marked by a chain-reaction shunt involving three carloads of dignitaries. Recently declared a 'National His-toric Civil Engineering Landmark', it is (in engineering terms) a magnificent relic, outdated almost as soon as built. By 1960 it was carrying seventy thousand cars per day – twenty-five thousand more than its planned capacity: today's drivers breathe in as they negotiate its cramped ten-foot lanes and horrendously tight ramps and curves. Still, it's soon over: eight miles, in LA terms, is the merest step. Greater Los Angeles covers 452 square miles – about 50 per cent more than the city of New York; set down in Britain, it would stretch from London to Birmingham. This is urbs on a different, Western scale. When, at the height of the Monica Lewinsky affair, the radio announced that her SUV (natch!) had flipped over on the Santa Ana Freeway, no more than forty miles from where I was just then driving, I felt I had only just missed her; not a feeling I get about accidents occurring at the London end of the M1 when I hit Junction 14, forty miles away.

This is not to say that Los Angeles has no pre-car history. It was first inhabited by Shoshone Indians, the fertile location of whose settlement on the banks of the Los Angeles River (near the existing North Main Street Bridge) was so admired by the Mexicans that in 1771 they decided to site a mission nearby. The end of the Mexican War in 1848 led to an Anglo influx, but Los Angeles remained a predominantly Mexican town until its connection to the Southern Pacific Transcontinental Railroad in 1876. After that, its wonderful climate and fertility began to attract settlers by the trainload. And when, in 1885, a second railroad – the Santa Fe – arrived and embarked upon a price war with the Southern Pacific, the stream of settlers became a flood. In 1900 there were 100,000 Angelenos, in 1910, 300,000, in 1920, 576,000, in 1930, 1,238,000.

But how were they to be accommodated? Although, given water, the soil burgeons into what Reyner Banham, bard of the freeways, called 'a reasonable facsimile of Eden',[3] southern California, sold to easterners as 'the land of perpetual spring', is naturally a desert with a few fertile areas around its limited natural water supplies. And that, in all centuries but ours, would have ruled it out as the site of a great city. 'Of the seven urban areas of the United Kingdom,' wrote the Goodman brothers,

> six coincide with coal beds; the seventh, London, was the port open to the Lowlands and Europe. When as children we used to learn the capitals and chief cities of the United States, we learned the rivers and lakes that they were located on, and then, if we knew which rivers were naviga- ble and which furnished water-power, we had in a nutshell the history of American economy . . . These are the kinds of technical and economic factors that have historically determined, with an iron necessity, the big physical plan of industrial nations and continents.[4]

No longer. Los Angeles, from the start, declared itself free of these old-fashioned constraints. It had oil, to be sure, and harbours, but that wasn't why people wanted to live there. They came not for reasons of grim economy but for sunshine: a city built, from the start, on hedonism. 'In 1916,' wrote Norman Bel Geddes, 'the mere mention of California stirred visions of sun- light and paradise. Everywhere described in statements, claims, opinions and advertisements as America's Garden of Eden, with perfect climate, gorgeous coastline, beautiful beaches, pastel blue hills, profusion of flowers and so on.'[5]

But perpetual sunshine is no use without water. And if, without access to water, the land was valueless, this meant (as astute and ruthless men like William Mulholland and Henry Huntington soon realized) that, with it, fortunes were guar- anteed. Los Angeles' water politics have ever since provided material for muckrakers and thriller writers; but the fortunes thus amassed soon smoothly acquired a patina of high-minded respectability. At the Huntington Library and Art Collection in San Marino, a heavily panelled and marbled monument to the gulf between luxury and comfort is surrounded by fabulous botanical gardens, appropriately bathed in a perpetual mist of water – drawn, these days, from the far-off Colorado River.

Water and real estate soon led to other, interlinked fiefdoms: power and transit. You bought your parcel of cheap land, brought in water and power, and built an electric rail line. *Then* you took your profit in the form of subdivisions for housing developments. It was speculators like Huntington who laid down the system of electric inter-urban railways which formed the skeleton of the Los Angeles we know today. But since they were expensive to construct, were privately rather than municipally owned and catered to a captive market, once built there was little incentive for improvement. There were constant complaints of inadequate services and overcrowding, and although some suburbs had direct rail links – for example, between Pasadena and Santa Monica – there was often no way of getting from suburb to suburb, or out to the hills or sea, without first going into the city centre; an annoyance anywhere, but particularly irksome in LA, where downtown was never (as in older-established cities further east) the unquestioned industrial or commercial hub. In Norman Bel Geddes' 1916 view, the reality was very far from the hype. 'Los Angeles, where the sun shines every day and every day is the same, is monotonous; a collection of houses nowhere near a carline . . .'[6]

For these far-flung Angelenos, the internal combustion engine answered a whole variety of prayers. By 1929, there were two automobiles for every three residents – that is to say, more or less every adult owned a car. And with this last constraint upon settlement removed, such was the rate of expansion (an average of 350 newcomers a day for ten years)[7] that the city authorities could barely keep abreast of the builders. 'When we faced the matter of subdivisions in the County of Los Angeles,' wrote planner Gordon Whitnall in 1924, 'subdivisions which were coming like a sea wave rolling over us . . . we reached the conclusion that it would be absolutely necessary to go out and try to beat the subdividers to it by laying out adequate systems of primary and secondary highways at least, thus obtaining the necessary area for highways and boulevards.'[8]

The result was a pattern of development quite different from that of any previous city. In London, New York, Chicago, despite enormous suburban development, the central hub, served by radiating networks of commuter railways, retained its commercial supremacy. Not so Los Angeles. Downtown's already weak pulling power was further reduced by hopeless congestion as the old Spanish mission town, whose narrow streets already accommodated the tracks of the local streetcar system and the inter-urban railways, became choked with numerous automobiles, both moving and parked. A city-centre parking ban, opposed by car owners but supported by shop-keepers, was imposed by the city council in April 1920. The effect on trade, however, was quite the opposite of what had been intended. As soon as the ban came into effect retail sales fell by 25–40 per cent. But lifting it (after nineteen days, at the request of the desperate shop owners) simply returned the situation to its previous unsatisfactory state. Clearly some other solution had to be found. Since trade could not come to the shops, the shops would have to move to the trade.

And so they did. Slowly at first, but with increasing con-viction, business of all kinds moved out to the suburbs; and, as these in turn became crowded, out again to yet fresher fields – ones with plenty of space for car-parking. When in 1929 Bullock's department store opened on Wilshire Boulevard, the main entrance of this ornate art-deco palace of consumption led not on to the street, as in older cities where customers rode in by train and shopped on foot, but on to the enormous parking lot. Downtown, with its cramped spaces, could offer nothing to compete. By 1930 it was in decline. Shops shut and did not reopen; the first slums appeared. Soon Los Angeles was established as a city with no centre – or rather a city of many centres, dispersed, sprawling, and reliant almost entirely on the automobile.

A popular myth, still persisting (for instance, in the film *Who Framed Roger Rabbit?*), tells how public transport in Los Angeles was destroyed in favour of the automobile by a conspiratorial combination of General Motors and the oil companies. But although conspiracy theory is always seductive, and especially so in LA, this is not the true story. The electric railways died not because big business decreed they should, but because customers voted with their automobiles. The Arroyo Seco Parkway had the backing of downtown merchants because they thought it would lure shoppers to the city centre. And as most freeways ran through downtown, they did indeed revivify the old centre's economic base. But, more importantly, this new, swift link encouraged Angelenos to move to the suburbs. When they saw the Parkway's effect on Pasadena house prices, the realtors, who had built the railways, vociferously switched their enthusiasm to freeways. Inexorably, in what Reyner Banham has christened 'the transportation palimpsest', the new mass transit system imposed itself upon the old. From the original *pueblo* (downtown), the north-western rail route along the Los Angeles River towards the San Fernando Valley became the Southern Pacific line, and then the Golden Gate Freeway. Another Southern Pacific line, running south-east towards Santa Ana, became the Santa Ana Freeway, yet another, the San Bernardino Freeway. The Los Angeles Independent Railroad, running westward towards Santa Monica, became the Santa Monica Freeway. The Los Angeles and San Pedro Railroad, south towards San Pedro, became the Harbor Freeway. East through the San Gabriel Valley, the Pasadena and Foothill Freeway follows the old Santa Fe route, and the Pomona Freeway, the Union Pacific. By the time the last streetcar ran between Watts and Long Beach in 1961, the service – infrequent, overcrowded, and useless to anyone (that is, almost everyone) not living near a streetcar line – had become virtually irrelevant. If you lived in Los Angeles, you drove.

The resulting agglomeration does not look like an industrial city. Indeed, to European eyes it hardly looks like a city at all. But it is now the largest manufacturing concentration in the United States: a monument to people's preference for living and working where they choose rather than where economic necessity dictates.

» » »

To descend from the Getty Museum on to the freeway itself is to experience, in its purest form, the lonely crowd. Henry Ford's great achievement was the transformation of a scatter of solitary farmers into cohesive communities: villages, cities, states, a nation. But less than a century later the automobile, in one of the paradoxical twists that litter its history, has become the instrument of our utter apartness. Jammed together, nose to tail, thousands upon thousands of solitary drivers are lost in their own worlds. One moment all is adrenalin, as we negotiate last-minute lane changes, or see our exit, suddenly upon us, fly past and recede into the distance; next moment we are stationary, crawling in a phalanx as the sun beats down and the air shimmers with the expelled heat of ten thousand air-conditioning systems, close-packed yet isolated as securely as grubs in the separate cells of a beehive. Nameless crimes may be in progress only six feet away; shut away behind black glass, music thumping, air-con on max, who knows what unnatural couplings, what grim extortions are taking place? The sporadic freeway shootings are surely nothing but the *Look at me!* tip of an unimaginable iceberg of secret sin. But Angelenos are unfazed. They eat, bank, visit the doctor, without leaving their cars; there is even a drive-in church, the Crystal Cathedral, home to the famous, or infamous, preacher Robert Schuler. And who knows whether, in the depths of some Ford Galaxy or Lincoln Continental, the service relayed on those giant screens is not the backdrop for some private satanic rite? The car frees us not merely from the constraints of distance, but from all other constraints, too. In this unshared space, as nowhere else, we can unashamedly be our nose-picking, farting, guzzling, cigarette-smoking selves.

This solitary journey echoes an increasingly atomized society: both in and out of our cars, life's journey is ever more lone. Robert Putnam's recent book *Bowling Alone* took its title from the finding that between 1980 and 1993 league bowling declined by 40 per cent, while the number of individual bowlers rose 10 per cent. A paper presented to the American Psychological Association[9] found that young Wall Street brokers at the start of the new century preferred jogging and masturbating to any form of shared leisure activity. The 5 million new homes scheduled to be built in Britain before 2010 reflect not population increase but a trend towards single living.

The prophet of this uncivic world of self-sufficient individuals was Ralph Waldo Emerson, who in the 1850s declared that 'the dream house is a uniquely American form because for the first time in history a civilization has created a utopian ideal based on the house rather than the city and the nation'.[10] This of course reflected the settler's life, in which community was a commodity often in scarce supply and the house, built slowly and lovingly by the toil of its inhabitants, both a declaration of civilization and a refuge from the inhospitable wilderness without. But it was also a question of climatic habit. In the sparsely furnished Mediterranean, life takes place outdoors and privacy is of relatively little account. By contrast, the inward-looking culture of interior décor is an essentially northern preoccupation, in which Scandinavians, survivors of the six-month night, reign supreme. Driven indoors by the weather, we concentrate upon curtains; in Britain, a land of cold winds and muddy puddles, an unbroken diet of home-decoration and gardening programmes fills the television screens night after night. And although the America of Emerson's dictum was, for the most part, a hot country, it possessed the social instincts of the cold north whence so many of its grandparents had fled, retreating, as soon as technology allowed it to do so, from the shared evenings of porch and *paseo* into its ideal home.

The car was very much part of this shift. When the garage replaced the porch as the average house's street frontage, it not only moved family life from the public front to the private back of the house, but walled it off from the street. A *Los Angeles Times* article of 1927 declared the walled back yard 'almost a necessity' for the house on a small lot; 'it provides a definite area for garden treatment, and gives the effect of shutting out the surrounding stretches of barren country or adjoining houses'.[11] The public parks and beaches, where once everyone flocked, were depopulated as individual Edens blossomed and private swimming-pools became prevalent. During the 1930s, Depression and the dustbowl increased homelessness and brought in the Okies, camping around their ramshackle cars wherever space permitted; their 'auto-camps', seen as an urban problem to be swept away, brought public space further into disrepute. Add in the anti-social effects of air-conditioning and television, and by 1955 a survey was able to report that of a sample of 773 families, over half were indifferent to or disliked being able to see the street from the inside of the house, while only 27 per cent felt it was important to be 'near houses of good friends'.[12]

The Los Angeles freeways, swinging across the city, literally imposed this shut-away northern culture upon the street-oriented Latino communities they bestrode and divided. On either side the city becomes mere carpet, traversed by the chariots of a strictly private heaven whose inhabitants hold the world at bay with the sinister 'armed response' signs that

68. The freeways as seen by those who live beneath them:
this mural is entitled 'Division of the Barrios'.

sprout on every suburban lawn – a message strangely at odds with the flowery 'welcome' flags often to be seen hanging over the front doors of those same houses. What unseen armies threaten these empty streets, and how will they be identified? If I knock on the door, shall I be greeted as one of the welcome elect, or shot? Curious to know, I called the armed-response companies. How often are they summoned out, and in what circumstances? Once a week, once a year? They weren't saying. Why not? 'Ma'am,' they told me crossly – the formal opening mode an immediate indicator of displeasure – 'this is not the kind of information we divulge.' But the fact of their existence is more significant than any statistic. The 'concept manager' at Ford Car Research who saw automobiles as 'small security vaults' in which the commuter could barricade herself against the criminal city centre[13] was expressing something funda-mental about the automobile culture. Once you start shutting yourself in, you *ipso facto* shut the world out.

The result is a congeries of private utopias without public spaces as other cities know them. 'It is interesting,' writes Charles Moore

> to consider where one would go, in Los Angeles, to have an effective revolution of the Latin American sort. Pre-sumably, that place would be in the heart of the city. If one took over the public squares, who would know? A march on City Hall would be inconclusive. The heart of the city would have to be sought elsewhere . . . The only hope would seem to be to take over the freeways.[14]

That would indeed be a recipe for revolution, though not, perhaps, of the kind Moore is discussing. What he means is that revolution requires assembly; and how can one assemble in cars? They negate the very idea, both because of their exis-tential separateness and because in the automobile city, built around their needs, 'there is' as Gertrude Stein famously said of Oakland, up the coast, 'no there, there'. Both spatially and psychologically, public life is an essentially pedestrian concept. And in Los Angeles pedestrianism is an eccentricity. When my husband asked how he might walk from the Huntington Museum to a street perhaps a mile distant, he was met with blank incomprehension – except from the car-park attendant, a person still, presumably from necessity rather than choice, acquainted with the use of feet.

For most Angelenos, though, pedestrianism has become theme-park material. In Universal Studios' crowded 'City Walk', the 'city street' has become a movie set, a perfectly impermeable front concealing a total absence of back, where the punters who wander among the shops, restaurants, street musicians and entertainers may relish the unaccustomed pleasures of urban loitering at $41 a throw. Of course one may happily loiter in (for example) Santa Monica, for free and with added seaside fun. But Santa Monica also contains poor people, pollution and cars: in other words, actual life. And in Los Angeles everyone knows that real life doesn't compare with the movies. A film set, that's where you get a safe, clean, smog-free pedestrian street. What, in any case, constitutes reality? In the home of Hollywood, is not a film-set as real as any other surrounding?

This complex perception of what, in southern California, is real and what unreal is confirmed by Los Angeles' one immediately identifiable gathering-place for pedestrians. For the single spot in southern California that could unequivocally be called a public space was built not by any architect or city planner but by a movie-maker: Walt Disney.

After twenty-five years the pleasure of entering Disneyland's relaxed acres remained one of the most vivid memories of my first visit to LA: a measure, perhaps, of how deep a need it fulfils. And if, on a second visit, the magic was somewhat abated (I had not remembered the crowds, the endless queuing,

69. City Walk.

the tackiness: I had grown older), enough still remained to delight, at least for a while. Disneyland, thinks Charles Moore, is 'enormously important and successful . . . because it recreates all the chances to respond to a *public* environment, which Los Angeles in particular does not have any longer . . . It has big and little drama, hierarchies of importance and excitement, with opportunities to respond at the speed of rocketing bobsleds . . . or of horse-drawn streetcars . . . All this diversity, with unerring sensitivity, is keyed to the kind of participation without embarrassment which apparently we crave.'[15] A mere $41 (for some reason this is the magic figure) buys a passport to an ideal land where people still stroll down Main Street, mill in the New Orleans Square, take a turn in the paddle steamer, float through the fibreglass jungle, ride the steam train, watch the procession for Chinese New Year without fear of pickpockets or muggings . . .

Part of the pleasure lies in the unabashed return to childhood – both its delights and its irresponsibilities. From the moment we step from our cars and allow ourselves to be ushered aboard the neat green-and-white train, we abandon ourselves to a shared fantasy, suspending disbelief just as when first we saw *Bambi* or *Snow White* – as see them we all did. Driving, any lapse in concentration may lead to death, or at the very least to missing your road; walking, you expose yourself to heat, dirt and the constantly touted dangers of the street. But Disney's little train, chugging you towards the turnstiles while its friendly attendants issue their precise instructions, transports you to another psychological country – infantile perhaps, but orderly, hygienic and safe. In Disneyland there is none of the street's nervousness or distrust of strangers. We are all here to enjoy ourselves, happy in the shared certainty of excellent sanitation, instantly recognizable participatory pleasure, a wide range of affordable baubles and plenty of polite, friendly, personable staff on hand to sort things out and take charge should any trouble occur. Just as in the master's films, we know that nothing really bad can possibly happen.

Charles Moore remarks that 'Curiously, for a public place, Disneyland is not free. But then, Versailles cost someone a great deal of money, too.'[16] However, set against Versailles at its peak, Disneyland is indubitably a reduced version of public life – hardly surprising, given that the whole place reflects the imagination of a man to whom Beethoven's Pastoral Symphony suggested gambolling hippos and pink and blue My Little Ponies with fluttering eyelashes. But, despite these images, or perhaps because of them, *Fantasia* became a universal hit. For Disneyland, like Versailles, encapsulates its culture. Versailles was about awe and exclusion: precedence, hierarchy, grandeur. It offered an incomparable experience, but only to those arbitrarily selected by birth. In Disneyland, by contrast, John DeLorean's 'great fruits of American life' are available to anyone who can afford the price of entry.

'The United States,' observes Stephen Greenblatt, 'lacks virtually all of those elements that, to European thinkers of the 18th and 19th centuries, were the preconditions of nationhood: Americans are not a Volk; there is no single unifying environment or climate; and the population did not share a set of culture heroes . . . around whom a national identity could be fashioned'.[17] What they did and still do share were and are commodities, both tangible and cultural: movies, brands, sporting heroes, objects of desire. And in an age of infinite physical mobility and cultural homogeneity, this has become true even in more ostensibly unified societies. History is controversial: your view of what happened is not necessarily mine. A commission on the future of multi-ethnic Britain recently questioned the use of the term 'British' because of its racial connotations of 'white colonialism'.[18] The once-rulers and once-ruled need a new concept to define what they now share. So the past, its sting removed, becomes 'heritage' – the Disneyfied, Fordian concept of history as theme park. Meanwhile the present is experienced virtually, inside our heads. Shut away inside our ideal homes, watching other people decorate their living-rooms on the telly, enclosed in our dream cars, though physically separate we inhabit a kind of public space of the mind: the freeway rider's Trafalgar Square.

» » »

Los Angeles, the first place fully to experience motoring's pleasures and possibilities, was also the first to recognize its costs. During the first half of the century southern California, with its pure, dry air and hot climate, was a haven for the bronchitic and tubercular. But during the 1940s, on some hot, still summer days, a brownish-yellow haze started to appear in LA's blue skies, and people began to find that on those days their eyes smarted and the air irritated their lungs: a condition caused, as we now know, by photochemical smog. The authorities blamed oil-burning factories and the local oil-refining industry, and during a crisis in 1947 shut many of them down. But although industry certainly did contribute to the problem, a team at the California Institute of Technology discovered that it was largely due to a combination of automobile emissions and California's hot, sunny climate. The sunlight, acting on unburned hydrocarbons and nitrogen oxides, produced ozone, a respiratory irritant, its effects exacerbated by Los Angeles' geographical situation in a basin surrounded by hills, with low wind speeds and onshore breezes. This topography made it particularly liable to 'temperature inversion'. On still, clear nights the slopes of the hills radiate heat and become cooler, chilling the air around them. The cool, dense air then slips down to the valley floor, where it lies beneath an upper layer of warm, lighter air; and the pollution is trapped.

In the late 1950s Los Angeles failed to satisfy federal air quality standards on more than three hundred days a year. It became the smog capital of the world. Now it fails the tests only sixty-five days a year, and it is hoped that the figure will soon drop to between twenty and forty. This has been achieved thanks to more than seventy specific control regulations, targeting not just cars but less obvious pollutants such as paint fumes. Even so, Los Angeles remains, after Houston, the most polluted city in the United States. For although per capita emissions have been reduced by 75 per cent, the population has increased from 2 million in 1930 to between 12 and 14 million today, almost all driving cars. The eventual target for cars is zero emissions, achievable for example by electric vehicles (though this takes no account of emissions from the power stations needed to produce all the extra electricity). California set a target for 1998 of 2 per cent zero emission vehicles lighter than 3,750 pounds (1,700 kilos – about the weight of an average saloon car); by 2003 the target is 10 per cent. But even so 90 per cent will go on polluting.

Smog now affects cities worldwide – and in heavily urbanized countries it is not to be escaped even in the countryside. Just when the weather seems most inviting death lurks in the air. In September 2000, a study funded by the World Health Organization suggested that 6 per cent of all deaths in Switzerland, France and Austria are now caused by the micro-particles emitted by car exhausts;[19] in Britain, ten thousand deaths a year are caused by air pollution, the peaks of death rates (from asthma and other respiratory diseases) coinciding with peaks in pollution.[20]

Pollution controls are now standard in many countries, although few regimes approach Los Angeles' fierceness. More problematic is the other great auto disbenefit: congestion. Many towns and cities teeter so near gridlock that the slightest disruption leads to paralysis. For example, in Bedford, England, a town whose main industry is education, the roads are clogged every morning and evening with school buses and parents' cars. A local train service also carries a number of pupils. This service is not very profitable, and one day the rail company decided to axe it. As a result of the extra road traffic, the town ground to a halt. Not a vehicle could move, and no one got to school before mid-morning. After concerted protests from headteachers and municipal authorities, the service was reinstated; without it, the town quite simply ceased to function.

This was an extreme situation. But road journeys everywhere now take far longer than they did ten or twenty years ago. The auto producers not only recognize this fact, but cater to it. At the Detroit Motor Show in January 2000, Ford unveiled its 24-7 high-tech vehicle, a personal computer on wheels which will enable the gridlocked driver to improve the stationary hour by checking her e-mail and stock readings. Since congestion is unavoidably with us, goes the thinking, it makes more sense to enjoy its benefits (quiet, privacy) than risk apoplexy by fuming over it.

The most obvious solution to congestion is (so it would seem) to build more roads, or widen existing ones. But every transport planner knows this doesn't work. Build new roads and they very soon fill up, in an endless spiral that might continue until the entire countryside was covered with asphalt – a situation not far distant in some parts of the world. Road builders John Laing once suggested that a good way to save space and reduce traffic noise would be to build urban motorways *on top of* houses. 'The noise level in the rooms nearest the top, immediately below the car parking floor, could be well within the limits proposed by the Wilson Committee for bedrooms. So long as a 50 mph limit was imposed, the noise level in buildings facing the motorway would also be acceptable,' they advised.[21]

Perhaps not surprisingly, this scheme has never been tried. However, there are other, less alarming possibilities. For instance, one popularly touted panacea is to pack the cars in tighter. At the moment minimum stopping-distance requirements mean that a typical motorway lane can carry only about two thousand vehicles per hour. But if the responsibility for guiding the car were removed from the driver and vested in an electronic control system, then the amount of traffic could be tripled.

This is not a new idea: it was mooted by Norman Bel Geddes, whose Futurama exhibit carried a working model of an 'automated highway'. But although GM developed the idea after the war, the necessary technology was not yet available. Now, however, it is a real possibility, using either a dedicated lane system or a mixed traffic system. Either way, the driver would specify the desired destination using an in-car computer, perhaps at the start of a journey, perhaps just before joining the automated highway. In one scheme the cars are steered by magnetic rods set in vertical holes down the centre of the lanes; another system has each car following the signal given out by the car ahead. Merging and demerging, however, are problematic. Computers monitoring the roadway might take on a supervisory role, assigning speeds and directing the passage of vehicles between the automated highway and local roadways – techniques successfully tested in California and Japan. But it is hard to see how the transition from the automatic mode to resumed self-drive can be achieved without danger. In Europe, meanwhile, the European Commission is funding a programme to modify heavy trucks, in which an 'electronic towbar' will allow one or more trailers to follow a manually driven truck, thus forming a platoon of heavy vehicles with a single human driver. In June 1999 DaimlerChrysler gave a public demonstration of this technology at the southern end of the Lake Constance Freeway in Switzerland. 'In the year 2015,' says DaimlerChrysler's head of machine understanding, 'road users will scarcely be able to believe how low-tech

70. Automated highway, 1998.

systems like traffic lights were once the primary means of controlling traffic.' However, traffic regulations have not yet caught up with the new technology, and would have to be be updated before it could be used.

But automated highways are far from being an ideal solution. On the contrary, they are an expensive and high-tech admission that the situation is out of control. They pack the cars in tighter, but do not reduce their numbers. And this is the only real way to reduce pollution and congestion. People must be prised out of their cars.

The first essential is obvious: excellent public transport. Unfortunately, most cities' public transport systems were laid down in the pre-car era, and are inadequate, outworn, or both. However, as the car's deleterious effect on city life becomes more apparent, public transport renewal is increasingly an urban priority. In Athens, a city whose climate and geographic location are comparable to LA's, car ownership rose over thirty years from thirty-six thousand to nearly 2 million. But now Athenians are rethinking their automotive enthusiasm. The city's buildings and monuments are being eaten away by pollution; from the Acropolis the city may still be made out, but only through a thick blanket of smog, or *nefos*. Asthmatics are advised not to visit Athens, where this smog killed an estimated six to ten people every summer day during the 1980s.[22] When at the end of January 2000 two new metro lines were opened, such was Athenians' joy that they marked the occasion by singing and dancing outside their new, white-marble stations. Katerina Evangelopoulou, an office clerk, spoke for many when she said, 'This is the sort of thing that can change a person's life.'[23] Or indeed save it.

Athens is an old city with a compact hub; if it is willing to make the investment, public transport, whether by metro, bus or park-and-ride, remains a realistic option. But in sprawling automobile cities like Los Angeles, this is not the case. Although

LA, unlike Detroit, does have trains and buses, using them is not easy. Dana Reed, a member of the California Transport Commission, took a month's vow of carlessness in July 1999: his diary was a record of frustration. On day three, attempting to take the Metro Rail subway to Hollywood, he ended up in the Wilshire district, miles from his destination: there are, it turns out, two Metro red lines, and like other novice riders he had failed to distinguish between them. On day five it took him five hours to make the journey from his house in Newport Beach to the Los Angeles apartment where he spends weeknights; on day fourteen, unclear directions at Union Station meant that he nearly missed the Metrolink train connecting with his plane at the airport . . . His diary entry for day twenty-eight began: 'Three days and counting. If I were ever to do this again I would choose to do it in February. There are only 28 days in February . . .'[24]

In the view of planning theorist Melvin Webber, the only viable option for public transport in a city like Los Angeles is 'a transit system which is like automobiles – if we could make an automobile into a transit vehicle for those that are carless we could meet the real costs of it. And the way to do that I think is by using all of this new high tech communications technology, to communicate between people who want rides and people who have got rides.'[25]

Ironically, such a system (though not radio-controlled) was once popular throughout America, and indeed originated in Los Angeles. On 1 July 1914, L. P. Draper picked up a passenger at a trolley stop in his Ford Model T and dropped him off a few blocks further on, charging him a nickel (5¢). The idea caught on and was labelled 'the jitney', after the slang term for a nickel. By the summer of 1915 62,000 jitneys were operating: 1,000 in San Francisco, 350 in Milwaukee, 500 in Dallas. Seattle had 500 jitneys carrying 49,000 passengers daily; Los Angeles, 1,500, carrying 150,000.[26]

The jitneys [writes Clay McShane] found an economic niche between cars, whether taxis or privately owned vehicles, and trolleys. A driver, usually a Model T owner, plied main streets leading to the central business district, picking up three or four passengers to take downtown for five or ten cents. Some jitneys operated with regular customers, offering door-to-door service . . . Some . . . were commuters themselves, picking up a few riders on the way to work in the morning and a few others on the way home at night . . . Jitneys also delivered the kind of crosstown service to shopping or recreational sites that trolley companies usually avoided.[27]

Riders liked jitneys for many reasons. They carried more than one passenger, so were cheaper than taxis; they were more flexible than trolleys, and much quicker. And they avoided the social problems the trolleys imposed. If you were black jitneys freed you from colour-bar problems; women need not fear the attentions of 'bustle-pinchers'. And suburban riders could preserve 'all the values associated with the suburban dream'[28] – chief among them the reassuring certainty that you would never, as in a city or a crowded trolley, be forced into intimacy with people you would rather avoid.

'Encouraging jitney use might have improved the efficiency of urban travel and reduced jams, by limiting the number of one-car, one-passenger trips,' thinks Clay McShane. But it never happened. Transit firms and taxi drivers, alarmed at this new competition, lobbied against the jitneys, insisting that they carry the same insurance and licences as full-time cabs. This destroyed their cost-effectiveness and within three years, it was all over: jitneys had been lobbied or sued out of existence in every big city in America.[29]

There is a modern form of jitney-riding: car-pooling. In Los

Angeles and Chicago, 17 per cent of travellers use car pools: the American average is 19 per cent. Special lanes are reserved for vehicles carrying two persons or more; in San Francisco pedestrians wait at the entrance to the Bay Bridge, offering entry to the car-pool lane in return for a ride. Solitary drivers trapped in the freeway's endless jams look on enviously as the lucky multi-occupant vehicles speed past.

Yet 80 per cent prefer to ride alone, despite the delays. Why? Because *they have the option*, and choose to exercise it in favour of privacy. The jitney riders did not own cars themselves, so for them this was a taste of automotive freedom at reduced prices; for those who sold space in their cars, the extra money was important. And in places where there still remains a large pool of such people, for instance Manila, Caracas, Tel Aviv, Teheran, jitney equivalents still ply under a variety of names (*sheruts*, *colectivos*). But in Europe and America almost everyone possesses their own car and cherishes its unsociable freedoms, while the monetary savings of car-pooling are insignificant – rarely enough to compensate for the constraint such arrangements may entail. For example, a number of people living on my street work in the same place, but all – including a husband and wife – drive there individually. Why? Because each has different working arrangements, and car pools, like all forms of shared transport, mean compromise: you are trapped in other people's schedules, perhaps leaving home before you would wish to, or staying on at work when you might otherwise have left. Of course this was always true when people relied on public transport; but now we have got used to the absolute flexibility, and absolute self-indulgence, that comes with owning a car. That is worth more than a few pounds in shared petrol costs, even with prices at Britain's record highs – 83p a litre for unleaded at the time of writing: that is $1.25, about two and a half times the current US price. Dana Reed reckoned that his Jeep Cherokee cost $290 a month to fuel and park in Los Angeles; in London that figure would be nearer $730. But even that is not enough to outweigh the various motivations of time and convenience that send seven people from the same street in to work at the same place every day in seven different cars.

In some places (though not Britain) the monetary savings made using public transport are substantial – more so than those of car-pooling. In Los Angeles, for example, Dana Reed's experimental month's fares and passes for buses and trains cost $55, against $290 in parking and gasoline.[30] But this takes no account of time. When you price in time – as only peasants and housewives do not – public transport soon seems less of a bargain. For any busy working person, $235 is a negligible amount when set against the time spent getting to stations or bus stops, waiting for buses and trains and (worst of all) transferring between them. A survey of 1,400 British motorists interviewed by the RAC in the autumn of 2000 (*before* the train crash that left Britain's railways in disarray throughout the winter of 2000–1) found the proportion of drivers saying they would make less use of their cars if public transport were to improve had fallen to an eight-year low of 36 per cent. One in five who had been willing to consider changing to public transport in 1997 rejected the idea three years later.[31]

The economists' reply would be that the price difference is evidently not enough – though how much would be enough is hard to say: the value of a car, like that of a good woman, is seemingly above rubies. In 1996 Britons paid, on average, £52 a week to keep a car on the road; by 2000 that had risen to £72 a week.[32] Even so, four out of five motorists interviewed by the RAC did not intend to buy a smaller car, though smaller cars attract less excise duty and use less fuel. Nearly half the RAC's respondents expected to have to pay £10 to drive into a city centre by 2010, and one in five expected it to cost £10 a day to park at the office. But they still expected to stay with their cars.

Nevertheless, there must come a cut-off point. If queues form, points out Andrew Oswald, Professor of Economics at Warwick University, elementary economics dictates that the product that attracts them (in this case, the road) must be too cheap. 'If only Britain would manage roads in the way it manages supermarkets!' he pleads.

Imagine what would happen if supermarkets gave away their products for free or nearly free. There would be queues outside every store. People would have to get up early and allocate periods in their diaries just to buy food.

It would be no use building wider front doors to these supermarkets (the let's build more roads approach), or having special paths into supermarkets that only certain people could use (the bus lane approach). As soon as the queue starts to shorten, other consumers would notice and come to the new wide-entrance supermarkets.

The supermarkets would be better advised to put prices on their goods. That is what they do – and it works. Britain's roads could be like this. They could flow without queues . . .[33]

There are various possibilities for road-pricing. If the aim was to cut out rush-hour jams, it would cost more to use a particular route at a particular time. If (as in the case of London and many other cities) the aim was to discourage drivers from entering the city centre at all, blanket tolls might be imposed, perhaps increasing the nearer you got to the centre. This is a pick-and-mix solution, easily tailored to suit the particular situation.

The objection to road-pricing is that it would raise business costs. But, Oswald points out, a road toll of, say, £5 would be negligible for a truck carrying a load worth £100,000 – a cost easily offset by the time gains resulting from free-flowing traffic.

On the other hand, it might well deter a casual shopper, or someone contemplating a ride to school because it's raining.

This sounds irresistibly simple, but the politics of road-pricing are delicate. When the interests of our motoring selves conflict with our other personae, wheels tend to win the day. For example, we refer to road deaths as 'accidents' and treat the perpetrators much more leniently than in cases of manslaughter – by definition equally accidental. The British Road Traffic Act of 1956, which established the offence of dangerous driving, was a direct response to the high acquittal rate for drivers charged with manslaughter. Jurors might find it hard to imagine killing in cold or even hot blood. But most of them are drivers. There but for the grace of God go they; if the penalty is too high they refuse to convict.[34]

Unsurprisingly, then, the reaction was ambivalent when, in November 1999, the British Secretary of State for the Environment proposed a raft of anti-congestion measures, including road-pricing, in the hope of shifting drivers on to public transport. The measures were welcomed by that section of the population that breathes urban air and uses cities. But the motoring lobby at once rounded upon the minister, accusing him of persecuting motorists – to such effect that he very soon announced a new road-building programme. And who were these motorists? Why, those very self-same air breathers and city dwellers: nearly 90 per cent of Britons live in areas classified as urban.

In the end the government declared that it supported road-pricing on principle, but would leave its implementation to the discretion of individual local councils. Unfortunately, for such a policy to work it must be introduced nationally, not city by city. Otherwise, if you must pay to drive into town A, you will simply drive to town B instead and do your shopping there. The minister doubtless knows this as well as anyone. But government's first concern is to remain in power; and this is not achieved by the imposition of unpopular policies. So national road-pricing is not introduced.

Another persistently unrealized panacea has been the electronic office. As computers began to play an ever larger part in commercial life, it quickly became clear that virtual meetings might substitute for the real thing. Constantly connected via phone, fax, video and computer, we would, it was confidently assumed, make fewer real-life journeys. The daily trip to the office in particular would become a thing of the past. In the RAC survey referred to earlier, seven out of ten motorists believed that within ten years most people now working in offices would be doing their work on computers at home, leaving rush-hour roads uncongested. And logically this makes sense. If you work in a shop or a factory your actual presence can't be done without, but for most office jobs this is no longer the case. Offices came into existence because information, stored in piles of paper, was physically moved around them. But that information is now held in computers; and virtual proximity obviates the need for physical proximity. Strictly speaking, offices should be on the decline.

Yet, contrary to all predictions, the office continues to flourish. Neither the horrors of commuting nor the boredom of routine deter people from slogging into the city every morning rather than working at their terminals in the comfort of their own homes. In part this reflects the creative tension of the office milieu. Ideas rarely spring unbidden; they are generated by contact with other ideas, sometimes in formal meetings, often unexpectedly over a cup of coffee. But it is also a social decision. Now that homes, cars and television so efficiently isolate us one from another, the office remains the last great arena of social life. By comparison the isolation of what the jargon horrendously terms 'telecottaging', in which you do your office work at home, connected to other telecottagers via your networked computer terminal, can be hard to take. At home, as any mother of young children can testify, it is easy, even when your activity is fascinating and rewarding, to feel marooned and cut off from the world. And few people's work is fascinating and rewarding enough to occupy them, unbroken, day after day. So despite all the forecasts, teleworking has not taken off. A study by the University of California at Davis puts the 'telecommunity' at perhaps 2 per cent of the American workforce.[35] A prize-winning 'televillage' near Crickhowell in Wales, purpose-built against the inevitability of new working habits, recently went into receivership when thirteen of its thirty-nine houses remained persistently unsold. Its designer remains certain that this is the wave of the future; demonstrably, however, the present has not yet caught up with it.

Meanwhile, in the city centres that once housed factories and workshops, great glass boxes now contain advertising agencies, television companies, management consultants and banks, each desk a monument to atavism in the shape of our unquenchable preference for meeting each other in the flesh; a preference for which we are prepared to spend hours every day sitting in traffic jams surrounded by others bound on the same quest. So far, indeed, is the virtual world from diminishing our desire for face-to-face contact that those wishing to launch e-commerce ventures and those prepared to finance them meet not on the web but at specially arranged cocktail parties. When, in November 2000, the British rail system failed, the proprietress of a Manchester e-venture appeared on television bewailing the cost to her enterprise, despite teleconferencing, of being unable to reach London to conduct business face to face. We wish – we need – to meet other people; and for most of us, work is how we do it.

Indeed (and quite counter-intuitively), telecommunications, far from decreasing the number of journeys we make, seem to have quite the opposite effect. 'It's often speculated,' says Melvin Webber

71. Traffic jam.

that as communication increases it will substitute for transportation [but] the work that we've done . . . suggests that
it doesn't work that way, that the more communication
the more contact, the more associations the more business
deals, the more friendships formed, the more reason to
take trips. And so communication is generating transportation, and then when you take a trip and talk to somebody,
then that generates more communication.[36]

In Webber's view, our seemingly infinite willingness to tolerate the car's uncomfortable effects means that congestion and
pollution are perhaps not such serious problems as some like
to suggest. Up to a point – a point evidently not yet reached
anywhere in the world – we are prepared to accept these problems as a price worth paying for our cars. In a 2000 survey by
the Automobile Association, 28 per cent of those surveyed oxy-
moronically described their car as 'environmentally friendly';
only 14 per cent thought the word 'polluting' applied to their
vehicle.[37]

When does a problem become 'serious'? Presumably, when
it passes the limits of bearability. But how do we define those
limits? For Webber they define themselves: when they are
breached, we change our behaviour. 'When persons find themselves in a traffic stream and find the cost of congestion too
high they accommodate to it by moving – they move their
house, or if it's an employer he moves his office or his factory
. . . Presently in [the US] there's a notion that congestion is
getting worse and worse and worse and I don't believe that,
I don't believe it's getting worse and worse. It's constantly
adapting to some level which is acceptable. We may not like
it but we'll tolerate it.'[38]

» » »

Melvin Webber's sanguine assumptions about congestion and pollution, like his views on the desirability or otherwise of suburbanization, rest upon the infallibility of the psychological marketplace. The question is not whether a phenomenon is good or bad, but whether people like it enough to buy it. If the answer is yes, they'll persist with it, live in suburbs and commute to work by car. If the answer is no, then (and not before) they'll change their habits – live near their work, or at the very least near a train station. It's up to them to choose. Choice: the twentieth century's watchword, the car's great gift, the luxury we possess and that our grandparents were denied.

But the history of the car belies Webber's genial certainties. Rather it is a story of hubris and nemesis, each triumph bringing in its wake some rude, unforeseen and mythically apposite come-uppance. The motorist's open road denies the street to all those not on wheels. The countryside, suddenly available to all, vanishes under asphalt; once-remote beauty spots, victims of too much love, are ruined by car parks and high-rise hotels. Freed from horse shit, cities choke on auto-mobile pollution. The ever-expanding acres of desirable automobile suburbs confine their inhabitants in the ideal homes for which they yearned, and imprison anyone unable to drive. Mobility for all founders in gridlock.

And now we are faced with the end of the story – or rather with alternative endings. Will the internal combustion engine, irresistible bringer of freedom and happiness, polluter of the air we breathe, destroyer of our cities and our countryside, put paid to our very existence through climate change? Or will the prospect of the imminent end of oil, finally percolating into consciousness, speed up invention in time to save us all – which is to say, *before* all that oil is burned?

Such questions are rarely, if ever, broached in the motoring columns, an absence made flesh at the 1999 Motor Show, where alternative technologies were notable for their total invisibility, and only one stand – Volvo, produced by socially conscious Swedes – so much as mentioned global warming. But as the twentieth century drew to a close, perceptions began to change. When the first British Motor Show of the new millennium opened in October 2000, one of the event's organizers declared that new technologies were at its centre. He opined that in twenty-five years' time there would be no more internal combustion engines, and drew a comparison with the situation in New York at the turn of the century. Then, the perceived health hazards of horse shit hastened the introduction and acceptance of the new, clean horseless carriage. Now, he observed, we faced a similar situation. The real crunch would come when people began to see very significant changes in climate and made the connection with the internal combustion engine.

As it happens, the year 2000 saw exactly such significant changes. One of the climatologists' forecasts was that higher temperatures would bring increased rainfall and more extreme weather of all sorts. And, bang on cue, even temperate Europe began to experience meteorological catastrophes. The millennium celebrations were marked by hurricanes across France; autumn saw record rainfall cause unprecedented floods throughout Britain; in the Italian Alps mudslides engulfed entire villages; two tornados hit England's sedate south coast. Was this enough crunch? If the year's other events were anything to judge by, the answer appeared to be no.

During the last weekend of August, the roads north to Calais are crowded with British holidaymakers driving home at the end of the summer holidays. But in August 2000 they found themselves stuck on the wrong side of the Channel. In late 1998, at the nadir of the Asian recession, the price of oil was less than $10 a barrel; by January 2000 it had risen to $30 as OPEC cut production. Fuel prices at the pump rose steeply; and French fishermen, unable either to absorb these costs or to charge more for their already expensive catches, decided to mount a blockade of the Channel ports on the busiest weekend of the year. Conditions rapidly became intolerable, and after a few days the fishermen were given a deal. But by then France's truckers had joined in, and almost all French oil refineries and fuel depots were blockaded. Within six days France was at a standstill. Four-fifths of petrol stations stood empty, regional airports were closed, and school buses and postal deliveries suspended. Finally, on 9 September, the government agreed to lower fuel tax, and the blockades were lifted, albeit grudgingly. The public punished the French government, whether for perceived weakness, for not giving enough or for simply presiding over the fiasco, by turning against the premier, M. Jospin, whose popularity rating at once fell twenty points.

Protests of this kind are not unusual in France, and the reaction on the British side of the Channel tends to veer between superiority (none of this blackmail for us!) and fury as truck drivers and tourists find themselves caught in endless tailbacks. On this occasion, however, the last finger had hardly wagged before Britain, too, found itself paralysed. British petrol prices are the highest in Europe, and, as in France, the high price of fuel threatens to tip many marginally profitable businesses over the edge. So British farmers and hauliers, impressed by the effectiveness of their French colleagues' tactics, decided to try the game for themselves.

On 8 September lorries and tractors began blockading refineries in Wales and north-west England; by the 9th the first forecourts were emptied of fuel. Motorists panicked and rushed to fill their tanks; a house near Manchester began to leak petrol and was revealed to be stacked with overflowing containers. Petrol stations throughout the country started to run short. Some introduced *ad hoc* rationing, some hiked their prices – in one case as high as £2 a litre. But motorists, undeterred, bought on. At the height of the panic, one person was reputed to have bid £102 for two gallons of petrol in an internet auction. So one paradoxical effect of the protests was to show that, however unwillingly, people will pay almost any-thing to remain mobile. Town centres, meanwhile, found a long-lost tranquillity. Walking down the Brompton Road towards Knights-bridge, normally a seething hell of noise, fumes and crowded, narrow pavements, I was struck by the delights of a long-lost London built for human pleasure. Buses, a mode of transport generally practical only when time is of no account, suddenly became an excellent way of getting about the city. It was an object lesson in the desirability of excluding private cars from city centres.

The protests soon began to affect more than just petrol supplies for private cars. Flexibility of supply, combined with the high price of storage, in terms of both space and commodi-ties, means that very little reserve stock is now held by traders in either fuel or food. Instead it must be trucked in, if not daily then every two or three days. Within a couple of days filling-stations ran dry, and emergency services were threatened with paralysis. Panic buying cleared supermarket shelves, local authorities began suspending non-urgent public services, hotels reported cancelled bookings. After five days postal services, banks and food supplies joined the catalogue of disruption. Schools closed in south Wales and west Yorkshire, and bus and train operators announced they would run out of fuel next day. Nevertheless, even despite this massive inconvenience, the end was judged worth the means. So close to our hearts is cheap automobility that public sympathy remained, as poll after poll confirmed, firmly on the protesters' side. Only when faced with the prospect of deaths as hospitals ran out of fuel and staff, did the blockades begin to break. By the 15th they were over – though the hauliers threatened to protest again if their concerns were not addressed within sixty days.

These protests were not confined to Britain and France.

Belgian truckers blocked main roads in Brussels and a refinery at Charleroi; in Holland there were blockades in Rotterdam and Breda. The action spread to Poland, Germany, Israel, Ireland, Italy, Norway, Sweden and Spain. And generally speaking, such is our dependence on wheels that the protesters got what they were looking for. In France the government bought its way to peace; in the Netherlands the government agreed a £200 million package of subsidies to the transport sector; in Belgium a £40 million aid package was agreed; in Spain there were rumours of a £150 million aid package to offset fuel prices; and in Israel the government agreed to adjust the price of diesel fuel each month, based on an international average.

In Britain, unusually, the protest ended without the government capitulating, though tax on low-sulphur fuel was reduced two months later. Nevertheless, like M. Jospin (who did give ground), Mr Blair saw his popularity plummet. In July, opinion polls had placed New Labour twenty points ahead of its Conservative rivals. But polls taken after the fuel protests showed the two parties running level – at one point, the Conservatives even notched up an eight-point lead. This did not last, but it showed the importance people attach to fuel prices: this was the first time since 1992 that the Conservative Party had overtaken Labour in the polls.

The government faced criticism from two opposing directions: populist and environmentalist. The populist camp took the protesters' side and declared the price of petrol and diesel too high. Most of what motorists pay for petrol in Britain goes to the government: in 2000 taxes stood at 71p for every pound spent on petrol. The government, declared this lobby, should abandon its intransigent stand and reduce taxes forthwith. Environmentalists, meanwhile, thought the high prices correct, but felt the government had failed to justify them vociferously enough. Pollution and congestion, went this argument, are ruining all our lives. The only way to alleviate them is to drive less; and without high fuel prices, this will never be achieved. There was some talk of global warming, but this was vague. Both groups, however, presented high fuel prices as a matter of choice, arbitrarily imposed by high-taxing governments and greedy oil producers.

It was also widely alleged that the oil companies, not displeased by this opportunity to show the politicians who, *in extremis*, calls the tune, were in no hurry to get supplies moving again. Who, indeed, could imagine a more dramatic demonstration of the extent to which our lives are dependent upon the internal combustion engine? But although motorists are the oil industry's *raison d'être*, pump prices represent a rather small proportion of its profits, while high taxes, by raising prices, reduce sales (as indeed they are intended to). As, day by day, the noose tightened, the oil companies, determined that any price reductions should come from the government's exchequer, not theirs, denied all responsibility for their tanker drivers' immobility. Meanwhile, in the third quarter of 2000, the profitability of British oil companies reached a fifteen-year high, the rise in oil and gas prices boosting returns in the North Sea sector to a phenomenal 36.4 per cent.[39]

So the arguments raged to and fro. Meanwhile, my unexpectedly delightful experience in Knightsbridge during that strange interlude was echoed in television reports and letters to newspapers up and down the country, all proclaiming the newfound delights of uncongested streets. If policies such as road-pricing meant such pleasures might be achieved on a permanent basis, surely (I thought) people might be more willing to put up with them – might even applaud them? Perhaps one unforeseen effect of the fuel protests would be to wean us, to some extent, from our cars.

But most, it seemed, did not share my perceptions. As soon as the oil began to flow, cars smothered the city once more, to sighs of relief. Automobility, like life, liberty and the pursuit of happiness, is, it seems, for twenty-first-century westerners a fundamental and inalienable right.

» » »

Earlier that year America had experienced its own similar fuel protests. In February 2000, three hundred angry truck drivers brought the centre of Washington to a standstill in reaction to a 55 per cent hike in the price of fuel. America's cheap energy prices reflect the fact that, unlike Europe, Americans pay little tax on fuel; any rise in crude-oil prices is therefore soon noticeable at the pumps. And during 1999, as we have seen, the price of crude oil tripled, rising from $10 to $30.

The US immediately opened talks in an attempt to persuade OPEC to open the taps; but to no avail. Although in July Saudi Arabia, the largest producer, announced that it wanted to bring the price down to $25 a barrel, and that crude-oil supplies would be increased by an additional five hundred thousand barrels a day if the price remained high, it continued to rise, hitting $33 by September. So when the unrest hit Europe, President Clinton took the opportunity to renew his plea to OPEC: they should increase production and lower prices in short order.

From the standpoint of the oil-consuming economies, Clinton's plea made obvious sense. Economic historians agree that the long burst of economic growth between 1945 and 1973 was due to the low level of oil prices, and that the oil-price collapse following the 1991 Gulf War underpinned the economic boom of the 90s. The IMF declared 2000 the best year in the global economy for a decade. But in a world nervously awaiting the next crash, there were worries that the rise in prices might be starting to undermine this happy picture. Many European governments agreed, as we have seen, to reduce prices in response to protests. The British government's insistence on maintaining high prices was greeted with fury. The US even went so far as to release oil from its strategic petroleum reserve in order to increase supplies and lower prices.

This was not the first time the world had had to cope with a sudden rise in oil prices. In 1973–4 oil prices tripled in response to an Arab embargo following the Yom Kippur War; in 1979, after the fall of the Shah of Iran, they doubled again. But the response at that time was in marked contrast to that of 2000. Where in 2000 Clinton wanted to increase supplies at any cost in order to maintain consumption, the reaction in the 70s was just the opposite: to lower consumption, reduce oil dependence and beef up conservation. What had changed in the ensuing thirty years, that today's response should be so dramatically different?

The austere mood of the 70s was set in 1972 by the publication of a report entitled *Limits to Growth*, the work of a group of businessmen and academics calling themselves the Club of Rome. This report, which sold 12 million copies in thirty-seven languages, prophesied that, if consumption patterns and population growth continued at the current high rates, the earth would strike its limits within a century. And although dismissed by both communists and capitalists, the former citing technology's infinite powers, the latter the infallibility of market mechanisms, it nevertheless affected public attitudes when the oil crisis hit. America abandoned its love affair with large cars and turned to compacts – there was even talk (though not much) of resuscitating the steam car. In Britain subsidies were introduced for those wishing to insulate their homes to reduce energy consumption. Throughout the world there was a surge of interest in self-sufficiency and low-energy housing. Autarky was the wave of the future.

Writing about the American auto industry in 1973, Emma Rothschild expressed the then zeitgeist. Even when it came to an object as beloved as the car, logic would prevail, and 'auto consumers, already discontented, will reject continued automotive growth before cities reach an apocalypse of immobility'.[40]

In the present situation of auto difficulty, social support for increased auto use is already fractured and disintegrated . . . The discontent of some consumers, particularly in large cities, where the disadvantages of auto-based planning are first apparent, seems in part a reaction against past extremes of auto enthusiasm . . . In the next ten or twenty years, the real costs of the present and historical structures of automotive support will become ever more evident – and ever more disruptive of auto expansion.

The waste left by auto development will seem less and less tolerable . . . Auto transportation is already seen as a major social expense by all government agencies concerned with preserving national resources, the natural environment, national energy supplies. The arguments of these agencies – the Office of Emergency Preparedness, for example, showing that given the need to conserve national fuel supplies, currently expected growth in automobile use would be 'unacceptable' – are persuasive . . .

American overinvestment in automobiles and in highway transportation involved perhaps the largest commitment of resources in the history of any country. Yet a reduction of the automotive system is possible – because the reasons for auto growth are historical, and contingent, and no longer compelling, and because, at least in large American cities, the auto system no longer works . . . Like [railroads] auto investments can be transformed, grassed over, used again . . .[41]

Today it is hard to believe anyone can seriously have envisaged such a scenario. For the mood has changed utterly. The central message of *Limits to Growth* was the necessity of increased state intervention to avoid worldwide recession – in transport terms, Rothschild's swing away from individual commuting in favour of public transport. But the 1980s saw events take an exactly opposite turn. Huge new oilfields in Alaska and the North Sea came on stream at the end of the 70s, and the resulting return of economic confidence led, in both Europe and the US, to an era of free-market triumphalism and detestation of state intervention in whatever form. In the UK these were the days of train-hating Mrs Thatcher's 'great car economy' – an obvious preference for a person convinced that 'there is no such thing as society'. As a result the real cost of private motoring in the UK did not change for twenty-five years, while during the same period average rail fares rose 50 per cent, and bus fares 80 per cent. Meanwhile, far from the Club of Rome's predicted 1990s depression, the world economy, fuelled by oil at $15 a barrel, roared ahead.

Thirty years (and billions of barrels) later, the prospect of oil famine, real enough in 1973 to set people not just thinking but acting, is never mentioned; it has become just another of the unfounded scares that have punctuated the history of motoring. In 1897, when the car was hardly even launched, a M. Marcel Desprez contacted the Automobile Club of France objecting to the petrol-driven engine on the grounds that 'if this fuel comes into use for vehicle propulsion, we shall sooner or later be brought face to face with an oil famine, because only 8,000,000 tons of oil are annually taken from the earth, while 400,000,000 tons of coal are annually mined'.[42] In 1921 it was feared that supplies of gasoline might run out within the next few years. Five billion barrels of oil had already been extracted from the American fields, and geologists estimated that only 6.5 billion barrels remained. 'You Are Throwing Half of Your Gasoline Away – Improper Carburetion Wastes Millions Every Year!' scolded Touring Topics, the magazine of the Automobile Club of Southern California.[43] But new reserves were discovered, both in America and elsewhere, banishing uncertainty just as the newly discovered fields in Alaska and the North Sea banished the post-1973 spectre of dependence on the unreliable Middle East.

The assumption seems to be that this will go on indefinitely. As more oil is needed, so more will be found. Despite current energy prices, therefore, as Edward Luttwak points out, 'the "new economy" companies . . . keep their offices brightly lit all night long. In part this serves to advertise their "24/7/365" culture of non-stop work to achieve the next software breakthrough, but in part it reflects an entire mentality in which profligacy has replaced austerity.'[44]

In automobile terms, the equivalent of twenty-four-hour lighting is size and speed. Although auto bodies have become substantially lighter as plastics replace steel, fuel consumption has not dropped, because horsepower levels of middle-range family cars are now twice as high as in the 1970s. The number of seconds it takes your car to accelerate from 0–60 mph, irrelevant in almost any driving situation, still figures on many ads and in all specifications. Industry experts canvassed by the Automobile Association in their survey of prospects for the first twenty years of the new millennium pointed out that 'nobody has dared move their brand to less acceleration and yet by doing so, you get enormous fuel economy benefits. They're still selling "go faster, go faster".'[45] In a recent article celebrating the Nissan Skyline GT-R34, a speedster at the top end of the market, the journalist overcame the machine's fundamental logical flaw – the fact that speed limits render most of its power irrelevant – by '[taking] it for a proper run. Down the motorway to Brighton, middle of the night, avoiding the speed traps.'[46]

Yet the trend is for ever larger and more powerful cars. In 1998 Volkswagen, having just acquired Rolls-Royce, announced that it was thinking of reviving the eighteen-cylinder Horch limousine favoured by millionaires, film stars and Adolf

Hitler in pre-war Germany. Six weeks later Daimler-Benz announced its new super-car, the Maybach, with an overall length of 5.77 metres, an engine capacity of almost six litres, and two matching sets of personalized golf clubs in the boot. GM, meanwhile, not to be outdone, weighed in with the $100,000 Hummer. This is a civilian adaptation of its Humvee military vehicle, designed to keep GM's Indiana factories in production now that the Cold War has ended. In the city the Hummer will do thirteen mpg, fifteen on the highway. Classified as a medium-duty truck, it is (like all SUVs) exempt from federal fuel-economy rules. It is taller, much wider and a full ton heavier than even GM's huge Suburban 4×4, has sixteen inches of ground clearance, and is designed to climb vertical walls up to twenty-two inches tall. This will be especially useful in New York City, where, according to Michael DiGiovanni, GM's general manager of Hummer operations, many potential buyers live. It is intended for 'successful achievers', people who per-ceive themselves as daring risk takers. 'They're daring in the sense that they may take a big stock-market position, like buying 20,000 shares of an e-commerce stock,' said Mr DiGiovanni. Mike Tyson, a differently successful achiever, bought six; a Houston manufacturer of 'hillbilly' novelty teeth bought two and plans to buy another for his nine-year-old daughter when she turns sixteen. 'I think it's a great first car for a kid,' he said.[47] And although Hummer owners are still the exception rather than the rule, more than 60 per cent of new car buyers in the US now prefer heavy SUVs to sedans;[48] sales of these vehicles in Britain doubled between 1995 and 1999. At the time of writing SUVs provided a quarter of Ford's profits.[49]

Meanwhile, as the fuel protests so dramatically showed, our pattern of living ties us ever more inextricably to our cars. Los Angeles, built around the automobile, is, as we have seen, unthinkable without it; and throughout the world cities are becoming more like Los Angeles. A recent comparison of the world's mega-cities showed that in Bangkok, Manila, Tokyo, São Paulo – even in the crowded Netherlands – suburbanization is taking place at American – that is to say low – densities.[50] In the twenty-first century, this is how people prefer to live.

Even where they do not yet live like this, they are fast learning to do so. Ten years ago, Beijing was a city of bicycles; now it is choked with cars, its pollution a byword. On China's official environmental website, a headline calls for a 'New Goal for Automobile Pollution Control'. A delegation of mayors from the larger Chinese cities recently visited the UK to consider ways of combating automobile pollution. Various measures were discussed – small engines, more efficient emissions controls, cleaner fuels. But the suggestion that China might return to the bicycle – as presumably it still could – was coldly received. On the contrary: we don't, they protested, have nearly *enough* cars. And this echoes another headline on the official website, which says 'China Must Encourage the Purchase of Automobiles'.[51] For China is looking to the future, and bicycles are the past. Bicycle production peaked in the early 1990s at one bike for every four Chinese, but fell 24 per cent year-on-year in the first half of 1996; a survey of cyclists in Shanghai (where one in two owned bikes) showed that nearly two-thirds would prefer a motorcycle despite the much higher cost.[52] Shanghai's ever-spreading new suburbs are being built at automobile densities.

China now stands where America did in the Model T era, Europe in the 50s, Japan in the 60s. With a vast first-time-buyer market virtually untapped, the car is poised to transform the economy. A network of almost-empty motorways waits only to be filled. The population of China is 1.2 billion, nearly a billion more than that of America; but where America, in 2000, boasted more than 70 million motor vehicles, there were only 15 million in China, one for every 135 people. And of those nearly two-thirds were buses or trucks, while most of the 5.3 million 'private' cars belonged to government bodies or firms.

Meanwhile one in five urban families could and would afford a car if one were available for 100,000 yuan – about £8,400.[53]

That such a car will soon be available can hardly be doubted; and in that case the Chinese will buy it. Why not? Why should the Chinese, the Africans and the rest of the developing world deny themselves the intoxicating pleasures of automobility simply because they came late to the game? We are all addicts now. Our motoring selves, it seems, really do take priority over all the rest; the British government's reluctance to portray itself as anti-car is nothing but the most basic political realism.

And this skewing of priorities perhaps explains the dog that so bizarrely and persistently fails to bark in the night: the absolute refusal of governments anywhere in the world to look beyond pollution and congestion to the deeper and more intractable causes of oil's current high price, and the reasons why that price is unlikely to drop.

Chapter Nine

Rolling Over

In 1956 M. King Hubbert, a research scientist with Shell, presented the Production Division, Southern District, of the American Petroleum Institute with some news they didn't want to hear. In his speech, he predicted that crude-oil production in the lower forty-eight states would rise for thirteen more years, then peak in 1969, give or take a year.

His audience was disbelieving. They preferred to put their faith in geologists like the eminent Stanford professor who, seven years earlier, had assured the United Nations that 'any failure of oil supply to meet world demand over the next several hundred years will certainly not be due to a lack of undiscovered reserves but rather a failure of the discovery effort for one reason or another'.[1] Hubbert had argued against him, but in more general terms, and the controversy had died down. Now reignited, it raged for almost twenty years. Then, in 1972, on cue, US crude oil production began to fall. Hubbert had been proved right.

M. King Hubbert was born in 1903 on a farm in San Saba County, Texas, 'probably the only part of Texas where there isn't any oil'.[2] He worked his way painfully to the University of Chicago, where his dean pointed out, after his first year, that he had picked no major subject, and that the university rules required him to do so. Hubbert, who wanted an education rather than a degree, 'had a very wide spectrum of interests, and I didn't want to be pinned down. I studied the college catalogue very carefully and found a little known provision for a joint major in geology and physics. That made it almost a necessity to minor in mathematics' – an ideal training, he believed, for a geophysicist. After two years at the wilder edge of prospecting in Texas (*Beds 50¢, baths 50¢, free baths for regular roomers*), he took a job as instructor in geophysics at Columbia, remaining for seven unhappy years. He joined Shell three weeks before his fortieth birthday – a crucial date: Shell had a hard rule that they would take on no one over the age of forty. By the time he made his first intervention at the United Nations in 1949, he had for some years enjoyed a free hand to research in any direction he wished.

At Chicago Hubbert had taken a course in economic geology, during which he plotted how production and consumption in iron and steel, the foundations of modern industry, fitted a curve. By the mid-1930s he had realized that in any large region, unrestrained extraction of a finite resource rises along a bell-shaped curve that peaks when about half the resource is gone. 'Curves don't keep going up. They go over the jump and back to zero. This is the one future point on the curve that you definitely know and it greatly facilitates the mathematics. The area beneath the curve is graphically proportional to the amount of development. The area beneath the curve can't exceed your estimate. It's a very simple but very powerful method of analysis.' By 1956 Hubbert had worked out a mathematical formula to express his theory and, to prove it, fitted his bell curve to American production statistics: this was the occasion of his controversial speech to the American Petroleum Institute. In 1958 he recommended that the US government should start importing and storing foreign oil. Instead, driven by military rather than economic imperatives, it embarked upon an expanded interstate highway programme. However, despite ever larger estimates of America's untapped oil reserves, culminating in the US Geological Survey's 1961 figure of 590 billion barrels, 'evidence from the field consistently followed [Hubbert's] predicted curve, confirming his modest 150–200 billion barrel estimate'.[3] And in 1973, when the Middle East cut back production, America was caught short.

Hubbert curves show that US and Canadian oil topped out in 1972; production in the former Soviet Union has fallen 45 per cent since 1987; the UK and Norway will reach their peak in 2002; and after that the world will rely principally on Iran, Iraq, Kuwait, Saudi Arabia and the United Arab Emirates. Bahrain's reserves are already exhausted; Iraq, holder of by far the largest amounts, hardly seems likely to go out of its way to oblige the West. Unless there is a global recession, it seems probable that world production of oil will peak around 2010; if the most optimistic estimates are used, that moment will be postponed ten years, to 2020. This is the moment known in the jargon as the Big Rollover. There will still be plenty of oil left – as much, in fact, as has already been extracted. But from then on production will begin to fall, and what is left will get progressively harder to extract.

Can this really be true? That in ten, or at the very most twenty years, half the world's supply of oil will have been used up and we shall be on the downward slope of Hubbert's curve? The answer to this question depends, as so often, upon whom you ask and exactly what you mean.

The kind of oil that gushes conveniently out of the ground is known in the jargon as 'conventional resources', and comes in three levels of certainty: proved reserves, probable reserves and possible reserves. Proved reserves consist of known reservoirs economically recoverable at current prices and levels of technology. Probable reserves are not definitely assured, but

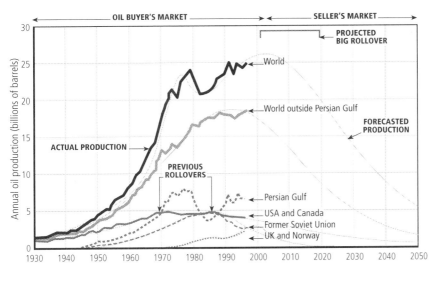

72. The Big Rollover: end of the buyer's market in oil.

are likely to exist outside the current boundaries of existing reservoirs and would be accessible by small extensions of drilling activity. Possible reserves are those that might be found in the field or basin if one is lucky – the amount varying according to how you make your predictions.

But vast quantities of oil do not gush. These are contained in oil shales and heavy oil and tar sands: 'unconventional' resources. Tar sands and heavy oil deposits probably contain more than 3.2 trillion barrels of oil, while oil shales may contain as much as 2.1 quadrillion barrels. Since world consumption in 2000 was about 20 billion barrels, this would be enough, despite rising demand, to keep the world in oil for the indefinite future. However, the oil contained in unconventional resources is not easy to access. It is so thick that it does not flow, and may only be separated by heat, either by 'roasting' the rock or adding steam. These processes are expensive, energy-consuming and (given current technologies and prices) not economic. They also tend to destroy the environment in particularly brutal ways. Tar sands are usually strip-mined: the extraction process creates a great deal of air pollution, and some of the sludge contains heavy metals and sulphur that must be removed – and dumped.

The oil industry (no doubt with an eye to its share prices) tends to be bullish when asked about remaining reserves. Chevron, for example, puts the amount of recoverable oil (that is: proved reserves *plus* probable reserves *plus* possible reserves *plus* undiscovered resources *plus* recoverable unconventional resources *plus* recoverable undiscovered unconventional resources) at about 10 trillion (10×10^{12}) barrels.[4] Other oil industry reports mentioned a figure of 1,020 billion barrels in proved reserves at the start of 1998. Dividing even this much smaller figure by the current production rate of about 23.6 billion barrels per year would indicate that crude oil should remain plentiful and cheap for forty-three more years – probably longer, because official charts showed reserves growing.[5]

'Unfortunately,' write Colin Campbell and Jean Laherrère, oil geologists who have worked in the industry for more than forty years, in Campbell's case for Texaco and Amoco, in Laherrère's for Total,

> this appraisal makes three critical errors. First, it relies on distorted estimates of reserves. A second mistake is to pretend that production will remain constant. Third and most important, conventional wisdom erroneously assumes that the last bucket of oil can be pumped from the ground just as quickly as the barrels of oil gushing from wells today. In fact, the rate at which any well – or any country – can produce oil always rises to a maximum and then, when about half the oil is gone, begins falling gradually back to zero.[6]

The OPEC nations tend, at least in public, to overestimate their reserves, because the more oil they claim there is, the more they may export. And it is always possible that big new fields will be discovered, although this is improbable: theoretical advances in geochemistry and geophysics now allow productive and prospective fields to be mapped with great accuracy, and large tracts, including much of the deepwater realm, are reliably dismissed as barren.

But while supplies are set to decline, demand heads ever upwards. Global demand for oil is currently rising at 2 per cent a year. Since 1985, energy use has risen by 30 per cent in Latin America, 40 per cent in Africa and 50 per cent in Asia. The US Energy Information Administration forecasts that worldwide demand for oil will increase 60 per cent (to about 40 billion barrels a year) by 2020.[7] By that time world production will almost certainly be well past its peak. In the words of M. King Hubbert, 'A child born in the middle [19]30s will have seen the consumption of 80 per cent of all American oil and gas in his lifetime; a child born about 1970 will see most of the world's [reserves] consumed.'[8] We have burned about 900 billion barrels of oil already; by Hubbert's method of reckoning, about 1,000 billion barrels remain. It seems reasonable to conclude that the recent price rises are no mere blip but the beginning of an inexorable trend, as increasing demand chases diminishing supplies.

People have known all this for a long time. In 1970, Esso forecast that global production would peak around 2000. In 1976 Britain's Department of Energy said that North Sea production would peak about the same time (as it has). But this has had no visible effect on policy. On the contrary, as we have seen, governments are urged to *decrease* fuel prices in order to subsidize the road haulage industry, while the OPEC countries, far from being encouraged to conserve their resources, are urged to open the taps in order to bring world oil prices down.

Why, since this information is not new, is there such apparent resistance to taking in its implications and acting upon them? One reason, of course, is its devastating significance for our way of life. An oil-scarce future is so unthinkable that we simply can't bring ourselves to imagine it. And this selective blindness is exacerbated because, as policy analyst David Fleming points out, 'the economic principles which explain how a market economy works tend to break down when applied to natural resources such as oil'.[9]

Fleming identifies four such principles. The first is to do with the rules of supply and demand. In a normal economic situation, 'if the price of something goes up, this gives a signal . . . to produce more of it; new producers will pile into the market until the price settles down again'. However, this does not hold for the oil market. Hubbert's 1956 opponents, with their blithe prophecies of undiscovered resources, were speaking at a time when such resources were indeed plentiful.

In those days oilfields were easily found, terrifically profitable and cheap to pump. Prospectors naturally crowded in; discoveries peaked around 1965. These discoveries provide most of the oil we are using today. But that was forty years ago. No more such huge and easily accessible fields now remain, and – unlike other comparably desirable economic commodities – no price rise, however steep, will bring them into being.

Another reason why economists fail to grasp the significance of the Big Rollover is because they think, rightly, that an enormous amount of oil will still remain in the ground after that date. But production will nevertheless start to decline – perhaps by as much as 3 per cent a year – while demand continues to rise. This means that oil, the foundation of our way of life, will become increasingly unavailable, while competition for supplies becomes correspondingly savage – so savage, indeed, that the market may find itself unable to cope with the consequences. It will go into 'contango', a situation in which the price of future supplies is forced up so high that they are only available to the very wealthiest.

The third point concerns the special nature of oil – its exceptional suitability as a transport fuel. No other fuel is at once so cheap and so energy-dense – that is, no other fuel will allow us to travel so far so light while paying so little. And this means that although in terms of total energy use the world depends less on oil than it once did (in the UK it has fallen from 45 to 33 per cent of total energy use since 1973), this is not the relevant statistic. All that matters is the volume of transport: and that has doubled. As Fleming observes, 'The world as a whole uses 30 per cent more oil now than it did in 1970, and the fact that its consumption of gas has risen many times over does not mean that it is less oil-dependent; it simply means that it has become dependent on gas, too.'[10]

The fourth fallacy is the notion that technological wizards will always pull a solution out of the hat in the nick of time –

what one oil-industry analyst refers to as the 'surprise' source: perhaps a new way of controlling nuclear reactions, or 'unidentified renewables'.[11] But to be ready in time, such sources should already be under intensive development. At present, for example, renewable energy accounts for 1.7 per cent of energy used in Britain. If it were to be given the highest possible priority, and combined with various forms of energy conservation, then a transition might be made in a minimum of twenty-five years. But if twenty-five years is the absolute minimum time to rebuild Europe's energy economy on renewables, we should be starting now. If we wait until oil becomes so expensive that everyone accepts the necessity of developing renewable forms of energy, then the only certainty is that we shall be twenty-five years too late.

» » »

Terrifying as the prospect of oil shortage may be, in another way it is fortunate that supplies are limited. Indeed, if we burn the last half of the world's oil at the same rate as we burned the first, we shall be in serious trouble. For oil depletion is not the only prospect too frightening to be contemplated by a public intent on seeing fuel prices reduced. Equally threatening, and intimately related, is the question of global warming – the greenhouse effect.

As everyone these days knows, energy from the sun drives the earth's weather and climate, and heats the earth's surface; in turn, the earth radiates energy back into space. Atmospheric gases – water vapour, carbon dioxide, methane and others – trap some of this outgoing energy, retaining heat like the glass panels of a greenhouse. Without this natural 'greenhouse effect' temperatures would be much lower than they are, and life as we know it impossible. But problems arise when the atmospheric concentration of greenhouse gases increases. And this is what has been happening since the beginning of the industrial revolution. In less than two hundred years we have burned peat, coal and oil that took millions of years to lay down as forests died and were transmuted. And the carbon dioxide those forests absorbed has been released into the atmosphere. Since the beginning of the Industrial Revolution, concentrations of carbon dioxide in the atmosphere have risen more than 30 per cent; methane has more than doubled (partly due to fossil fuel burning, but also because of increases in rice culture and cattle, both generating methane from rotting vegetation); nitrous oxide, a potent greenhouse gas produced by industry, motor transport and agriculture, has risen about 15 per cent.[12] And they are still rising, carbon dioxide at a rate of 4 per cent a decade.[13]

It is still uncertain exactly how the earth's climate responds to these gases. But the world's temperature is unquestionably rising. Global mean surface temperatures have increased between 0.6 and 1.2°F since the late nineteenth century. In another of the interlocking ironies that mark auto history, it seems clear that smog and pollution for a while masked this effect. But clean-air laws, while relieving the world's asthmatics and bronchitics, now expose city dwellers to dramatically increased solar radiation. The ten warmest years on record all occurred within the twentieth century's last decade and a half, 1998 being the warmest of all. Snow cover in the northern hemisphere and floating ice in the Arctic Ocean have decreased; glaciers are melting. The Intergovernmental Panel on Climate Change (IPCC), which for some time projected further global warming of 2–6°F by the year 2100, recently revised its estimates upwards: it now predicts a worst-case scenario of 8°C – that is, 15°F. Even the low end of this projection 'would probably be greater than any seen in the last 10,000 years'.[14]

In 1992, the first Climate Change Convention at Rio set a target of stabilizing emissions at the level of 1990 by 2000. But this has not happened. On the contrary, because of the US economic boom we bought larger cars, travelled further to work, took more and farther-flung holidays, and ate more exotic foods shipped in from the other side of the world. As a result, carbon dioxide emissions in 2000 were up 18 per cent since 1990.

Meanwhile, in accordance with climatologists' predictions, rainfall has increased by about 1 per cent, with more frequent extreme 'rainfall events' and 'weather events'. The insurance industry, which invariably signals the emergence of a genuine risk by a sudden reluctance to cover it,[15] is becoming chary of hitherto once-in-a-lifetime climatic events. In September 2000, after torrential rain caused catastrophic floods in Sussex, a spokesman for the Association of British Insurers, which thinks it 'certain that climate change is occurring', announced that cover would henceforth be unobtainable 'in places where there is a habitual risk'.[16] Similarly, it is suggested that within the foreseeable future property in Indonesia and parts of the south-eastern United States may become uninsurable against extreme weather events.

Some, while recognizing that changes in climate may be occurring, insist they have nothing to do with fuel consumption and the resulting emissions. The Global Climate Coalition, a group of US lobbyists financed by the auto and energy industries, dismisses the whole notion as a liberal scare story. But whatever the ultimate cause of all this (perhaps, some argue, the normal cycle of meteorological uncertainty following the end of the Little Ice Age that lasted from 1450 to 1900, though the IPCC, for many years unwilling to commit itself on this issue, has now stepped firmly down off the fence, insisting that human activity must be seen as the principal cause of global warming)[17] there is little doubt that increased carbon dioxide in the atmosphere will exacerbate any warming effect.

Cars and trucks account for a considerable proportion of greenhouse gases: 30 per cent of all US carbon dioxide emissions,[18] and, once the energy used in refining and transporting

Test drive
the Shogun now.

Exceptional conditions call for an exceptional vehicle. Happily, we've just launched the new Mitsubishi Shogun.

With a new monocoque body with built-in frame to increase size but not weight. A new advanced four-wheel-drive system that takes hell or high water in its stride.

From as little as £22,995 on the road, it won't burst your bank, either.

To arrange a test drive, call 0845 070 2000.

Or wait for the next Boat Show.

IDENTIFY YOURSELF
The new Mitsubishi SHOGUN

MITSUBISHI
MOTORS

73. Beat the floods – drive your SUV through them.

fuel is included, not far off that figure in Britain.[19] In Britain today, the average car, doing average mileage, dumps four tons of carbon dioxide into the atmosphere each year; a heavy, gas-guzzling SUV about twice that; an average house, ten tonnes; a Mediterranean holiday for four, including air travel, four tons; the food on the average family's table, seven tonnes.[20] And although better traffic management may go some way to improve efficiency (in 1996 traffic engineers reported that drivers in Los Angeles and New York City alone wasted 600 million gallons of gasoline annually just sitting in traffic, which translates into about 7.5 million tons of carbon dioxide)[21] it is clear that both the preservation of our habitat and the conservation of precious oil point in the same direction. We urgently need to develop more eco-friendly automobiles, burning fewer, if any, fossil fuels.

This urgency has not penetrated to the motoring public. When the Automobile Association, in 2000, asked its members their views on the shape of motoring in 2020, only one in ten of the drivers interviewed thought their car would achieve a hundred mpg by then, and only 3 per cent that the petrol/diesel engine would have been replaced by new technologies. Alarmingly, UK industry experts were even less adventurous: they saw environmental issues 'almost entirely as a matter of reducing vehicle weights to reduce overall emissions'.[22] Nevertheless, at the 2000 Motor Show, some new trends were, at last, apparent.

The simplest and best-known of these was in fact not new at all: welcome back, the electric car. Two were on show in Birmingham. Ford offered an electric 'city car', the Thinkmobile, but although it is available in Scandinavia the UK won't see it until 2002. Peugeot does an electric version of its 106: this is available, but at £13,500 costs around £6,000 more than the standard version.

But shall we take any more kindly to the electric than did our grandfathers? Camille Jenatzy's *Jamais Contente*, the first car to break the hundred-kph barrier, was an electric; but generally speaking electrics were, as we have seen, viewed as tame ladies' cars for tame ladies. And none of the limitations that made the internal combustion engine such an easy winner have been overcome. You still can't go far or fast in an electric. Ford's tiny Thinkmobile has a maximum range of fifty-three miles, restricting it firmly to the city; an 80 per cent recharge takes four to six hours. Bigger cars with more batteries go further, but are still restricted. The Nissan Altra EV, available in California, has a top speed of seventy-five mph and a 120-mile range; GM's sleek EV-1 goes slightly further. However, both need four to six hours' recharge for every ninety minutes' driving, which in California terms could make even a shopping trip problematic. Small-battery technology (developed for laptop computers and mobile phones) means that some problems of bulk and weight have been solved – the desirably streamlined EV1 is glamorous enough for a film producer living in Los Angeles to know he 'had to have one' as soon as he saw it. And electrics are cheap to run – top-up for the Nissan costs only $2 (£1.50), for the Think only 40p (70¢). But they suffer, as they always did, from what one user terms 'dicklessness – lack of phallic expansion'. Not for nothing does (or did) a leading brand of Italian motor oil rejoice in the name *Woom!*. There is no *woom* in electrics: on the contrary, they are so silent that, like a bicycle, they must announce their coming with a bell.

All this sounds trivial, but, as every advertiser will tell you, it is no minor defect. Lack of virility did for the mini-van, or 'people mover', which became identified with 'soccer moms' and has now been overtaken by phallic expansion incarnate in the shape of the SUV. The sense of power, for women as well as men, constitutes (as we have seen) a large part of the car's attraction; and sexual empowerment is very much part of that. The equation of car and penis is a cliché, but autos, it seems, may swing both ways. Take, for instance, the Alfa Romeo 166. Only 5 per cent of these particular cars, it seems, are bought by women. Why? Because, according to Alfa's spokeswoman (referring apparently to what one journalist describes as 'the pubic triangle in the middle of the bonnet'), 'When a man sees the front of this car coming towards him, it reminds him of a woman.'[23] In a recent Alfa ad this equation was made even more explicit, the radiator's horizontal bars echoed by a bodice in which the model's breasts peeked between horizontal ribbons. Either sex will do, but sex there must be. And the electric car is not sexy.

There are some modifications of the internal combustion engine already in widespread use – for example, adaptations to liquid petroleum gas or compressed or liquefied natural gas. Both these are cheaper and less polluting than petrol, and LNG, which is suitable for larger vehicles, is much quieter-running than diesel. But for fuel economy and pollution control, more important than any of these alternatives is the 'hybrid' – a car that can use both an internal combustion engine and an electric power source, switching from one to the other as economy dictates: electricity for stop-start urban driving, petrol for longer runs.

Hybrids were conceived as a way to compensate for the limitations of battery technology. Where the range of electric cars is always limited by the bulk, weight and storage capacity of the batteries they must carry, hybrids have an on-board generator powered by their internal combustion engine, so that the batteries are recharged whenever the engine cuts in. This, too, is an old idea: Los Angeles' Petersen Automotive Museum contains a 1917 Woods 'duo-power' coupé which operated on this same principle. But the automatic technology necessary for maximum efficiency is a more modern development.

74. The irresisitible Alfa.

Hybrids seem certain to come into their own when, as is inevitable, petrol prices rise even further and high fuel consumption is penalized. Everyone is working on them, though only two – the Honda Insight and the Toyota Prius – are in general use at the time of writing. In energy-poor Japan, the Prius, launched in 1997, has already sold forty-three thousand. In 2000, two hundred were available in the UK; two thousand were promised for 2001.

Hybrid technology is cleaner than that of a normal internal combustion engine: the Prius emits only 10 per cent of the carbon dioxide of a comparable family saloon, and imperceptible levels of oxides, nitrogen and carbon monoxide. It is also far more economical. My Peugeot delivers about forty miles per gallon; the average SUV will give you fifteen if you're lucky, thirteen in town. The two-seater Insight can, under test conditions, deliver 103 mpg, though a more realistic figure would be somewhere in the eighties; the larger Prius uses more fuel, but still offers fifty-seven mpg in town. Ford are even planning a hybrid SUV, the Escape, available in 2005, which will deliver about forty mpg in urban driving, an improbable combination of size and machismo with environmental awareness and super-low emissions.

Electrics and hybrids are less polluting *in situ*; and hybrids are far more energy-efficient than ordinary internal combustion engines. But hybrids offer at best a way of stretching what resources remain, while electrics, though undoubtedly resulting in cleaner cities, merely displace the pollution problem, from the streets to the power station. If all cars suddenly transferred from petrol to electricity, power-station emissions would inevitably rise proportionately as the stations worked to supply the increased demand. And if those power stations were run on fossil fuel, then this would be an outstandingly inefficient way of using it, though electric cars are less inefficient than petrol-powered at converting energy into motion. This

75. Woods 'duo-power' hybrid, 1917.

'driveline efficiency' in internal combustion engines is about 25 per cent; older electric cars are perhaps 60 per cent efficient from battery to wheels, and with modern electronic systems the figure is nearer 80 per cent. But fossil-fuelled power stations are only a little more than 30 per cent energy-efficient (the other 70 per cent goes up in steam through the cooling towers) while a further 10 per cent of electrical energy is lost in transmission along the lines. So electrics, as well as being impractical, are (unless supplied by nuclear or renewable power) an unsatisfactory solution in energy and emissions terms, too. In the long term we must find some way of powering our vehicles that is both renewable and non-polluting, either directly or at one remove.

There are a number of alternative fuels, in development or already available, which will power existing internal combustion engines. And in the case of at least one, biodiesel, we revisit an old friend: the universal soybean, apple of Henry Ford's eye. Sauce, milk, protein, suits, plastics – that it should produce fuel, too, was perhaps inevitable.[24] 'Biodiesel' is a cleaner-burning diesel fuel made from natural, renewable resources such as new or used vegetable oils and animal fats. It is biodegradable, requires minimal engine modification when used either blended with ordinary diesel or on its own, and is potentially cleaner burning than the diesel it replaces. SoyDiesel, made by reacting methanol with soya oil, is currently the main form, but peanuts, sunflower seeds, cottonseed and rapeseed are other potential sources.

Another biological fuel is ethanol, already widely used in Brazil. It is grain alcohol, made by fermenting a mash of corn or other carbohydrate-rich plant, distilling it to a pure state and denaturing it to make it unfit for human consumption. The grain is then used for livestock feed, and the other by-product, carbon dioxide, may be collected and used in carbonated drinks. Like biodiesel, ethanol can be used in modified internal combustion engines, and is renewable. And although like biodiesel it is still expensive by comparison with ordinary petroleum products, this will not always be true. Generally speaking, new technologies begin with niche markets and progress to become competitive with existing resources, getting cheaper as they do so: for example, electricity in the US achieved a 25 per cent cost reduction for every doubling in take-up.[25]

These fuels do not entirely solve the problem of emissions, but they substantially reduce them: compared with emissions from existing cars, methanol will cut carbon dioxide by 25 per cent, as well as liberating us from dependence on oil and oil producers. There is, however, one fuel that will eliminate carbon dioxide emissions altogether: hydrogen.

In theory, hydrogen has everything to recommend it. Stored on board in liquid or gaseous form, an electrochemical fuel cell combines it with oxygen from the air to produce electricity. This drives the car, and the only emission is water vapour. Hydrogen is abundant, ubiquitous, non-polluting; it may be separated and compressed using well-known technologies. BMW already runs a fleet of hydrogen-powered cars, fuelled from the world's first publicly available robot-operated hydrogen fuel station at Munich Airport. BMW sees the way forward as an internal combustion engine that burns hydrogen: it thinks that this is the only way to deliver the acceleration and responsiveness drivers want. But internal combustion engines are notoriously inefficient, converting only 20 per cent of fuel energy into traction. DaimlerChrysler is looking in another direction: its New Electric Car, operating on liquid hydrogen with an efficiency of 80 per cent, covers 280 miles on a full tank; has a top speed of ninety mph and carries five passengers and their luggage.

Unsurprisingly, the auto and energy industries see hydrogen as the fuel of the future. GM says its 'long-term vision is of a hydrogen economy'. A Deutsche Shell director predicts

50 per cent of all new vehicles, and 20 per cent of the existing fleet, will be hydrogen vehicles by 2020. Ford, whose president William Clay Ford Jr dropped out of the Global Climate Coalition in October 1999, is scheduling its seventy-mpg Prodigy fuel-cell hybrid for production in 2003. Shell says it would take at most two years to convert many thousands of gasoline filling-stations to hydrogen. Even Sheikh Yamani, Oil Minister of Saudi Arabia between 1962 and 1986, is a hydrogen enthusiast. In July 2000 he forecast that world oil prices would drop sharply in about five years, and later crash definitively, because of competition from hydrogen fuel cells. 'This is coming before the end of the decade and will cut gasoline consumption by almost 100 per cent,' he said. Hence, perhaps, Saudi Arabia's desire to increase oil production now, while demand lasts. 'Thirty years from now, there will be a huge amount of oil – and no buyers,' Yamani said. 'Thirty years from now, there is no problem with oil. Oil will be left in the ground.'[26] The Stone Age, he added, did not come to an end because people ran out of stones. If this is true, then we have nothing to worry about, and can dismiss David Fleming's doomsday scenarios. But is it, and can we?

The key to hydrogen cars is the fuel cell. Like a battery, a fuel cell delivers electrical power from a chemical reaction. Unlike a battery, however, the reactants are stored *outside* the fuel cell. A battery must be recharged or replaced once its internally stored reactants are used up: this limits the range of battery-powered vehicles, which are also slow to recharge. A fuel cell, on the other hand, will produce electricity as long as its reactants – hydrogen and oxygen – are delivered to it; and refuelling is quick. So fuel-cell cars can combine the electric's zero emissions with the internal combustion vehicle's range, performance and flexibility.

Fuel-cell technology, though still experimental, is well advanced. It is not new – the fuel cell was invented nearly two hundred years ago, by a Welsh physicist called Sir William Grove. But like many inventions it was ignored because at the time there were no obvious uses for it. It came into its own with the advent of space travel, when it was used in the US's Gemini spacecraft; and in the mid-1990s an important breakthrough occurred when a small company, Ballard Power Systems of Vancouver, Canada, dramatically improved its power-to-volume ratio from a meagre 167 watts per litre to 1,000 watts per litre. Ballard's latest cell delivers 1,310 watts per litre – powerful enough to make a seventy-five-kilowatt (hundred brake horsepower) engine that fits comfortably inside a car.

Now all the large auto makers are concentrating on fuel cells. For example, Ford is combining in a fuel-cell alliance with DaimlerChrysler, Ballard, ARCO, Shell and Texaco, the California Air Resources Board and the California Energy Commission. The technology will soon be generally available, and, as always with new technologies, it will quickly become both cheaper and more refined.

But Sheikh Yamani need not yet worry about bankruptcy. For one large obstacle remains. Where is the hydrogen supply to come from? Oil comes pouring out of the earth, conveniently ready to use. Hydrogen does not. No hydrogen mines await discovery, no hydrogen wells lurk beneath the ocean bed. Though all around us, it is inextricably mixed up with other elements. Hydrogen is the hydro in hydrocarbons; water is made of hydrogen and oxygen.

The obvious way to make hydrogen is by electrolysing water so that it splits into its component elements. However, electrolysis uses energy – more, in fact, than you get back from the hydrogen produced. Consequently, if the normal fossil-fuelled power-station supply is used to make hydrogen, not only will the net result be negative in energy terms, but – as with electric cars – the huge demand will increase power-station emissions, and hence – however clean hydrogen-powered vehicles them-selves may be – global warming.

The ideal answer would be to generate the necessary electricity by renewable power sources – solar energy or wind energy. But it will require enormous investment and a long lead time before the necessary stations are built. Meanwhile Amory Lovins, long-time advocate of the ultra-light Hypercar, has prepared a 'Strategy for the Hydrogen Transition'. This rests its hopes on photovoltaic (PV) fuel cells, which convert light energy directly into electricity.

PVs were originally developed for use in space, where the only other practical energy source was nuclear and cost was no object. They are clean, silent and reliable, require no maintenance, have no moving parts. They are already with us, perhaps powering your watch or calculator; they provide electricity for pumping water and powering communications equipment in isolated spots. They may also be used to provide electricity for buildings, built in as wall cladding or roof panels, though cost has been a barrier. Between 1976 and 1988 – years when people used PV panels for industrial appliances and consumer goods – the cost of making these panels fell 15 per cent a year in real terms. Then interest declined. But now PVs are more generally interesting: the US Department of Energy hopes to double the efficiency of modules and reduce their manufacturing cost by a factor of three, reducing costs to 6¢ per kilowatt hour by 2010. This would approach parity with conventional sources – at the time of writing, 2.5p, or 3.5¢, per kilowatt hour.

Lovins's strategy posits an integration of hydrogen tech-nology between buildings and transport. It 'relies on existing technologies, can begin immediately, and proceeds in a logical and viable sequence'.[27] Buildings use more than half of all energy in developed countries, and much of this – especially where distribution grids are old or congested – could already be competitively provided by PV, while opening up the market in this way would soon cut costs. The price of PV cladding, to produce the electricity, is already about the same as that of granite or aluminium, both routinely used in high-quality office buildings. Hydrogen could be made in the building, using a mass-produced 'hydrogen appliance', and this, in off-peak hours, would supply vehicles – particularly those whose drivers worked or lived near those same buildings. And while the vehicles were parked at the buildings, they in turn could be used as plug-in power plants. In this way energy use and supply would be fully integrated, and hydrogen fuelling could be made practical with no need for vast new power plants or a new distribution infrastructure.

But such systems, however ingenious, will not be quick to set up. The necessary technology (in particular the 'hydrogen appliances') must be developed. And this is true of all the various alternative fuel possibilities. It will take time to prepare for the transition. Plant must be built and fuel-cell technology developed; land must be set aside for biomass – the crops to produce ethanol and biodiesel; huge distilleries must be constructed. These are all complex and expensive processes – far more complex and expensive than digging a hole in the ground and selling the oil that gushes up from it.

The only country truly prepared for what may happen is Iceland, 'the Bahrain of the North',[28] where electricity is generated from hydropower and geothermal energy and the population is only 276,000. Thorsteinn Sigfusson, Professor of Physics at the University of Iceland, and chairman of Iceland New Energy, declares that within twenty years his country can become the first in the world to run on hydrogen without recourse to fossil fuels.

Iceland, significantly, has no fossil fuel resources of its own. Elsewhere, better-cushioned governments have hardly begun to think about such projects. On this front, too, we have moved backwards since the 1970s, when not only did frightened governments begin to think in terms of long-term energy policy, but the auto companies and oil companies redefined themselves as 'total transportation organizations' and 'total energy companies'.[29] Since then, however, complacency has set in.

Will it be shattered in time? We put our faith in experts. But because, in David Fleming's words, the problem 'falls outside the mind-set of market economics', they – and therefore we – fail to see what's in front of our nose. Far from urgently reducing our dependence on the internal combustion engine, devoting our best energies to the development of renewable technologies, rearranging our settlement patterns into higher densities and conserving energy, we appear to be engaged in a race to see who can use the most fuel in the shortest possible time.

The Big Rollover, according to those willing to forecast, will happen 'somewhere between 2003 and 2020'.[30] Oil scarcity will affect the poorest first – paraffin is already too expensive for some in the least prosperous countries. But the time will come when it affects all but the richest. And at that point – indeed, well before it – the problem will become not just technological but urgently political. Shall we pierce the barrier of unthinkability and economic taboo, or must we wake up one day to a crisis that need never have been unforeseen? How long will it take for every city to equip itself with some form of cheap and reliable public transport, for the biomass fields to be planted, the photovoltaic claddings attached, the solar stations built?

In the words of L. B. Magoon of the US Geological Survey, 'Hang on tight, if we don't recognize the problem soon and deal with it, it's going to be quite a ride!'[31]

» » »

Seventy years before Freud hit upon his metaphor of mechanical 'accessory organs', in *Civilisation and Its Discontents*, Samuel Butler, in *Darwin Among the Machines*, elaborated with characteristic verve his scenario of machine suzerainty. 'That the time will come when the machines will hold the real supremacy over the world and its inhabitants is what no person of a truly philosophic mind can for a moment question,' he wrote. 'Our opinion is that war to the death should be instantly proclaimed against them . . . If it be urged that this is impossible under the present condition of human affairs, this at once proves that the mischief is already done, that our servitude has commenced in good earnest . . . and that we are not only enslaved but are absolutely acquiescent in our bondage.'[32]

And there, it appears, we have arrived. The air is foul, the weather deteriorating, the roads impassable, the future (to put it mildly) uncertain. But we are true addicts: we know we imperatively shouldn't, but we can't, *can not*, resist. Eighty-six per cent of British car owners interviewed in 2000 said they would find it hard to adjust their lifestyles if they were deprived of their cars;[33] in America the figure would probably be even higher. Travel on demand is built into every iota of our existence; practically, economically, emotionally, we are incapable of imagining life without our darling destroyers. With my wheels outside the door I am happy; in one of life's habitual paradoxes, the mere possibility of escape renders escape unnecessary. But as soon as the car is absent – borrowed, under repair – my feet start to itch, I feel trapped, enclosed, intolerably confined. True child of my time, my car is necessary to my well-being. As Adam and Eve learned to their cost, knowledge is corrupting. We have known freedom, and nothing can undo that knowledge.

This state of affairs cannot last. Travel, whether to work or play, is going to become a luxury; the days of driving out to watch the sunset, of running the kids to school because it's easier, are numbered. As oil gets scarce it will be comman-deered – by the military, the rich, the airlines – and the era of cheap and universal travel will be over. Even in highly taxed Britain, a litre of petrol, at 83p, is still cheaper than a litre of mineral water. Whatever our future fuel, whether it be hydro-gen, biomass or some technology as yet unthought-of, it will cost much, much more than that.

The internal combustion engine has allowed us to set up home regardless of those constraints that kept our forebears tied to the immediate vicinity of their food and livelihood. But what do we do when our lifeline is cut? Will the millions living in automobile suburbs suddenly find themselves marooned, their property devalued while city-centre prices rise? Will the slums move from the centre of cities, suddenly desirable once more, to the outer settlements? Or will the high cost of trans-port make those cities so expensive to feed and service that none but the wealthiest can afford to live or work there? Per-haps we shall be finally forced into the long-forecast, long-resisted seclusion of the teleworker, cultivating our vegetable gardens while our magic carpets, too expensive for all but the most essential journeys, are reserved for those occasions when needs truly must.

Notes

One / A Visit to the Motor Show

1. Leisure services and goods £59.80 per week, food and soft drinks £58.90, housing £57.20, motoring £51.70, out of a total expenditure of £352.20. National Statistical Office figures reported in the *Guardian*, 25 Nov 1999.

2. The Automobile Association, *The Great British Motorist 2000*, p. 12.

3. For a discussion of this see Schafer and Victor, 'The Past and Future of Global Mobility', *Scientific American*, Oct 1997.

4. Schafer and Victor, 'The Future Mobility of the World Population', Discussion Paper 97-6-4 in the Co-Operative Mobility Program, Center for Technology, Policy and Industrial Development, Massachussetts Institute of Technology. Some of the findings were also presented in the *Scientific American* article referred to in the previous note.

5. Marsh and Collett, *Driving Passion*, p. 160.

6. Ibid.

7. Freud, *Civilisation and its Discontents*.

8. At the last count, Britain registered 1.1 fatalities per 100 million vehicle-kilometres, as against 1.2 in the United States, 3.3 in Belgium, 6.1 in Poland

and 9.6 in Hungary. Pucher and Lefèvre, *the Urban Transport Crisis in Europe and North America*, p. 26.

9. Red Cross, *World Disasters Report*, 1998.

Two / Paris to Bordeaux

1. Maxim, *Horseless Carriage Days*, p. 175.

2. Plowden, *The Motor Car and Politics 1870–1970*, p. 24.

3. Young, *The Complete Motorist*, pp. 270–1.

4. Quoted Rolt, *Horseless Carriage*, p. 20.

5. Quoted ibid., p. 21.

6. Maxim, op. cit., p. 5.

7. Ibid., p. 1.

8. Ibid, p. 2.

9. Ibid., p. 5.

10. Not that this noticeably increased his wealth, as her family cut her off without a penny, disapproving of either the match or the lady: the Baronne van Zuylen has her own niche in social history as a masterful member of the lesbian circle surrounding Natalie Barney.

11. Maxim, op. cit., pp. 80–1.

12. Quoted Berger, *The Devil Wagon in God's Country*, p. 88.

13. McShane, *Down the Asphalt Path*, p. 126.

14. *Horseless Age*, Jul 1897.

15. Belloc, *The Road*, p. 193.

16. *Autocar*, 21 Jun 1895.

17. *Le Figaro*, 12 Jun 1895.

18. Plowden, op. cit., p. 43.

19. Young, op. cit., pp. 223–4.

20. Maxim, op. cit., p. 175.

21. *Le Figaro* 14 Jun 1895.

22. Ibid.

23. *The Engineer*, 21 Jun 1895.

24. Laux, *In First Gear*, p. 26.

25. Ibid., p. 23.

26. *New York World*, 17 Nov 1895.

27. Maxim, op. cit., p. 16.

28. Ibid., p. 11.

29. Figuier, *Merveilles de la Science*, p. 7.

30. Maxim op. cit. pp. 51–4.

31. Laux, op. cit., p. 23.

32. *Motor*, vol. 1, 9 Jul 1902.

33. Veblen, *The Theory of the Leisure Class*, p. 41.

34. Dorfman, *Thorstein Veblen and His America*, p. 6.

35. *Motor*, vol. 1, Feb–Mar 1904.

36. Quoted Brandon, *The Dollar Princesses*, p. 16.

37. Marsh K. Powers in *Outlook*, 12 Apr 1922, quoted Michael K. Berger, 'The Car's Impact on the American Family', in Wachs, ed. *Men, Women and Wheels*, pp. 59–60.

38. Quoted Scharff, *Taking the Wheel*, p. 19.

39. *Motor* Jul 1904.

40. Veblen op. cit., p. 77.

41. Geoffrey Miller, 'Waste is Good', *Prospect*, Feb 1999.

42. Ibid.

43. Quoted Hall, *Cities of Tomorrow*, p. 25.

44. McShane, op. cit., p. 62.

45. Ibid., p. 1.

46. Ibid., p. 118.

47. Ibid., p. 176.

48. Ibid.

49. Maxim, op. cit., p. 103.

50. Plowden, op. cit., p. 38.

51. *New York Times*, 16 Nov 1905.

52. McShane, op. cit., p. 176.

53. Montagu of Beaulieu, *The Gordon-Bennett Races*, p. 59.

54. McShane, op. cit., p. 198.

55. Ibid., pp. 181–2.

56. Rolt, op. cit., p. 71.

57. Plowden, op. cit. p. 43.

58. Ibid., p. 42.

59. Ibid.

60. McShane, op. cit., p. 133.

61. *New York Times*, 3 Oct 1904.

62. *Horseless Age*, London, Aug 1897.

63. McShane, op. cit. p. 183.

64. Montagu of Beaulieu, op. cit., p. 34.

65. *Motor*, vol. 1, 9 Jul 1902.

66. Vanderbilt, *Log of my Motor*, pp. 96–7.

67. Ibid.

68. Ibid.

69. Ibid., pp. 138–40.

70. *New York World*, 17 Nov 1895.

71. *Horseless Age*, New York, vol. 1 no. 2, Dec 1895.

72. *Autocar*, Apr 1897.

73. *Literary Digest*, 14 Oct 1899.

74. John Adams, *The Social Implications of Hypermobility*, OECD, 1999, quoted the *Guardian*, 15 Dec 1999.

75. Ibid.

76. Young, op. cit. p. 230.

77. Lynd and Lynd, *Middletown in Transition*, p. 265.

78. Adams op. cit.

Three / Greenfield Village to the Rouge

1. John B. Rae, 'Why Michigan?' in Lewis and Goldstein, eds., *The Automobile and American Culture*, pp 1–9.

2. Interview, *Manchester Guardian*, 16 Nov 1940.

3. Quoted Nevins and Hill, 'Ford: The Times, The Man, The Company', vol. 1, p. 149.

4. McShane, *Down the Asphalt Path*, p. 107, drawing on the account of George S. May, *A Most Unique Machine*.

5. Nevins and Hill, op. cit., p. 156.

6. Ibid., p 152.

7. Waldemar Kaempffert, 'The Mussolini of Highland Park', *New York Times Magazine*, 8 Jan 1928.

8. Nevins and Hill, op. cit., pp. 156–7.

9. *New York World*, 17 Nov 1895.

10. Nevins and Hill, op. cit., p. 167.

11. Quoted Nevins and Hill, op. cit., pp. 174–5.

12. Quoted Ibid., p. 177.

13. Nevins and Hill, op. cit., p. 215.

14. Ibid.

15. Ford, *My Life and Work*, p. 50.

16. Nevins and Hill, op. cit., p. 205.

17. Ibid., p. 217.

18. Ibid., p. 218.

19. Quoted Nevins and Hill, op. cit., p. 218.

20. Leonard, *The Tragedy of Henry Ford*, p. 20.

21. Ibid., p. 224.

22. *Writings of Thomas Jefferson*, quoted Brandon, *Singer and the Sewing Machine*, p. 103.

23. Hultén, *The Machine as Seen at the End of the Mechanical Age*, p. 52.

24. Bugatti, *The Bugatti Story*, p. 29.

25. Nevins and Hill, op. cit., p. 385.

26. *Motor World*, 7 Jul 1910.

27. Quoted Wik, *Henry Ford and Grass-Roots America*, p. 235.

28. Quoted ibid., p. 233.

29. Nevins and Hill, op. cit., p. 276.

30. Ibid., p. 277.

31. Wik, op. cit., p. 236.

32. Quoted Flink, *America Adopts the Automobile*, p. 37.

33. Wik, op. cit., p. 235.

34. *American Agriculturalist*, 1 Oct 1908; Wik, op. cit., p. 236.

35. Quoted Nevins and Hill, op. cit., p. 336.

36. Kaempffert, op. cit.

37. Sorensen, *My Forty Years with Ford*, p. 26.

38. Wilson, *The American Earthquake*, p. 220.

39. Ford, op. cit., p. 66.

40. Quoted Nevins and Hill, op. cit., p. 339.

41. Quoted ibid., p. 355.

42. Quoted ibid., p. 390.

43. Quoted ibid., p. 391.

44. Thanks to Nick Humphrey for this one.

45. Wilson, op. cit., p. 234.

46. Rockford, Illinois, dealer, *Ford Times* 1, 15 Apr 1908.

47. Ibid.

48. White, *Farewell, My Lovely* in *Essays* pp. 162–8.

49. *Ford Times*, 15 Apr 1908.

50. Nevins and Hill, op. cit., p. 396.

51. Sorensen, op. cit., p. 117.

52. Ibid., p. 118.

53. Ibid., pp. 130–1.

54. Quoted Sorensen, op. cit., p. 131.

55. Dos Passos, *The Big Money*, U.S.A. p. 784.

56. Taylor, *The Principles of Scientific Management*.

57. Ibid.

58. Ibid.

59. Nevins and Hill, op. cit., p. 468.

60. Ibid., p. 469.

61. Ibid., pp. 507–8.

62. Sorensen, op. cit., p. 137.

63. Mumford, *The Pentagon of Power*, p. 169.

64. Nevins and Hill, op. cit., pp. 527, 538.

65. Quoted Nevins and Hill, op. cit., p. 523.

66. Ibid., p. 523.

67. Ford, op. cit., pp. 103, 105.

68. Quoted Lewis, The Public Image of Henry Ford.

69. The Shelley Report, quoted Rothschild, *Paradise Lost*, p. 131.

70. Lynd and Lynd, *Middletown in Transition*, p. 30.

71. Ibid., p. 74.

72. Ibid., p. 33.

73. Quoted Nevins and Hill, op. cit., p. 528.

74. Wilson, op. cit., p. 223.

75. Laux, *In First Gear*, pp. 191–2.

76. Nevins and Hill, op. cit., p. 514.

77. Sorensen, op. cit., pp. 138–9.

78. Ibid., p. 149.

79. Nevins and Hill, op. cit., p. 533.

80. Ibid.

81. Lewis, op. cit., p. 71.

82. Ibid.

83. Sorensen, op. cit., pp. 141–2.

84. Ibid.

85. Nevins and Hill, op. cit., p. 540.

86. Marquis, *Henry Ford*, p. 154.

87. Ford pamphlet, 1915: *Factory Facts from Ford.*

88. Ibid.

89. Leonard, op. cit.

90. *Factory Facts from Ford.*

91. Wilson, op. cit., p. 238.

92. Dos Passos, op. cit., p. 810.

93. Ford, op. cit., p. 95.

94. Lewis, op. cit., p. 118.

95. Nevins and Hill, 'Ford: The Times, the Man, the Company', vol. 2, pp. 338–9.

96. Hall, *Cities of Tomorrow*, pp. 364–7.

97. Lochner, *Henry Ford*, p. 1.

98. Quoted Wik, op. cit., p. 5.

99. Quoted Nevins and Hill, op. cit., vol. 2, p. 339.

100. Wik, op. cit., p. 5.

101. Nevins and Hill, op. cit., vol. 1, p. 574.

102. Ibid., p. 575.

103. Wilson, op. cit., p. 234.

104. Nevins and Hill, op. cit., vol. 1, p. 577.

105. Wik, op. cit., p. 7.

106. Maxim, *Horseless Carriage Days*, p. 174.

107. White, op. cit., p. 162.

108. Dakota farmer, quoted Wik, op. cit., p. 67.

109. Oklahoma farmer, quoted ibid., p. 62.

110. Ford, *My Life and Work*, p. 193.

111. Quoted Wik, op. cit., p. 1.

112. Farmer, quoted Berger, *The Devil Wagon in God's Country*, p. 42.

113. Berger, op. cit., p. 57.

114. Kaempffert, op. cit.

115. Scharff, *Taking the Wheel*, p. 142.

116. Berger, op. cit., p. 66.

117. Lynd and Lynd, op. cit., pp. 254–6.

118. Ibid., p. 261.

119. Wik, op. cit., p. 65.

120. *Ford News*, 1915.

121. Tobin, 'Henry Ford and His Village Industries in South-East Michigan', p. 55.

122. *Ford News*, 1942.

123. Dos Passos, op. cit., p. 814.

124. Nevins and Hill, op. cit., vol. 2, p. 138.

125. W. J. Showalter, 'The Automobile Industry: An American Art That Has Revolutionized Methods in Manufacturing and Transformed Transportation', *National Geographic Magazine*, vol. 44 no. 4, pp. 337–413.

126. Lynd and Lynd, op. cit., p. 251.

Four / Letchworth, Pasadena, Poundbury

1. Richard Sennett, *The Fall of Public Man*, pp. 131–2.

2. Clark, 'Transport: Maker and Breaker of Cities', *Town Planning Review* 28, 1957. See also Roberts and Steadman *American Cities and Technology*, p. 203.

3. Roberts and Steadman, op. cit., p. 204.

4. Hall, *Cities of Tomorrow*, p. 36.

5. Lawrence Veiller, quoted Hall, op. cit., p. 36.

6. Hall, op. cit., p. 37.

7. McShane, *Down the Asphalt Path*, pp. 42–3.

8. Ibid., p. 45.

9. Ibid., p. 49.

10. Ibid., p. 52.

11. Quoted Jacobs, *The Death and Life of Great American Cities*, p. 341.

12. McShane, op. cit., p. 52.

13. Warner, *Streetcar Suburbs*, p. 17.

14. Howard, *To-morrow: A Peaceful Path to Real Reform*, quoted Hall, op. cit., pp. 93–4.

15. Quoted Hayden, *The Grand Domestic Revolution*, p. 231.

16. See Ruth Brandon, *The New Women and the Old Men*, London, 2000.

17. Wells, *A Modern Utopia*, 1905.

18. Brochure, Letchworth Garden City Heritage Museum.

19. Quoted Hall, op. cit., p. 97.

20. Mrs E. B. Pearsall, *Co-operative Howes at Letchworth*.

21. Flink, *The Automobile Age*, p. 140.

22. Quoted McShane, op. cit., p. 226.

23. Martin Wachs, 'Men, Women and Urban Travel', in Wachs and Crawford, eds., *The Car and the City*, p. 89.

24. Jackson, *To the Crabgrass Frontier*, p. 89.

25. Ibid., p. 115.

26. Quoted Preston, *Automobile Age Atlanta*, p. 74.

27. Quoted Jackson, op. cit., p. 163.

28. Lewis and Goldstein, eds., *The Automobile and American Culture*, p. 93.

29. Jackson, op. cit., p. 284.

30. Frank Parsons, quoted McShane, op. cit., p. 123.

31. Flink, op. cit., p. 80.

32. Preston, op. cit., pp. 80–4.

33. Hall, op. cit., pp. 277–8.

34. Goodman and Goodman, *Communitas*, pp. 176–7.

35. Quoted Longstreth, *The Drive-in, the Supermarket and the Transformation of Commercial Space in Los Angeles, 1914–1941*, p. 14.

36. Longstreth, op. cit., p. 79.

37. Ibid.

38. Ibid., pp. 77–8.

39. Ibid., p. 170.

40. Wright, *The Disappearing City*, 1932, quoted Longstreth, op. cit., p. 130.

41. Jackson, op cit., p. 285.

42. Department of Housing and Urban Development's 'State of the Cities' report, 1998, quoted Jackson, op. cit.

43. Ibid. Jackson gives no date, but the quote is used in association with an exhibition he organized in 1983.

44. Quoted Jackson, op. cit., p. 168.

45. Quoted Hall, op. cit., p. 59.

46. Hall, op. cit., p. 61.

47. Wachs, op. cit., p. 87.

48. As it happens, the notion of purdah was integral to the suburban ideal as it was first established. In the late eighteenth century a group of wealthy London merchants belonging to evangelical Christian sects, who aspired to landed estates and wished to isolate their wives and children from the evils of urban life, decided to move to Clapham, then a country village on the outskirts of the city. From this reassuringly remote location the men fought

doughtily for social reform whilst the ladies supported them in modest and healthful seclusion, helped by plenty of servants, friends within walking distance and all services delivered to the door.

49. Quoted Hayden, op. cit., pp. 10–11.

50. Cowan, *More Work for Mother*, p. 108.

51. Ibid., p. 109.

52. Ibid.

53. For a full and fascinating discussion of these ideas, see ibid., especially Chapter 3, 'The Invention of Housework'.

54. Scharff, *Taking the Wheel*, p. 40.

55. Ibid.

56. *Motor*, Apr 1904.

57. Quoted Scharff, 'Gender, Electricity and Automobility', in Wachs and Crawford, op. cit., pp. 79–80.

58. Quoted Scharff, op. cit., p. 21.

59. Cuneo, *A Woman's Experience in the Glidden Tour*.

60. *New York Times*, 3 Oct 1913.

61. McShane, op. cit., p. 157.

62. White, *Farewell, My Lovely*, in Essays.

63. Sharff, 'Gender, Electricitity and Automobility', in Wachs and Crawford, op. cit., p. 81.

64. Ibid., pp. 82–3.

65. Ibid., p. 83.

66. Quoted Scharff, op. cit., p. 82.

67. Quoted Berger, 'The Car's Impact on the American Family', in Wachs and Crawford, op. cit., p. 70.

68. Quoted Wachs, 'Men, Women and Urban Travel', in Wachs and Crawford, op. cit., p. 94.

69. Quoted Goodman and Goodman, op. cit., p. 21.

70. Arthur Miller, 'Are You Now or Were You Ever . . . ?', *Guardian*, 17 Jun 2000.

71. Hayden, op. cit., p. 25.

72. Friedan, *The Feminine Mystique*, p. 15.

73. Ibid., p. 37.

74. Ibid., pp. 38–41.

75. US Bureau of the Census, *Women in the American Economy*, quoted Sandra Rosenbloom, 'Why Working Families Need a Car', in Wachs and Crawford, op. cit., p. 39.

76. Calthorpe, *The Next American Metropolis*, p. 18.

77. Rosenbloom, op. cit., p. 40.

78. Calthorpe, op. cit., p. 18.

79. Rosenbloom, op. cit., p. 40.

80. Calthorpe, op. cit., p. 17.

81. Rosenbloom, op. cit., p. 47.

82. Ibid., pp. 50–1.

83. Goodman and Goodman, op. cit., p. 22.

84. Automobile Association, *The Great British Motorist 1998*, pp. 2, 6.

85. Jacobs, op. cit., p. 10.

86. Quoted Scott London, 'The City of Tomorrow: A Conversation with Peter Calthorpe', http://www.scottlondon.com/insight/scripts/calthorpe.html.

87. Robert Cervero, 'Why Go Anywhere?', *Scientific American*, Sept 1995, pp. 92–3.

88. Calthorpe, in Open University film, *Los Angeles and the Car*, 1998.

89. Ibid.

90. Cervero, op. cit., pp. 92–3.

91. Ibid.

92. Calthorpe, *The New American Metropolis*, p. 147.

93. Brodsly, *L.A. Freeway*, p. 36.

94. In conversation with Philip Steadman, Open University film, 'Los Angeles and the Car'.

95. Ibid.

96. For a discussion of Disney's manoeuvrings see Richard Foglesong, 'Walt Disney World and Orlando: Deregulation as a Strategy for Tourism', in Judd and Fainstein, eds., *The Tourist City*, p. 90.

97. Ibid., p. 92.

98. Ibid., p. 102.

99. David Brady and Sylvia Oliande, 'A Visit to Celebration', http://www.primenet.com/~dbrady/oliande/celebration.html.

100. Foglesong, op. cit., p. 102.

101. Hogan, 'Celebration', http://xroads.virginia.edu/~MA98/hogan/celebration/main.html.

102. Quoted the *Observer Magazine*, 7 May 2000.

103. Hogan, op. cit.

104. Ibid.

105. The *Guardian*, 12 Jun 2000.

106. Ibid.

107. Ibid.

108. Foglesong, op. cit., p. 96.

109. Figures from the Department of Housing and Urban Development's 'State of the Cities' report, 1998.

110. Prof. Melvin Webber, 'Los Angeles and the Car', Open University film.

111. Ibid.

Five / Berlin

1. Brand, *Whole Earth Catalog*, 1974, p. 643.

2. R. J Overy, 'Cars, Roads and Economic Recovery in Germany, 1932–1938', *Economic History Review*, 28 Aug 1975, p. 469 n. 3.

3. Ibid., p. 469.

4. Table taken from Overy, op. cit., p. 477.

Fiscal year	Military expenditure (million marks)	Motor transport (million marks)
1932/3	766.2	814.0
1933/4	1,360.0	1,139.0
1934/5	1,900.0	1,618.0

5. Ibid, pp. 473–8.

6. GB Admiralty figures, quoted Hall, *Cities of Tomorrow*, p. 280.

7. Hall, op. cit., p. 280.

8. Overy, op. cit., pp. 475–6.

9. This account is taken largely from Nelson, *Small Wonder*, pp. 24–32.

10. Overy, op. cit., p. 469.

11. Ibid., p. 472.

12. *Manchester Guardian*, 5 Jan 1939.

13. Nelson, op. cit., p. 52.

14. Rules concerning applications for a Volkswagen Savings Book, Karl Ludvigsen, *An Investigation of the Design and Performance of Civilian and Military Volkswagens 1938–46*, see B.I.O.S. *People's Car*, pp. 136–7. Original undated, but this would have been issued from 1938 on.

15. Ibid., p. 2.

16. Ibid.

17. Ibid., p. 7.

18. Ibid., p. 9.

19. The *Guardian*, 19 Jun 2000.

20. Ford, *My Life and Work*, p. 19.

21. Lewis, op. cit., p. 139.

22. Lee, *Henry Ford and the Jews*, p. 149.

23. Ford, op. cit., p. 7.

24. Quoted Lewis, op. cit., p. 137.

25. Quoted Lee, op. cit., p. 13.

26. J. and S. Pool, *Who Financed Hitler?*, p. 87.

27. Lee, op. cit., p. 14.

28. Ibid.

29. Quoted Pool, op. cit., p. 111.

30. Ford was not the only American industrialist to be received into this order. Thomas J. Watson, chief executive of IBM, also received its Merit Cross. IBM's German subsidiary Dehomag was instrumental in helping Hitler locate Jews for extermination, running his censuses and surveys on its punch-card tabulators: a technology as essential to Auschwitz as to Roosevelt's first social security programme.

31. Waldemar Kaempffert, 'The Mussolini of Highland Park', *New York Times*, 8 Jan 1928.

32. Huxley, *Brave New World*, Penguin edition, 1958, pp. 175, 179.

33. Lee, op. cit., p. 99.

34. Quoted Lewis, op. cit., ch. 11.

35. *The Guv'nor*, BBC Home Service, 29 Dec 1959.

36. Interviewed in *System, 'The Magazine of Business'*, in 1924.

37. Quoted Adeney, *Nuffield*, p. 67.

38. *Daily Express*, 1927, Quoted Adeney, op. cit., p. 121.

39. Quoted Adeney, op. cit., p. 125.

40. Quoted ibid., p. 126.

41. Adeney, op. cit.

42. Ibid., p. 127.

43. Newspaper cutting, Morris archive, Nuffield College, Oxford.

44. Morris archive.

45. Thomas, *Out on a Wing*, p. 176.

46. In the same letter, to the then Bishop of London, that contained his infinitely misquoted *aperçu* that 'Power tends to corrupt and absolute power corrupts absolutely.'

47. Ian Buruma, *Voltaire's Coconuts*, London, 2000, p. 220.

48. Ford, op. cit., pp. 7–8.

Six / Harley Earl vs Norman Bel Geddes

1. Sloan, *My Years with General Motors*, p. 151.

2. Scharff, *Taking the Wheel*, p. 123.

3. Parlin and Bremier, *The Passenger Car Industy: Report of a Survey*.

4. Scharff, op. cit., p. 124.

5. Sorensen, *My Forty Years with Ford*, p. 218.

6. Sloan, op. cit., p. 151.

7. Ibid., p. 167.

8. Ibid., p. 239.

9. Ibid., pp. 267–8.

10. Bayley, *Harley Earl and the Dream Machine*, p. 22.

11. Sloan, op. cit., p. 269.

12. Quoted Bayley, op. cit., pp. 42–3.

13. Bayley, op. cit., p. 45.

14. Ibid., p. 46.

15. Ibid.

16. Sloan, op. cit., p. 273.

17. Ibid., pp. 272–3.

18. Ibid., p. 273.

19. Bayley, op. cit., p. 52.

20. Ibid., p. 78.

21. Nader, *Unsafe at Any Speed*, p. 216.

22. Bayley, op. cit., p. 12.

23. Ibid., p. 20.

24. Ibid., p. 46.

25. Ibid., p. 62.

26. Berger, *The Devil Wagon in God's Country*, p. 43.

27. Ibid.

28. Flink, *The Automobile Age*, p. 153.

29. Wik, *Henry Ford and Grass-Roots America*, p. 183.

30. Ibid., p. 184.

31. Ibid., p. 185.

32. John Tobin, 'Henry Ford and His Village Industries in South-East Michigan'.

33. Parlin and Bremier, op. cit., p. 15.

34. James J. Flink, 'The Ultimate Status Symbol: The Custom Coachbuilt Car in the Interwar Period', in Wachs and Crawford, eds., *The Car and the City*, p. 163.

35. Lynd and Lynd, *Middletown*, pp. 265–9.

36. Parlin and Bremier, op. cit.

37. Meikle, *Twentieth Century Limited*, p. 19.

38. Ibid., p. 68.

39. Lynd and Lynd, quoted Meikle, op. cit., p. 4.

40. Bayley, op. cit., p. 61.

41. Ibid., p. 79.

42. Ibid., p. 60.

43. Geddes, *Horizons*, p. 47.

44. Ibid., p. 40.

45. Ibid., p. 54.

46. Ibid.

47. Quoted Meikle, op. cit., p. 143.

48. Meikle, op. cit., p. 145.

49. Quoted Flink, *The Automobile Age*, p. 238.

50. Memo, 24 and 25 October 1933, Geddes papers, Harry Ransom Humanities Research Center, University of Texas at Austin.

51. Geddes papers.

52. Marks, *The Dymaxion World of Buckminster Fuller*, p. 21.

53. Ibid., pp. 18–19.

54. Ibid., p. 28.

55. Ibid., p. 31. A film of the Dymaxion Car performing this manoeuvre may be viewed on http://www.thirteen.org/archive/bucky/car.html.

56. Ibid., p. 29.

57. Hickerson, Robert L., *Hubbert's Prescription for Survival: A Steady State Economy*, http://hubbertpeak.com/hubbert/index.html.

58. Folke T. Kihlsted, 'Utopia Realized: The World's Fairs of the 1930s', in Corn, ed., *Imagining Tomorrow*, p. 100.

59. Ibid., p. 98.

60 Geddes to Carl Austrian, Geddes papers.

61. Geddes, *Miracle in the Evening*, p. 127.

62. Ibid., p. 129.

63. Geddes, *Horizons*, p. 5.

64. Ibid., pp. 4–5.

65. Ibid., p. 291.

66. Ibid., p. 24.

67. Belloc, *The Road*, p. 197.

68. Geddes, *Magic Motorways*, p. 157.

69. Ibid., p. 31.

70. Ibid.

71. Ibid., p. 267.

72. http://www.moller.com/skycar.

73. *New Scientist*, 26 Aug 2000, p. 17.

74. Geddes papers.

75. Ibid.

76. Quoted Cohen, *Scenes of the World to Come*, p. 34.

77. Le Corbusier, *The City of Tomorrow*, pp. 183–4.

78. Ibid., p. 286.

79. Meikle, *The City of Tomorrow, 1937*, p. 15.

80. Geddes, memo, 1937, Geddes papers.

81. Le Corbusier, *Towards a New Architecture*, p. 264.

82. Geddes papers.

83. Geddes, *Magic Motorways*, pp. 144, 219.

84. Memo, 17 January 1938, Geddes papers.

85. *New York Herald Tribune*, 18 Jul 1939.

86. Presentation notes, Geddes papers.

87. *New York Herald Tribune*, 18 Jul 1939.

88. Ibid.

89. Hughes, *American Visions*, p. 462.

90. Calthorpe, in conversation with Scott London, 'Insight and Outlook', http://www.scottlondon.com/insight/scripts/calthorpe.html.

91. Ibid.

92. H. M. Waite to Geddes, 18 May 1944, Geddes papers.

93. Rexford J. Tugwell, 'Parts of a New Civilization', *Saturday Review of Literature*.

Seven / Detroit to Dunmurry

1. Anne Dingus, 'On its Twentieth Anniversary, We Look Back at the Making of Texas' most Famous Roadside Attraction', *Texas Monthly Magazine*, Jul 1994.

2. Quoted Keats, *The Insolent Chariots*, p. 49.

3. Keats, op. cit., p. 49.

4. Szudarek, *How Detroit Became the Automotive Capital*.

6. Kerouac, *On the Road*, p. 230.

7. Ibid., p. 236.

8. Interview, *Front Row*, BBC Radio 4, 12 Sept 2000.

9. Nader, *Unsafe at Any Speed*, p. 222.

10. Quoted Nader, op. cit., p. 228.

11. Nader, op. cit., pp. 224–5.

12. Ibid., pp. 224–6.

13. Ibid., pp. 217–18.

14. Ibid., pp. 219–20.

15. Ibid., pp. 220–1.

16. Wright, *On a Clear Day You Can See General Motors*, pp. 54–5.

17. Ibid., p. 51.

18. Marsh and Collett, *Driving Passion*, p. 188.

19. Noble and Green, *Thrust*, p. 13.

20. T. E. Lawrence, *The Mint*, London, 1978, p. 228.

21. Wright, op. cit., pp. 75–6.

22. Ibid., pp. 78–9.

23. Ibid., p. 75.

24. Nader, op. cit., p. 18.

25. Wright, op. cit., p. 93.

26. Fallon and Srodes, *DeLorean*, p. 38.

27. Ibid.

28. Quoted Fallon and Srodes, op. cit., p. 39.

29. 'Crashworthiness as a Cultural Ideal', in Lewis and Goldstein, eds., *The Automobile*, p. 332.

30. Fallon and Srodes, op. cit., p. 40.

31. Ibid., p. 39.

32. Rothschild, *Paradise Lost*, p. 67.

33. Ibid., p. 70.

34. Ibid., p. 68.

35. Fallon and Srodes, op. cit., p. 50.

36. Jean Lindamood, 'A Star is Born', *Automotive News*, 1981.

37. Fallon and Srodes, op. cit., p. 51.

38. Wright, op. cit., p. 31.

39. Ibid.

40. Lindamood, op. cit.

41. Quoted Fallon and Srodes, op. cit., p. 58.

42. Ed Lapham, 'Where the Money Was – Shades of Billy Durant', *Automotive News*, 1981, quoted Clarke, ed., *DeLorean Gold Portfolio 1977–1995*, p. 49.

43. Fallon and Srodes, op. cit., p. 105.

44. Ibid., p. 115.

45. *The Times*, 22 Nov 1983.

46. Fallon and Srodes, op. cit., pp. 132–3.

47. Mike Knepper, 'Busted Dream', in Clarke, op. cit.

48. Ibid., p. 164.

49. Ibid., p. 163.

50. Quoted Clarke, op. cit., p. 49.

51. See e.g. reports in *The Times*, 25 and 26 Oct 1983.

52. Interview, Clarke, op. cit., p. 170.

53. Quoted Fallon and Srodes, op. cit., p. 47.

Eight / Rolling Alone

1. D. H. Lawrence on Walt Whitman, in Lawrence, *Studies in Classic American Literature*.

2. Charles Moore, 'You Have to Pay for Public Life', in Moore and Allen, *Dimensions*, pp. 128–9.

3. Banham, *Los Angeles*, p. 31.

4. Goodman and Goodman, *Communitas*, pp. 11–12.

5. Geddes, *Miracle in the Evening*, p. 159.

6. Ibid.

7. Hise and Deverell, *Eden by Design*, p. 8.

8. *Proceedings of the Sixteenth National Conference of City Planners*, 7 Apr 1924.

9. Presented in August, 2000.

10. Quoted Jackson, *To the Crabgrass Frontier*, p. 288.

11. Quoted Drummond Buckley, 'A Garage in the House', in Wachs and Crawford, eds., *The Car and the City*, p. 137.

12. Cornell University, cited Buckley, op. cit., pp. 139–40.

13. Rothschild, *Paradise Lost*, p. 19.

14. Quoted Brodsly, *L.A. Freeway*, p. 7.

15. Moore, op. cit., p. 111.

16. Ibid.

17. Stephen Greenblatt, 'The Inevitable Pit', *London Review of Books*, 21 Sept 2000.

18. *The Future of Multi-Ethnic Britain, The Parekh Report*, London 2000.

19. *The Lancet*, 31 Aug 2000.

20. Department of the Environment, reported in the *Guardian*, 20 Jan 2001.

21. Aird, *The Automotive Nightmare*, p. 111.

22. Derek Elsom, *Smog Alert*, pp. 194–200.

23. The *Guardian*, 28 Jan 2000.

24. Dana Reed 'Experiment with Public Transit Becomes Ordeal', *Los Angeles Times*, 30 Jul 1999.

25. Melvin Webber, in conversation with Philip Steadman.

26. McShane, *Down the Asphalt Path*, pp. 194–5.

27. Ibid.

28. Ibid., p. 115.

29. Ibid., p. 196.

30. Reed, op. cit.

31. RAC survey, reported in the *Guardian*, 24 Jan 2001.

32. Family Expenditure Survey, quoted the *Observer*, 17 Sept 2000.

33. Andrew Oswald, 'If only Britain would manage roads in the way it does supermarkets', the *Guardian*, 9 Oct 2000.

34. Marsh and Collett, *Driving Passion*, p. 155.

35. Melvin Webber in conversation with Philip Steadman, 1998.

36. Ibid.

37. The Automobile Association, *2020 Vision: What the Drivers of Today's New Cars Think Motoring Will Be Like Twenty Years From Now*, Basingstoke, 2000, p. 17.

38. Melvin Webber in conversation with Philip Steadman.

39. Official figures, in the *Guardian*, 11 Jan 2001.

40. Rothschild, op. cit., p. 93.

41. Ibid., pp. 248–51.

42. *Horseless Age*, New York, Jan 1897.

43. *Touring Topics*, Oct 1920, May 1921.

44. Edward Luttwak, 'Truckers' Tantrums: The Embarrassing Truth', *London Review of Books*, 5 Oct 2000.

45. Automobile Association, op. cit., p. 18.

46. Miranda Sawyer, 'Sex Drive', *Observer Life* magazine, 23 Jan 2000, p. 67.

47. *New York Times*, 6 Aug 2000.

48. Luttwak, op. cit.

49. 'US Reels at Car Giants', "betrayal"', the *Observer*, 10 Sept 2000.

50. Melvin Webber, 'Los Angeles and the Car'.

51. www.enviroinfo.org.cn.

52. Andrew H. Spencer, 'Decision Time for Transport in the Cities', *China Review*, Spring 1998, issue 10.

53. John Gittings, 'China Wants the Car Economy But Not the Fumes', the *Guardian*, 16 Nov 2000.

Nine / Rolling Over

1. *New York Times*, 23 Aug 1949.

2. In conversation with R. D. Clark, *Geophysics*, Feb 1983, pp. 16–24.

3. Tribute to M. King Hubbert, American Academy of Sciences, 'Letter to Members', vol. 19 no. 4, Apr 1990.

4. Craig Moore, 'Oil-Based Economies and the Future: Part 1, How Much Oil is There?' http://energyindustry.about.com.

5. Campbell and Laherrère, 'The End of Cheap Oil', http://dieoff.com/page140.html.

6. Ibid.

7. Ibid.

8. See graph of 'The Global Production for Oil', ibid.

9. Fleming, 'After Oil', *Prospect*, Nov 2000.

10. Ibid.

11. G. Dupont-Roc, 'The Evolution of the World's Energy System 1860–2060', Shell International, London.

12. Figures given by the United States Environmental Protection Agency.

13. Report of Intergovernmental Panel on Climate Change (IPCC), 22 Jan 2001.

14. Ibid.

15. In the early 80s, we tried to insure our house against nuclear accident – an eventuality calculated by the industry at odds of a million to one against. No insurance company would cover us. The risk, they said, was simply too remote – perhaps the first and only time any business has declined to take money on the grounds that it is too easy a profit.

16. 'Inland Flooding Risks: Issue Facing Insurers', Association of British Insurers, Sept 2000.

17. IPCC report, 22 Jan 2001.

18. Climate Action Network report, *What's New About Global Warming*.

19. The Department of the Environment, Transport and the Regions (DETR) figure is 20 per cent, but this is just for driving.

20. Figures calculated by Robert and Brenda Vale and John Willoughby, based on DETR figures.

21. Texas A and M University, reported in the *San Francisco Chronicle*, 10 Dec 1966.

22. The Automobile Association, *2020 Vision*, p. 18.

23. The *Guardian*, 1 Feb 1999.

24. Soy is evidently the original of Beachcomber's legendary all-purpose product, Snibbo.

25. Dupont-Roc, op. cit., p. 12.

26. Rocky Mountain Institute, 'Recent Hypercar News', 9 Oct 2000.

27. Rocky Mountain Institute, 'A Strategy for the Hydrogen Transition', http://www.rmi.org.

28. 'Kicking the Habit', *New Scientist*, 25 Nov 2000 – an excellent overview of developments in this area.

29. Rothschild, *Paradise Lost*, p. 18.

30. L. B. Magoon, 'Are We Running Out of Oil?', http://www.hubbert-peak.com/magoon.

31. Ibid.

32. Samuel Butler, 'Darwin among the Machines', 1863. *Notebooks of Samuel Butler* ed. Henry Festing Jones, London, 1921, pp. 42–6.

33. RAC survey, autumn 2000, reported in the *Guardian*, 24 Jan 2001.

Bibliography

Abrams, M., *The Newspaper-reading Public of Tomorrow*, London, 1964.

Adeney, Martin, *Nuffield: A Biography*, London, 1993.

Adorno, Theodor, *Minima Moralia*, tr. E. F. N. Jephcott, London, 1978.

Aird, Alisdair, *The Automotive Nightmare*, London, 1972.

Allen, F. L., *The Big Change*, New York, 1952.

Andrews, P. W. S. and Elizabeth Brunner, *The Life of Lord Nuffield*, Oxford, 1955.

Appleton, Victor Jr, *Tom Swift and His Electric Runabout or The Speediest Car on the Road*, New York, 1910.

Automobile Association, *The Great British Motorist*, Basingstoke, 1998, 1999, 2000.

Ballard, J. G., *Crash!*, London, 1973.

Banham, Reyner, *Los Angeles: The Architecture of Four Ecologies*, New York, 1971.

Bayley, Stephen, *Harley Earl and the Dream Machine*, London, 1983.

   Sex, Drink and Fast Cars, The Creation and Consumption of Images, London, 1986.

   Harley Earl, London, 1990

Baudrillard, Jean, *America*, tr. Chris Turner, London, 1989.

Belasco, Warren James, *Americans on the Road: From Autocamp to Motel, 1910–1945*, Cambridge, Mass., 1979.

Bellamy, Edward, *Looking Backwards*, Toronto, 1887.

Belloc, Hilaire, *The Road*, London, 1924.

The Highway and its Vehicles, London, 1926.

Benson, Allan L., *The New Henry Ford*, New York and London, 1923.

Berger, K. T., *Zen Driving*, New York, 1988.

Berger, Michael, *The Devil Wagon in God's Country: The Automobile and Social Change in Rural America, 1893–1929*, Hamden, Conn., 1979.

Black, Angus, *A Radical's Guide to Self-Destruction*, New York, 1971.

Black, Stephen, *Man and Motor Cars*, London, 1966.

Blumenthal, Albert, *Small-town Stuff*, Chicago, 1932.

Bottles, Scott, *Los Angeles and the Automobile*, Berkeley, Calif., 1987.

Boyle, Kevin and Victoria Getis, *Muddy Boots and Ragged Aprons: Images of Working Class Detroit 1900–1930*, Detroit, Mich., 1997.

Brand, Stewart, *Whole Earth Catalog*, Berkeley, Calif., 1974.

Whole Earth Epilog, Berkeley, Calif., 1974.

Brandon, Ruth, *Singer and the Sewing Machine*, London, 1976.

The Dollar Princesses, London, 1980.

BIOS (British Intelligence Objective Sub-committee) *People's Car, a facsimile of B.I.O.S. final report no. 998, 'Investigation into the Design and Performance of the Volkswagen or German People's Car'*, reprinted with a new introduction by Karl E. Ludvigsen, London, 1996.

Brodsly, David, *L.A. Freeway*, Berkeley, Calif., 1981.

Buchanan, C. D., *Mixed Blessing: The Motor in Britain*, London, 1958.

Calthorpe, Peter, *The Next American Metropolis: Ecology, Community, and the American Dream*, New York, 1993.

Campbell, Colin J. and Jean H. Laherrère, 'The End of Cheap Oil', *Scientific American*, Mar 1998.

Carson, Richard Burns, *The Olympian Cars*, New York, 1976.

Cervero, Robert, *America's Suburban Centers: The Land Use-Transportation Link*, Boston, Mass., 1989.

'Why Go Anywhere?', *Scientific American*, vol. 273 no. 3, pp. 92–3 (1995).

Chambless, Edgar, *Roadtown*, Detroit, Mich., 1918.

Cheney, Sheldon and Martha Cheney, *Art and the Machine: An Account of Industrial Design in Twentieth-Century America*, New York, 1936.

Clark, Colin, 'Transport: Maker and Breaker of Cities', *Town Planning Review* 28 (1957).

Clarke, R. M. (ed.), *DeLorean Gold Portfolio 1977–1995*, Cobham, Surrey, n.d.

Cohen, Jean-Louis, *Scenes of the World to Come*, Montreal, 1995.

Collier, Peter and David Horowitz, *The Fords: An American Epic*, London, 1988.

Le Corbusier, *The City of Tomorrow*, tr. F. Etchells (1929), reprinted London, 1971.

    Towards a New Architecture, tr. F. Etchells (1927), reprinted London, 1982.

    The Radiant City, 1933, reprinted London, 1967.

Corn, Joseph J. (ed.), *Imagining Tomorrow: History, Technology and the American Future*, Cambridge, Mass., 1988.

Cowan, Ruth Schwartz, 'Two Washes in the Morning and a Bridge Party at Night', *Women's Studies*, 3.

    More Work for Mother, New York, 1983.

Cray, Ed, *Chrome Colossus: General Motors and Its Times*, New York, 1980.

Cuneo, Joan Newton, *A Woman's Experience on the Glidden Tour*, New York, 1907.

Davies, Mike, *City of Quartz*, New York, 1992.

Dettelbach, Cynthia, *In the Driver's Seat: The Automobile in American Literature and Popular Culture*, Westport, Conn., 1976.

Donovan, Frank, *Wheels for a Nation*, New York, 1965.

Dorfman, Joseph, *Thorstein Veblen and His America*, London, 1935.

Dos Passos, John, *U.S.A.*, New York (1938), Library of America edition, 1996.

Douglas, Mary, *In the Active Voice*, London, 1982.

Duffus, Robert L., *The Innocents at Cedro: A Memoir of Thorstein Veblen and Some Others*, Clifton, NJ, 1944.

Eaglesfield, Barry with C. W. P. Hampton, *The Bugatti Book*, London, 1954.

Ehrenburg, Ilya, *The Life of the Automobile* (Berlin, 1929) tr. Joachim Neugroschel, London, 1985.

Ehrenreich, Barbara, and Deirdre English, *For Her Own Good: 150 Years of the Experts' Advice to Women*, London, 1979.

Elsom, D., *Smog Alert: Managing Urban Air Quality*, London, 1996.

Exner, Virgil M. Sr and Virgil M. Exner Jr, 'Reminsicences', *Automotive Design: oral history project*, Dearborn, Mich., 1989.

Fallon, Ivan and James Srodes, *DeLorean: The Rise and Fall of a Dreammaker*, London, 1983.

Faulkner, William, *Intruder in the Dust*, New York, 1948.

Figuier, Louis, *Merveilles de la Science: La Photographie*, Paris, 1860, reprod. New York, 1979.

Fleming, David, 'After Oil' *Prospect* magazine, London, Nov 2000.

Flink, James J., *America Adopts the Automobile, 1890–1914*, Cambridge, Mass., 1975.

  The Car Culture, Cambridge, Mass., 1975.

  The Automobile Age, Cambridge, Mass., 1988.

Flower, Raymond and Michael Wynn Jones, *100 Years on the Road: A Social History of the Car*, London, 1981.

Ford, Henry with Samuel Crowther, *My Life and Work*, London, 1922.

  Today and Tomorrow, London, 1926.

Friedan, Betty, *The Feminine Mystique*, New York and London, 1963.

Freud, Sigmund, *Civilisation and its Discontents*, London, 1930.

Frostick, Michael, *The Cars that Got Away: Ideas, Experiments and Prototypes*, London, 1968.

  Advertising and the Motor Car, London 1970.

Garreau, Joel, *Edge City: Life on the New Frontier*, New York, 1991.

Geddes, Norman Bel, *Horizons*, London, 1934.

  Magic Motorways, New York, 1940.

  Miracle in the Evening, Garden City, NY, 1960.

Goodman, Paul and Percival Goodman, *Communitas*, Chicago, 1947.

Gowing, Laurence and Richard Hamilton, preface to exhibition catalogue, *Man, Machine and Motion*, Durham, 1955.

Greenleaf, William, *Monopoly on Wheels*, Detroit, Mich., 1961.

Hall, Peter, 'Squaring the Circle: Can We Solve the Clarkian Paradox?', *Environment and Planning B – Planning and Design*, 1994.

Cities of Tomorrow, updated edition, Oxford, 1996.

Hayden, Dolores M., *The Grand Domestic Revolution: A History of Feminist Designs for American Homes, Neighborhoods and Cities*, Cambridge, Mass., 1981.

The Power of Place: Landscape as Public History, Cambridge, Mass., 1995.

Hise, Greg and William Deverell, *Eden by Design: the 1930 Olmsted-Bartholomew Plan for the Los Angeles Region*, Berkeley and Los Angeles, Calif., 2000.

Hornbostel, Wilhelm and Nils Jockel (eds.), *Käfer der Erfolkswagen*, Munich, 1997.

Hughes, Robert, *American Visions*, London, 1997.

Hultén, K. G. Pontus, *The Machine as Seen at the End of the Mechanical Age*, MOMA catalogue, New York, 1968.

Huxley, Aldous, *Brave New World*, London, 1932.

Hyndman, H. M., *The Coming Revolution*, London, 1884.

Jackson, Kenneth, *To the Crabgrass Frontier*, New York, 1985.

Jacobs, Jane, *The Death and Life of Great American Cities*, New York, 1961.

Jeansonne Glen, 'The Automobile and American Morality'. *Journal of Popular Culture*, 8 (1974).

Jeffreys, Rees, *The King's Highway*, London, 1949.

Jewell, Derek (ed.), *Man and Motor: The 20th Century Love Affair*, New York, 1967.

Judd, Dennis R. and Susan S. Fainstein (eds.), *The Tourist City*, New Haven, Conn., 1999.

Jukes, Peter, *A Shout in the Street: The Modern City*, London, 1990.

Keats, John, *The Insolent Chariots*, New York, 1958.

Kerouac, Jack, *On the Road*, London, 1958.

Kipling, Rudyard, *Traffics and Discoveries*, London, 1904.

Labatut, Jean and Wheaton J. Lane (eds.), *Highways in Our National Life*, Princeton, NJ, 1950.

Lacey, Robert, *Ford: The Men and the Machines*, London, 1986.

Lane, Rose Wilder and Helen Dore Boylston, *Travels with Zenobia: Paris to Albania by Model T Ford*, Columbia, Miss., 1983.

Laux, James M., *In First Gear: The French Automobile Industry to 1914*, Liverpool, 1976.

Lawrence, D. H., *Studies in Classic American Literature*, New York, 1923.

Leavitt, Helen, *Superhighway – Superhoax*, Garden City, NY, 1970.

Lee, Albert, *Henry Ford and the Jews*, New York, 1980.

Leonard, Jonathan, *The Tragedy of Henry Ford*, New York, 1932.

Lewis, David L., *The Public Image of Henry Ford: An American Folk Hero and His Company*, Detroit, Mich., 1976.

Lewis, David L. and Laurence Goldstein (eds.), *The Automobile and American Culture*, Ann Arbor, Mich., 1983.

Lichtenstein, Claude, *The Esthetics of Minimized Drag: Streamlined: A Metaphor for Progress*, Baden (Switzerland), 1993.

Ling, James, *America and the Automobile*, Manchester, 1990.

Lochner, Louis B., *Henry Ford: America's Don Quixote*, New York, 1925.

Loeb, Harold, *Life in a Technocracy: What it Might Be Like*, New York, 1933.

Longstreth, Richard, *City Center to Regional Mall: Architecture, the Automobile, and Retailing in Los Angeles, 1920–1950*, Cambridge, Mass., 1998.

The Drive-in, the Supermarket and the Transformation of Commercial Space in Los Angeles, 1914–1941, Cambridge, Mass., 1999.

Lynd, Robert S. and Helen M. Lynd, *Middletown: A Study in Contemporary American Culture*, New York, 1929.

Middletown in Transition, New York, 1937.

Macmanus, Theodore F. and Norman Beasley, *Men, Money and Motors: The Drama of the Automobile*, New York, 1930.

Marks, Robert W., *The Dymaxion World of Buckminster Fuller*, New York, 1960.

Marquis, Samuel S., *Henry Ford: An Interpretation*, Boston, 1923.

Marsh, Peter and Peter Collett, *Driving Passion: The Psychology of the Car*, London, 1986.

Maxim, Hiram Percy, *Horseless Carriage Days*, New York, 1937.

May, George S., *A Most Unique Machine: The Michigan Origins of the American Automobile Industry*, Grand Rapids, Mich., 1975.

McLuhan, Marshall, *Understanding Media*, London, 1964.

McShane, Clay, *Down the Asphalt Path: The Automobile and the American City*, New York, 1994.

    The Automobile: A Chronology of its Antecedents, Development and Impact, Chicago, 1997.

Meikle, Jeffrey, *Twentieth Century Limited: Industrial Design in America 1925–1939*, Philadelphia, Penn., 1979.

    The City of Tomorrow, 1937, London, 1984.

Meyer, Stephen, *The Five-Dollar Day: Labour Management and Social Control in the Ford Motor Company, 1908–1921*, Albany, NY., 1981.

Montagu of Beaulieu, Lord, *The Gordon-Bennett Races*, London, 1963.

Moore, Charles and Gerald Allen, *Dimensions*, New York, 1976.

Morley, Christopher, *Streamlines*, New York, 1934.

Morris, W. R., 'Policies that Have Built the Morris Motor Business', *System*, vol. XLV no. 2, Feb 1924.

Mumford, Lewis, *The City in History*, London, 1961.

    The Highway and the City, New York, 1963.

    The Pentagon of Power, New York, 1970.

Musselman, M. M., *Get a Horse!: The Story of the Automobile in America*, New York, 1950.

Nader, Ralph, *Unsafe at Any Speed: The Designed-in Dangers of the American Automobile*, New York, 1965.

Nelson, W. H., *Small Wonder: The Amazing Story of the Volkswagen*, Boston, Mass., 1967.

Nevins, Allan and Frank Ernest Hill, 'Ford: The Times, the Man, the Company', New York, vol. 1, 1954; vol. 2 1957; vol. 3, 1963.

Noble, Richard and David Tremayne with Andy Green, *Thrust*, London, 1998.

North, Richard, *The Real Cost*, London, 1986.

O'Connell, J. and A. Myers, *Safety Last*, New York, 1965.

Papachristou, Judith, *Women Together: A History in Documents of the Women's Movement in the United States*, New York, 1976.

Parlin, Charles Coolidge and Fred Bremier, *The Passenger Car Industry – Report of a Survey*, Philadelphia, Penn., 1932.

Pearson, Lynn F., *An Architectural and Social History of Co-Operative Living*, London, 1988.

Pettifer, Julian and Nigel Turner, *Automania: Man and the Motor Car*, London, 1984.

Pipp, E. G., *Henry Ford: Both Sides of Him*, Detroit, Mich., 1926.

Plowden, E., *The Motor Car and Politics 1870–1970*, London, 1971.

Pool, J. and S. Pool, *Who Financed Hitler?*, London, 1979.

Post, Emily, *By Motor to the Golden Gate*, New York, 1916.

Preston, Howard L., *Automobile Age Atlanta: The Making of a Southern Metropolis*, Athens, Ga, 1979.

Pucher, John, and Christian Lefèvre, *The Urban Transport Crisis in Europe and North America*, London, 1996.

Rae, John B., *The American Automobile*, Chicago, 1965.

The Road and Car in American Life, Cambridge, Mass., 1971.

Ramsey, Alice Huyler, *Veil, Duster and Tire Iron*, Covina, Calif., 1961.

Roberts, Gerrylynn and Philip Steadman, *American Cities and Technology*, Milton Keynes, 1999.

Rolt, L. T. C., *Horseless Carriage: The Motor-car in England*, London, 1950.

Rothschild, Emma, *Paradise Lost: The Decline of the Auto-Industrial Age*, New York, 1973.

Rudofsky, Bernard, *Are Clothes Modern?*, New York, 1947.

Saunier, Baudry de, Charles Dollfus and Edgar Geoffroy, *Histoire de la locomotion terrestre*, Paris, 1935.

Schafer, Andreas and David Victor, *The Future Mobility of the World Population*, Discussion Paper 97-6-4, Center for Technology, Policy and Industrial Development, Massachusetts Institute of Technology, 1997.

Scharff, Virginia, *Taking the Wheel: Women and the Coming of the Motor Age*, New York, 1991.

Sennett, Richard, *The Fall of Public Man*, Cambridge, 1977.

Serrin, William, *The Company and the Union*, New York, 1973.

Sillitoe, K. K., *Planning for Leisure*, London, 1969.

Simmonds, William Adams, *Henry Ford: A Biography*, London, 1946.

Singerman, David, *Red Adair: An American Hero*, London, 1989.

Sloan, Alfred, *My Years with General Motors*, New York, 1965.

Sloan, Alfred P. Jr and Boyden Sparks, *Adventures of a White-collar Man*, New York, 1941.

Sorensen, Charles E. with Samuel Williamson, *My Forty Years with Ford*, New York, 1956.

Starr, Kevin, *1940 – Inventing the Dream: California Through the Progressive Era*, New York, 1985.

Stein, Gertrude, *The Autobiography of Alice B. Toklas*, New York, 1960.

Steinbeck, John, *The Grapes of Wrath*, New York, 1939.

    Cannery Row, New York, 1945.

Strasser, Susan, *Never Done: A History of American Housework*, New York, 1982.

Sward, Keith, *The Legend of Henry Ford*, New York, 1949.

Tarkington, Booth, *The Magnificent Ambersons*, New York, 1918.

Taylor, A. J. P., *The Origins of the Second World War*, London, 1961.

Taylor, Frederick Winslow, *The Principles of Scientific Management*, New York, 1911.

Thomas, Miles First Viscount, Nuffield Memorial Paper, Institution of Production Engineers, 1964.

    Out on a Wing, London, 1964.

Tobin, John, *Henry Ford and His Village Industries in South-East Michigan*, unpublished thesis, Henry Ford Greenfield Museum archive, Dearborn, Mich., 1995.

Totman, Richard, *Mind, Stress and Health*, London, 1990.

Vanderbilt, Suzanne, 'Reminiscences', *Automotive Design: oral history project*, Mich., Dearborn, 1986.

Vanderbilt, William Kissam, *Log of My Motor: A Record of Many Delightful Days Spent in Touring the Continent*, privately printed 1908, 1912.

Vanek, Joann, 'Time Spent in Housework', *Scientific American*, Nov 1974.

Veblen, Thorstein, *The Theory of the Leisure Class*, introd. C. Wright Mills, London, 1953.

von Hartz, John, *New York Street Kids: 136 Photographs*, selected by the Children's Aid Society, New York, 1978.

Wachs, Martin, *Men, Women and Wheels*, paper for Transportation Research Dept, Washington, D.C., 1987.

Wachs, Martin and Margaret Crawford, *The Car and the City: The Automobile, the Built Environment and Daily Urban Life*, Ann Arbor, Mich., 1992.

Warner, Sam Bass, *Streetcar Suburbs: The Process of Growth in Boston*, Cambridge, Mass., 1962.

Webber, Melvin, 'Order in Diversity, Community without Propinquity', in L. Wingo Jr (ed.), *Cities and Space: The Future Use of Urban Land*, Baltimore, Md, 1963.

'The Post-City Age', *Daedalus*, vol. 97 no. 4 (1968).

Wharton, Edith, *A Backward Glance*, New York, 1934.

White, E. B., *Essays*, London, 1977.

White, Lawrence, *The Automobile Industry Since 1945*, Cambridge, Mass., 1971.

Wik, Reynold M., *Henry Ford and Grass-Roots America*, Ann Arbor, Mich., 1973.

Williamson, A. M., *The Lightning Conductor*, New York, 1900.

Wilson, Edmund, *The American Earthquake*, New York, 1971.

Wolfe, Tom, *The Kandy-Kolored Tangerine-Flake Streamline Baby*, New York, 1965.

Wright, J. Patrick, *On a Clear Day You Can See General Motors*, Chicago, 1979.

Wright, Priscilla Hovey, *The Car Belongs to Mother*, Boston, 1939.

Young, Clarence, *The Motor Boys in Mexico*, New York, 1906.

Young, Filson, *The Complete Motorist*, London, 1904.

Index

Page numbers in *italics* refer to
captions/illustrations

accidents:
    to children 48–50, 53, 54–8, 60–2,
        309, 313
    with cyclists 48–9
    dangers of car design elements
        309–10
    to public 49–52, 60–2
    in road races 53–8
Acton, Lord 234
Addams, Jane 124
Adenauer, Chancellor 213
Adeney, Martin 231
advertising 168–70
aircraft 253–7, 280
    racing against motorbike 315
Alaska, oil fields 382
Alfa Romeo 402, *403*
Algonac *Courier* 107
Amarillo, Texas 302
Ambassador car 6
Amboise 28
American Agriculturist 81
American Automobile Association 44
American Petroleum Institute 388
American Society of Mechanical
    Engineers 97

Anderson, John 79
Angoulême 28
anti-Semitism 214–16, 232–3, 235, 236
Apple Computer 183–4
Arbuckle, Fatty 242
Architectural Record 152
ARCO 409
Arts and Crafts movement 135–6, 140,
    141, 142, 144
assembly line 93–9, 95, 98, 99, 102–5
Astor family 42
Athens 362
Atlanta, Georgia 152
Atlanta Constitution 152
Atlantic Monthly 46
Austria 3, 358
Auto-Union 203–4
Autocar 58–9
Automobile Association (AA) 51, 372,
    383, 400
Automobile Club of America 51
Automobile Club of France 21, 382
Automotive News 327, 335

Back to the Future (film) 337
ball bearings 20
Ballard, J. G. 307
Ballard Power Systems 409
Bangkok 385